Fodor's InFocus

S0-ARO-502

FLORIDA KEYS

14
TOP EXPERIENCES

The Florida Keys offer terrific experiences that should be on every traveler's list. Here are Fodor's top picks for a memorable trip.

1 Key West Architecture

Built on stilts to keep things cool, Key West's clapboard Conch houses feature porches with gingerbread trim. Many have been converted into atmospheric bed-and-breakfasts. (Ch. 5)

2 Kayaking and Canoeing

Whether you prefer sea kayaking, canoeing through calm and wildlife-rich mangrove waters, or stand-up paddle boarding, the Keys provide the setting and the perfect outfitter. (Ch. 2)

3 Key Lime Pie

You're going to need a lot of time and appetite, because key lime pie is everywhere, and everyone claims to make the best. (Ch. 5)

4 Dolphin Adventures

From watching them in the wild or captivity, to getting in the water to swim and interact with them, experiencing dolphins is a classic Keys adventure. *(Ch. 2)*

5 The Cuba Connection

Cuba looms large in Key West, which was settled by cigar-making immigrants. El Meson Pepe and El Siboney are two restaurants that serve Cuban delicacies. *(Ch. 5)*

6 Duval Street

Do the Duval Crawl in Key West. There are no rules: stop for a drink, simply wander, or shop instead of drink. But you aren't allowed to go fun-free. *(Ch. 5)*

7 Key Largo's Christ of the Deep

Just outside of John Pennecamp Coral Reef State Park on Key Largo, the submerged 9-foot-tall statue makes a divine underwater sight. *(Ch. 2)*

8 Ernest Hemingway's Home

You'll see his name all over Key West, but the best place to start is this historic home, where descendants of his six-toed cats still prowl. *(Ch. 5)*

9 Highway 1

Despite the traffic, the Overseas Highway (aka U.S. 1) is an engineering marvel and the only way to reach the southernmost point in the U.S. *(Ch. 2)*

10 Beaches

Keys beaches, including Bahia Honda State Park, Marathon's Sombrero Beach, and Key West's Fort Zachary Taylor Historic State Park, can be beautiful. *(Ch. 4, 3, 5)*

11 The Dry Tortugas

Seaplanes and fast ferries deliver you to Dry Tortugas National Park, known for its birding, snorkeling, and historic Fort Jefferson. *(Ch. 5)*

12 Fresh Seafood

You don't have to catch your own to relish the lobster, yellowtail snapper, hogfish, and mahi-mahi that are signatures of the Florida Keys. You'll find fresh seafood everywhere. *(Ch. 3)*

13 Fishing

Jump on a party or charter boat for offshore or back-bay fishing. Or cast a line from one of the Keys' many bridges. *(Ch. 4)*

14 Sunset at Key West's Mallory Square

Not only does the setting sun put on a fabulous show, but local musicians, magicians, and performance artists also join the act every evening. *(Ch. 5)*

CONTENTS

ABOUT THIS BOOK

Fodor's Ratings

Everything in this guide is worth doing—we don't cover what isn't—but exceptional sights, hotels, and restaurants are recognized with additional accolades. Fodor's Choice★ indicates our top recommendations; ★ highlights places we deem highly recommended. Care to nominate a new place? Visit Fodors.com/contact-us.

Trip Costs

We list prices wherever possible to help you budget well. Hotel and restaurant price categories from $ to $$$$ are noted alongside each recommendation. For hotels, we include the lowest cost of a standard double room in high season. For restaurants, we cite the average price of a main course at dinner or, if dinner isn't served, at lunch. For attractions, we always list adult admission fees; discounts are usually available for children, students, and senior citizens.

Hotels

Our local writers vet every hotel to recommend the best overnights in each price category, from budget to expensive. Unless otherwise specified, you can expect private bath, phone, and TV in your room. For expanded hotel reviews, facilities, and deals visit Fodors.com.

Restaurants

Unless we state otherwise, restaurants are open for lunch and dinner daily. We mention dress code only when there's a specific requirement and reservations only when they're essential or not accepted. To make restaurant reservations, visit Fodors.com.

Credit Cards

The hotels and restaurants in this guide typically accept credit cards. If not, we'll say so.

Ratings
- ★ Fodor's Choice
- ★ Highly recommended
- ☾ Family-friendly

Listings
- ⊠ Address
- ⊠ Branch address
- ⌻ Mailing address
- ☎ Telephone
- 🖷 Fax
- ⊕ Website

- ✉ E-mail
- 🎟 Admission fee
- ☉ Open/closed times
- Ⓜ Subway
- ✢ Directions or Map coordinates

Hotels & Restaurants
- 🛏 Hotel
- ⇗ Number of rooms
- ⦿ Meal plans

- ✕ Restaurant
- ⌕ Reservations
- 🏛 Dress code
- ⊟ No credit cards
- Ⓢ Price

Other
- ⇨ See also
- ☞ Take note
- ⅄ Golf facilities

Experience the Florida Keys

WORD OF MOUTH

"The beauty of Key West is that if you stay in Old Town, everything you want to do (including sunset celebrations, restaurants, water sports and other tourist activities) will be within walking distance."

—SusanCS

"Marathon is a great little place. Lots of inexpensive, interesting places to eat and it is a short drive to Key West."

—islandgirl355

WHAT'S WHERE

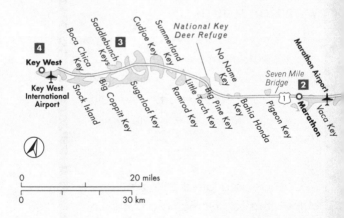

Gulf of Mexico

National Key Deer Refuge

Key West

Key West International Airport

Marathon Airport

Seven Mile Bridge

Marathon

0   20 miles

0   30 km

1 The Upper Keys. As the doorstep to the islands' coral reefs and blithe spirit, the Upper Keys introduce all that is sporting and sea-oriented about the Keys. They stretch from Key Largo to the Long Key Channel (MM 106–65).

2 The Middle Keys. Centered around the town of Marathon, the Middle Keys hold most of the chain's historic and natural attractions outside of Key West. They go from Conch (pronounced *konk*) Key through Marathon to the south side of the Seven Mile Bridge, including Pigeon Key (MM 65–40).

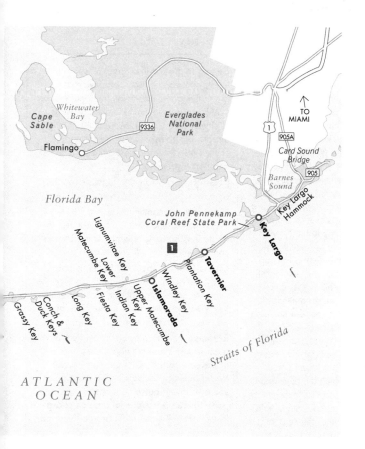

3 The Lower Keys. Pressure drops another notch in this laid-back part of the region, where wildlife and the fishing lifestyle peak. The Lower Keys go from Little Duck Key south through Big Coppitt Key (MM 40–9).

4 Key West. The ultimate in Florida Keys craziness, the party town Key West isn't the place for those seeking a quiet retreat. The Key West area encompasses MM 9–0.

FLORIDA KEYS PLANNER

Activities	Logistics
The Keys are all about being on and in the water. **Diving** in particular draws water sports enthusiasts to explore the clear waters and vibrant reefs and sea life. Dive shops up and down Overseas Highway sell dive trips, instruction, and equipment. **Fishing**, too, is spectacular, bringing the rod-and-reel crowd in search of big game such as marlin, tarpon, and dolphinfish as well as flats dwellers, most notably the easily spooked bonefish. On land, exploring **Key West** is the most popular pastime. Visitors do the "Duval Crawl" through the pubs and bars of Old Town. On its fringes, the island holds some of the Keys' best beaches, although they are all manmade. For a more serious crowd, plenty of museums, galleries, and historic sites offer cultural stimulation.	**Getting to the Islands:** You can fly into Key West, but because flights are few, many prefer flying into Miami International Airport (MIA) and driving the 110-mile Overseas Highway (aka U.S. 1). Marathon has an airport, but it's served only by charter flights. There's also ferry service from Marco Island and Fort Myers Beach. **Hassle Factor:** Medium to high, depending on how far you have to drive. **Nonstops:** You can fly nonstop to Key West from Atlanta (Delta), Fort Lauderdale (United), Miami (American), Tampa (American, United), or Fort Myers (Cape Air). **On the Ground:** There are both bus and shuttle services from the Miami airport to the Keys; the Lower Keys Shuttle runs between Key West and Marathon, offering cheap service and multiple stops. **Renting a Car:** It's possible to get by without a car in Key West, but you'll need one virtually everywhere else. It's usually cheaper to rent in either Fort Lauderdale or Miami if you are driving down from one of those airports. There are substantial drop-off charges if you rent in Key West but drop off your car in Miami.

Where to Stay

The Keys offers accommodations for every type of vacationer, from fishing lodges to luxury hotels to the famed historic B&Bs of Key West.

Resorts: Name-brand destination resorts such as Westin and Marriott take care of guests' every need with swimming pools, beaches, spas, restaurants, and concierges who will arrange tours and activities. Smaller resorts have a mom-and-pop feel—some every bit as luxurious as the big guys, others ultra-casual.

B&Bs: Government incentives to turn headed-for-decrepit historic homes into lodging led to Key West's abundance of guest houses and B&Bs. They range from all-men gay properties and little bohemian enclaves to elegantly turned-out mansions with no luxury spared. Other keys have a few more fine choices away from the Key West crowds and clamor.

Fishing Lodges: It's easy to find a fishing lodge in the Keys, outside of Key West. Some are simple and some more luxurious, with marina facilities on site or close by.

Hotel and Restaurant Costs

Prices in the restaurant reviews are the average cost of a main course at dinner or, if dinner is not served, at lunch; taxes and service charges are generally included. Prices in the hotel reviews are the lowest cost of a standard double room in high season, excluding taxes, service charges, and meal plans (except at all-inclusives). Prices for rentals are the lowest per-night cost for a one-bedroom unit in high season.

Pick the Right Key

1

Key Largo is great for diving and luxurious resorts and condo rentals; its proximity to the Everglades also makes it a destination for birders.

Islamorada is known for sportfishing (and at times celebrity spotting, particularly for those celebs who like game fishing).

Big Pine Key is great for fishing on a smaller scale or for kayaking.

Key West is known for cultural attractions, nightlife, dining, and great B&Bs; it's also the most popular gay destination in the Keys.

Marathon, while not bucolic or beautiful, has lots of mid-range accommodations, pretty good food, and great access to water sports.

Bahia Honda Key has the best beach in the Keys, hands down.

IF YOU LIKE

Water Sports

Fishing, snorkeling, scuba diving, and glass-bottom-boat tours top the list of Keys activities, but you'll find all manner of water sports from kayaking and stand-up paddle boarding to swimming and sailing.

Bahia Honda State Park, Bahia Honda Key. Not only does this state park boast the Keys' best white-sand beach, it's also the place to go snorkeling and kayaking.

Dry Tortugas National Park. A fast ferry makes the 2¼-hour trip each way from Key West to the reefs and historic fort on Garden Key. Once there, the snorkeling is fabulous.

Fishing trips. Party boats and charter captains in all the major keys take you where the fish are biting. You have your choice of back bay and deep-sea excursions.

John Pennekamp Coral Reef State Park, Key Largo. One of the most popular stops for snorkelers and divers, it also offers glass-bottom-boat tours to the reef that rims it.

Looe Key Reef, Lower Keys. One of the most stunning stretches of reef and marine life in the Keys, it is also the setting for the annual Underwater Music Festival.

Seafood

You don't have to eat seafood in the Keys, but it's so fresh that it's hard to resist. Talented chefs, however, prepare a variety of cuisines besides the trademark fish-heavy Keys style.

Ambrosia, Key West. The undisputed master of sushi in these parts, it makes the ultimate use of local fresh fish.

B.O's Fish Wagon, Key West. It doesn't get any funkier than this broken-down food truck that has grown into a junkyard-chic restaurant.

El Meson de Pepe, Key West. Authentic Cuban cuisine is easy to find in Key West, but this one has the best setting for watching the sunset at Mallory Square.

The Fish House, Key Largo. The very definition of Keys dining, it sports an old-island look, casual appeal, and focus on what's fresh from the deep.

Little Palm Island Restaurant. This top-of-the-toque dining experience includes a boat ride to a South Seas–style resort, gourmet food with island flair, and candlelight dining waterside.

Pierre's, Islamorada. Here is one fine example of how Keys chefs know their way around fine Continental cuisine.

Nightlife

You don't have to wait for nightfall to get started on Key West's celebrated party scene. The other keys, too, claim their favorite watering holes—usually (and appropriately) on the water.

The Garden of Eden, Key West. Bare it all at this upstairs clothing-optional spot.

Green Parrot, Key West. Another Key West classic—in fact, the town's oldest bar—it hosts live entertainment nightly at Mile Marker 0.

La Te Da Bar, Key West. For purely Keys style entertainment, catch the hilarious drag shows here.

Lorelei Cabana Bar, Islamorada. Teetering at the edge of a marina, its sunset entertainment draws the fishing and party crowds.

Sloppy Joe's, Key West. The first name in nightlife in Old Town, it jams day and night with live music.

Snapper's, Key Largo. Live bands play daily at this marina-side spot, where the food is as good as the cocktails.

Culture

Don't discount the Keys' serious side. The islands offer both history and arts in the most surprising places.

Ernest Hemingway Home and Museum, Key West. The unofficial patron saint of Key West, Nobel Prize–winning author Ernest Hemingway lived, fished, and wrote in Key West for more than ten years—one of several celebrated writers who have migrated here.

History of Diving Museum, Islamorada. It peeks into the development of scuba diving with 13 galleries of hands-on exhibits.

Key West Forts. Explore Fort Zachary Taylor Historic State Park and East and West Martello Towers to learn Key West's military importance in times past.

Key West Museum of Art and History, Key West. Housed in the late-19th-century customs house, the museum hosts changing art exhibits and permanent displays about island bygones.

Pigeon Key, Marathon. Take a ferry boat to this five-acre key that once held the Keys' railroading operations and housed its workers. Check out the railroad museum and Bahamian architecture.

WHEN TO GO

In high season, from mid-December through mid-April, traffic is inevitably heavy. From November to mid-December, crowds are thinner, the weather is superlative, and hotels and shops drastically reduce their prices. Summer is a second high season, especially among families, Europeans, bargain-seekers, and lobster divers.

Florida is rightly called the Sunshine State, but it could also be dubbed the "Humidity State." From June through September, 90% humidity levels are not uncommon. Thankfully, the weather in the Keys is more moderate than in mainland Florida. Temperatures can be 10°F cooler during the summer and up to 10°F warmer during the winter. The Keys also gets substantially less rain than mainland Florida, mostly in quick downpours on summer afternoons. In hurricane season, June through November, the Keys gets its fair share of warnings; pay heed and evacuate earlier rather than later, when flights and automobile traffic get backed up.

Festivals and Events

Many of the Keys' biggest events have to do with fishing, diving, and being water-bound. Fishing tournaments start in December with the **Islamorada Fishing Club Sailfish Tournament** in the so-called Sportsfishing Capital of the World. Come spring and summer, different target fish inspire the **Islamorada All-Tackle Spring Bonefish Tournament** in April and **Big Pine & Lower Keys Dolphin Tournament** in June. (Dolphinfish, aka mahimahi, is the catch of the latter.)

Key Largo celebrates Easter Keys-style during its **Underwater Easter Egg Hunt** followed in July by another signature below-the-surface tradition, the **Underwater Music Festival** on Looe Key Reef.

Next in importance comes seafood. Three biggies take place during the winter season, starting in late January with the **Florida Keys Seafood Festival** in Key West and **Key Largo Stone Crab & Seafood Festival.** In March, the **Original Marathon Seafood Festival** has been happening since the 1970s. To celebrate lobster season, Key West throws its **Lobsterfest** each August.

Finally, the islands celebrate their culture and heritage at such hallmark events as **Sculpture Key West,** a winter-long outdoor exhibition; Marathon's annual **Pigeon Key Art Festival** in February; and the 10-day **Conch Republic Independence Celebration** in Key West every April. Two of Key West's most publicized events include the **Hemingway Days** in July, with its highly competitive Hemingway look-alike contest, and October's manic **Fantasy Fest.**

KIDS AND FAMILIES

Families who love beaches, snorkeling, kayaking, and sea creatures will revel in the Keys. Although many smaller resorts and B&Bs discourage children, plenty of family resorts have kids programs and activities. Key West's wild party scene may seem the least attractive to families, yet it too boasts family resorts, beaches, and age-appropriate attractions.

Upper Keys
Key Largo Grande Resort & Club and **Marriott's Key Largo Bay Beach Resort** offer the best family amenities in a beachfront destination resort setting with planned activities. **John Pennekamp Coral Reef Resort** also provides snorkel and glass-bottom-boat tours, kayak rentals, and safe beaches. In Islamorada to the south, the climate is more upscale, but **Cheeca Lodge** has always been a family favorite, given its private beach and eco-educational Camp Cheeca.

Take the kids to **Robbie's Marina** in Islamorada, and have lunch at **Hungry Tarpon** before you feed sardines to the truly hungry tarpon. **Theater of the Sea** entails more marine life interaction, including rays, dolphin, and sea lions.

Middle Keys
Hawk's Cay, north of Marathon, is a perfect match for families with its villas, pirate-themed pool, kids program, and dolphin encounters. For more dolphin interactions, check out **Dolphin Research Center** or **Dolphin Cove**. Families will also feel at home at **Tranquility Bay** in Marathon, where they can play on the beach and spread out in a townhouse behind picket fences. Don't miss **Crane Point Museum, Nature Center & Historic Site** and **Pigeon Key** for easy-to-absorb lessons in history and the environment.

Lower Keys & Key West
Budget at least a half-day to spend beaching, snorkeling, kayaking, and hiking at **Bahia Honda State Park**. It's also a good place to rent a cabin (if you reserve early). Go in the morning or evening to try to spot the tiny deer at **National Key Deer Refuge** on Big Pine Key. In Key West, family lodging choices include the **Hyatt Key West Resort**, **Southernmost Hotel**, and **The Reach Resort**—all boast beach access and distance from the Duval Street hubbub. Casual seafood restaurants such as the **Half Shell Raw Bar** welcome children, and the **Key West Butterfly & Nature Conservatory**, **Key West Aquarium**, **Conch Train**, **beaches**, and **Eco-Discovery Center** give families many days' worth of entertainment and enlightenment.

FLORIDA KEYS' BEST BEACHES

Because the Bahama Islands steal the Keys' offshore sand, the region has fewer natural beaches than one might expect. But the ones it does have are award-winning, specifically those at Bahia Honda State Park.

Also, just because a beach is not natural, doesn't mean it should be overlooked. Some of the Keys' public man-made beaches provide solid recreation and sunning options for visitors looking to work on their tan. Many resorts additionally provide their own private beachfronts.

The Keys may not have a surplus of beaches, but one nice perk is the availability of camping on some of them. It's one of many ways to enjoy nature while on the beach. Another is keeping an eye out for sea turtles. From April through October female sea turtles lay their eggs in the sand for a nearly two-month period of nesting. ■TIP→ **Don't let pests ruin your day at the beach. To avoid the stings of sea lice, remove your swimsuit and shower thoroughly upon exiting the water. Sand fleas (aka no-see-ums) are tiny insects with big teeth that are most likely to attack in the morning and around sunset.**

Long Key State Park

The beach at Long Key State Park at MM 67.5 is a typical Middle Key beach. Rather than a sandy beach, what you see are more like sand flats, where low tide reveals the coral bedrock of the ecosystem. Here you can snorkel or fish (bonefishing is quite popular) during the day and then be lulled to sleep by the sound of gentle sea waves if you spend the night camping. (The beach is accessible only to day-trippers and campers.)

Sombrero Beach

Something of a local hangout—especially on weekends, when it can get crowded—Sombrero Beach in Marathon is worth getting off the beaten Overseas Highway path for (exit at MM 50 onto Sombrero Beach Road). Families will find much to do on the man-made coved beach and its grassy green, manicured lawn, playground area, and clear, calm waters. Separate sections also accommodate boaters and windsurfers.

Bahia Honda State Park

This state park at MM 37 holds three beaches, all of different character. These are hands-down the best beaches in all of the Keys. Sandspur Beach is the most removed from crowds, with long stretches of powdery sands and a campground. Loggerhead Beach is closer to the park's concession area, where you can rent snorkel equipment and kayaks. Like Sandspur, it faces the Atlantic Ocean, but waves are typically wimpy. Near Loggerhead, Calusa

1

Beach on the Gulf side near the marina is popular with families, offering a small and safe swimming venue and picnic facilities, as well as camping.

Higgs Beach, Key West

Situated on Atlantic Boulevard, this is as urban as beaches in the Keys get, with lots of amenities, activities, and distractions. Visitors can check out a historic site, eat at a popular beachfront Italian restaurant, rent a kayak, play volleyball or tennis, or at the playground—and all within walking distance of the long sweep of manmade beach and sparkling clear, shallow, and calm water.

Fort Zachary Taylor Historic State Park

This man-made beach is part of a Civil War–era fort complex at the end of Southard Street, and is arguably the best beach in Key West, with its typically small waves, swaying Australian pines, watersports rentals, and shaded picnic grounds. It also hosts, from mid-January through mid-April, an alfresco collection of oversize art called Sculpture Key West, which changes annually and showcases artists from across the country.

BIRDING IN THE KEYS

The Florida Keys beaches can be great places to look to the skies and waters for all varieties of birds. Permanent residents include shorebirds—plovers, ruddy turnstones, willets, and short-billed dowitchers; wading birds—roseat spoonbills, great blue herons, great white egrets, snowy egrets, tri-colored herons, and white ibis; brown pelicans; osprey; and turkey vultures. In the autumn, hawks migrate through the region, while in winter ducks and white pelicans make their debut. In the summer, white-crowned pigeons are commonly seen.

GREAT ITINERARIES

If You Have 3 Days

Spend your first morning diving or snorkeling at John Pennekamp Coral Reef State Park in **Key Largo.** Celebrate sunset with dinner at a waterside restaurant. On Day 2 savor the breathtaking views on the two-hour drive to Key West. Along the way stop at Crane Point Museum, Nature Center and Historic Site in **Marathon.** Another worthwhile detour is Bahia Honda Key State Park on **Bahia Honda Key,** where you can stretch your legs on a nature trail or snorkel on an offshore reef. Once you arrive in **Key West,** watch the sunset at the Mallory Square celebration. The next day, take a trolley tour of Old Town, stroll Duval Street and visit a museum or two, or spend some beach time at Fort Zachary Taylor Historic State Park.

If You Have 7 Days

Spend your first day as you would in the above itinerary, but stay both the second and third nights in **Islamorada,** fitting in some fishing, boating, or kayaking excursions from Robbie's Marina and a visit to Theater of the Sea. On the fourth morning head to **Marathon.** Visit Crane Point Museum, Nature Center and Historic Site and walk out on the Old Seven Mile Bridge or take the ferry to Pigeon Key. Spend the night and head the next morning to Bahia Honda State Park on **Bahia Honda Key** for snor-

keling, kayaking, fishing, hiking, and beaching. Spend the night in a waterfront cabin or in the campground. On your sixth day, continue to **Key West,** and get in a little sightseeing before watching the sun set at Mallory Square and spending the night and your last day visiting the sites, shops, restaurants, and bars in one of America's most lauded vacation spots.

If You Have 10 Days

To the seven-day itinerary add a few hours on Sombrero Beach in **Marathon** on Day 4, and spend the night in a local resort. Devote Day 6 to either snorkeling or diving at Looe Key Reef and a visit to the National Key Deer Refuge on **Big Pine Key.** Spend the night in the Lower Keys before heading to **Key West.** On Day 7, take a break from driving at Fort Zachary Taylor Historic State Park beach. Explore the fort and nearby Eco-Discovery Center. Book ferry passage to **Dry Tortugas National Park** for Day 8 to snorkel and explore the fort. Spend the remaining couple of nights and days sampling Key West's attractions and nightlife.

The Upper Keys

2

WORD OF MOUTH

"The Casa Morada [in Upper Matecumbe Key] was lovely. It is a boutique hotel one block off U.S. 1, but feels like you are in another world. The staff couldn't have been nicer or more helpful. The room came with a lovely breakfast buffet served on an outdoor terrace down by the water. Bottled water and snacks in the refrigerator in the suite were complimentary."

—theatrelover

By Chelle
Koster
Walton

DIVING AND SNORKELING RULE IN THE UPPER KEYS,
thanks to the tropical coral reef that runs a few miles off the
Atlantic coast. Divers of all skill levels benefit from accessible dive sites and an established tourism infrastructure.
Fishing is another huge draw, especially around Islamorada,
known for its sportfishing in both deep offshore waters
and in the backcountry. Offshore islands accessible only
by boat are popular destinations for kayakers. In short, if
you don't like the water you might get bored here.

Other nature lovers won't feel shortchanged. Within 1½
miles of the bay coast lie the mangrove trees and sandy
shores of Everglades National Park, where naturalists lead
tours of one of the world's few saltwater forests. Here
you'll see endangered manatees, curious dolphins, and
other marine creatures. Although the number of birds has
dwindled since John James Audubon captured their beauty
on canvas, bird-watchers will find plenty to see, including
the rare Everglades snail kite, bald eagles, ospreys, and a
colorful array of egrets and herons. At sunset flocks take
flight as they gather to find their night's roost, adding a
swirl of activity to an otherwise quiet time of day.

ORIENTATION AND PLANNING

GETTING ORIENTED

The best way to explore this stretch, or any stretch, of the
Florida Keys is by boat. As soon as possible you should
jump on any seaworthy vessel to see the view of and from
the water. And make sure you veer off the main drag of U.S.
1. Head toward the water, where you'll often find the kind
of laid-back restaurants and hotels that define the Keys.
John Pennekamp Coral Reef State Park is the region's most
popular destination, but it's certainly not the only place to
get in touch with nature.

PLANNING

GETTING HERE AND AROUND

Airporter operates scheduled van and bus pick-up service
from all Miami International Airport (MIA) baggage areas
to wherever you want to go in Key Largo ($50) and Islamorada ($55). Groups of three or more passengers receive
discounts. There are three departures daily; reservations are
preferred 48 hours in advance. The SuperShuttle charges
about $160 for up to 10 passengers for nonstop trips from

TOP REASONS TO GO

■ **Snorkeling.** The best snorkeling spots in these parts are to be found around the awe-inspiring Christ of the Abyss east of John Pennekamp Coral Reef State Park in the Florida Keys National Marine Sanctuary.

■ **Sunsets.** Find a comfortable place to watch the sunset, keeping an eye out for the elusive green flash.

■ **Aquatic Mammals.** Get up close and personal with a

dolphin or sea lion at Theater of the Sea or a number of other dolphin attractions.

■ **Boating.** Start with a visit to Robbie's Marina on Lower Matecumbe Key in Islamorada, a salty spot to find everything from fishing charters to kayak rentals.

■ **Nightlife.** It's not a disco, but you can dance the night away to music by local bands at Lorelei's Cabana Bar.

Miami International Airport to the Upper Keys. Shared-ride trips are also available. For trips to the airport, place your request 24 hours in advance.

ESSENTIALS
Transportation Contacts Airporter ☎ *305/852–3413, 800/830–3413.* **SuperShuttle** ☎ *305/871–2000* ⊕ *www.supershuttle.com.*

RESTAURANTS
The Upper Keys are full of low-key eateries where the owner is also the chef and the food is tasty and never too fussy. The one exception is Islamorada, where you'll find more upscale restaurants. Restaurants may close for a two- to four-week vacation during the slow season between early September and mid-November.

HOTELS
In the Upper Keys the accommodations are as varied as they are plentiful. Most lodgings are in small, narrow waterfront complexes with efficiencies and one- or two-bedroom units. These places offer dockage and often arrange boating, diving, and fishing excursions. There are also larger resorts with every type of activity imaginable and smaller boutique hotels where the attraction is personalized service. Depending on which way the wind blows and how close the property is to the highway, there may be some noise from U.S. 1. If this is an annoyance for you, ask for a room as far from the traffic as possible. Some properties require two- or three-day minimum stays during holiday

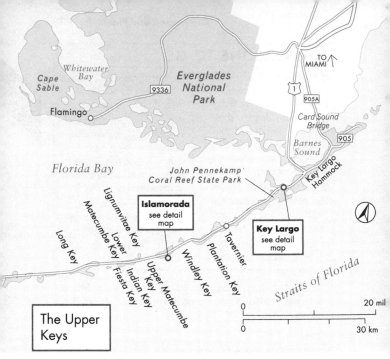

The Upper Keys

and high-season weekends. Conversely, discounts apply for midweek, weekly, and monthly stays. Campgrounds and RV parks with full hookups charge around $50.

HOTEL AND RESTAURANT PRICES

Prices in the restaurant reviews are the average cost of a main course at dinner or, if dinner is not served, at lunch, excluding taxes and service charges. Prices in the hotel reviews are the lowest cost of a standard double room in high season, excluding taxes, service charges, and meal plans (except at all-inclusives). Prices for rentals are the lowest per-night cost for a one-bedroom unit in high season.

KEY LARGO

56 miles south of Miami International Airport.

The first of the Upper Keys reachable by car, 30-mile-long Key Largo is the largest island in the chain. Key Largo—named Cayo Largo ("Long Key") by the Spanish—makes a great introduction to the region. This is the gateway to the Keys, and an evening of fresh seafood and views of the sunset on the water will get you in the right state of mind.

The history of Largo reads similar to that of the rest of the Keys: a succession of native people, pirates, wreckers, and developers. The first settlement on Key Largo was named Planter, back in the days of pineapple and later key lime plantations. For a time it was a convenient shipping port, but when the railroad arrived Planter died on the vine. Today three communities—North Key Largo, Key Largo, and Tavernier—make up the whole of Key Largo.

What's there to do on Key Largo besides gaze at the sunset? Not much if you're not into diving or snorkeling. Nobody comes to Key Largo without visiting John Pennkamp Coral Reef State Park, one of the jewels of the state park system. Water sports enthusiasts head to the adjacent Key Largo National Marine Sanctuary, which encompasses about 190 square miles of coral reefs, sea-grass beds, and mangrove estuaries. If you've never tried diving, Key Largo is the perfect place to learn. Dozens of companies will be more than happy to show you the ropes.

Fishing is the other big draw, and world records are broken regularly in the waters around the Upper Keys. There are plenty of charter companies to help you find the big ones and teach you how to hook the elusive bonefish, sometimes known as the ghost fish.

On land, Key Largo provides all the conveniences of a major resort town, including restaurants that will cook your catch or prepare their own creations with inimitable style. You'll notice that some unusual specialties pop up on the menu, such as cracked conch, spiny lobster, and stone crab. Don't pass up a chance to try the local delicacies, especially the key lime pie.

Most businesses are lined up along U.S. 1, the four-lane highway that runs down the middle of the island. Cars whiz past at all hours—something to remember when you're booking a room. Most lodgings are on the highway, so you'll want to be as far back as possible. Look at MM 95 for the mural painted in 2011 to commemorate the 100th anniversary of the railroad to the Keys.

GETTING HERE AND AROUND

Key Largo is 56 miles south of Miami International Airport, the mile markers ranging from 106 to 91. The island runs northeast–southwest, with the Overseas Highway, divided by a median most of the way, running down the center. If the highway is your only glimpse of the island, you're likely

CLOSE UP

The Mile Marker System

Getting lost in the Keys is almost impossible once you understand the unique address system. **Many addresses are simply given as a mile marker (MM) number.** The markers are small, green, rectangular signs along the side of the Overseas Highway (U.S. 1). They begin with MM 126, 1 mile south of Florida City, and end with MM 0, in Key West.

Keys residents use the abbreviation BS for the bay side of Overseas Highway and OS for the ocean side. From Marathon to Key West, residents may refer to the bay side as the gulf side.

---

to feel barraged by its tacky commercial side. Make a point of driving Route 905 in North Key Largo and down side streets to get a better feel for it.

ESSENTIALS
Visitor Information Key Largo Chamber of Commerce ✉ *MM 106 BS, 10600 Overseas Hwy.* ☎ *305/451–4747, 800/822–1088* ⊕ *www.keylargochamber.org.*

EXPLORING

Dagny Johnson Key Largo Hammock Botanical State Park. American crocodiles, mangrove cuckoos, white-crowned pigeons, Schaus swallowtail butterflies, mahogany mistletoe, wild cotton, and 100 other rare critters and plants inhabit these 2,400 acres, sandwiched between Crocodile Lake National Wildlife Refuge and Pennekamp Coral Reef State Park. The park is also a user-friendly place to explore the largest remaining stand of the vast West Indian tropical hardwood hammock and mangrove wetland that once covered most of the Keys' upland areas. Interpretive signs describe many of the tropical tree species along a wide 1-mi paved road (2-mi round-trip) that invites walking and biking. There are also more than 6 mi of nature trails accessible to bikes and wheelchairs. Pets are welcome if on a leash no longer than 6 feet. You'll also find restrooms, information kiosks, and picnic tables. ✉ *0.5 mi north of Overseas Hwy., Rte. 905 OS, North Key Largo* ☎ *305/451–1202* ⊕ *www.floridastateparks.org/keylargohammock* ⚟ *$2.50* ☉ *Daily 8–sundown.*

Key Largo

KEY
- **1** Restaurants
- ① Hotels
- Dive Site
- Boat Launch

Restaurants

Alabama Jack's, **1**

Ballyhoo's, **8**

Chad's Deli & Bakery, **11**

The Fish House, **5**

The Fish House Encore, **4**

Harriette's Restaurant, **9**

Key Largo Conch House, **7**

Mrs. Mac's Kitchen, **2**

Rib Daddy's Steak & Seafood, **6**

Snapper's, **10**

Sundowners, **3**

Hotels

Amy Slate's Amoray Dive Resort, **2**

Azul Del Mar, **3**

Coconut Bay Resort & Bay Harbor Lodge, **8**

Coconut Palm Inn, **12**

Dove Creek Lodge, **11**

Key Largo Grande Resort & Beach Club, **1**

Kona Kai Resort, **9**

Largo Lodge, **5**

Marriott's Key Largo Bay Beach Resort, **4**

The Pelican, **6**

Popp's Motel, **10**

Seafarer Resort, **7**

Florida Keys Wild Bird Center. Have a nose-to-beak encounter with ospreys, hawks, herons, and other unreleasable birds at this bird rehabilitation center. The birds live in spacious screened enclosures along a boardwalk running through some of the best waterfront real estate in the Keys. Rehabilitated birds are set free, whereas about 30 have become permanent residents. Free birds—especially pelicans and egrets—come to visit. A short nature trail runs into the mangrove forest (bring bug spray May to October). ⊠ *MM 93.6 BS, 93600 Overseas Hwy., Tavernier* ☎ *305/852–4486* ⊕ *www.fkwbc.org* ☞ *Free, donations accepted* ⊙ *Daily sunrise–sunset.*

MAKING MOVIES. The 1948 film noir classic *Key Largo*, starring Humphrey Bogart and Lauren Bacall, was the most famous movie filmed in the Florida Keys, but not the only one. Others have included *Beneath the Twelve Mile Reef, PT 109, License to Kill, True Lies, Speed 2,* and *Red Dragon*. Key Largo is also where the steamboat used in the film *The African Queen* came to live in 1983. On display at MM 100, it recently underwent a $60,000 restoration to enable it to do tours.

Ⓒ **Jacobs Aquatic Center.** Take the plunge at one of three swimming pools: an 8-lane, 25-meter lap pool with a diving well; a 3- to 4-foot-deep pool accessible to people with mobility problems; and an interactive play pool with a waterslide, pirate ship, waterfall, and sloping zero entry instead of steps. ⊠ *MM 99.6 OS, 320 Laguna Ave., at St. Croix Pl. (at Key Largo Community Park)* ☎ *305/453–7946* ⊕ *www.jacobsaquaticcenter.org* ☞ *$8–$10* ⊙ *Daily 10–6, (10–7 in summer).*

★ **Fodor's**Choice **John Pennekamp Coral Reef State Park.** This state
Ⓒ park is on everyone's list for close access to the best diving and snorkeling sites in the Sunshine State. The underwater treasure encompasses 78 square miles of coral reefs, seagrass beds, and mangrove swamps and lies adjacent to the Florida Keys National Marine Sanctuary, which contains 40 of the 52 species of coral in the Atlantic Reef System and nearly 600 varieties of fish, from the colorful stoplight parrot fish to the demure cocoa damselfish. The park's visitor center has a 30,000-gallon floor-to-ceiling fish tank surrounded by smaller ones, so you can get a closer look at many of the underwater creatures. When you want to head out to sea, a concessionaire rents kayaks and powerboats, as well as snorkeling and diving equipment. You

can also sign up for snorkeling and diving trips ($30 and $55, respectively, equipment extra) and glass-bottom-boat rides to the reef ($24). One of the most popular excursions is the snorkeling trip to see *Christ of the Deep,* the 2-ton underwater statue of Jesus. The park also has short nature trails, two man-made beaches, picnic shelters, a snack bar, and a campground. ⊠ *MM 102.5 OS, 102601 Overseas Hwy.* ☎ *305/451–1202 for park, 305/451–6300 for excursions* ⊕ *www.pennekamppark.com, www.floridastateparks. org/pennekamp* ⊠ *$4.50 for 1 person in vehicle, $8 for 2–8 people, $2 for pedestrians and cyclists or extra people* ☉ *Daily 8–sunset.*

WHERE TO EAT

★ **Fodor's** Choice ✕ **Alabama Jack's.** *Seafood.* Calories be damned—
$ the conch fritters here are heaven on a plate. The crab cakes, made from local blue crabs, earn hallelujahs, too. The conch salad is as good as any you'll find in the Bahamas and a third of the price in trendy Keys restaurants. This weathered, circa-1950 restaurant floats on two roadside barges in an old fishing community. Regulars include weekend cyclists, Miamians on the lam, and boaters, who come to admire tropical birds in the nearby mangroves, the occasional crocodile in the canal, or the bands that play on weekend afternoons. ■ **TIP→ It's about a half-hour drive from Key Largo, so you may want to plan a visit for your drive in or out.** Jack's closes by 7, when the mosquitoes start biting. ⑤ *Average main: $11* ⊠ *58000 Card Sound Rd.* ☎ *305/248–8741* ⌧ *Reservations not accepted.*

$$$ ✕ **Ballyhoo's.** *Seafood.* Occupying a historic Conch house with an outdoor patio, this place is all about the fish (including the nicely nautical fish-house decor). Yellowtail snapper, one of the moistest, most flavorful local fish, is served ten different ways on the all-day menu, including blackened, stuffed with crab, and Parmesan-crusted. During stone-crab season (mid-October to mid-May) get in on the all-you-can-eat special. Typically Keys, the service is uneven at best, but the black beans and rice and the burgers settle the score. ⑤ *Average main: $21* ⊠ *MM 97.8 median, 97800 Overseas Hwy.* ☎ *305/852–0822* ⊕ *www.ballyhoosrestaurant.com* ⌧ *Reservations not accepted.*

$ ✕ **Chad's Deli & Bakery.** *American.* It's a deli! It's a bakery! It's a pasta place! By day, Chad's serves monster sandwiches in pita wraps, rolls, or subs. It also offers pizza (try the garlic chicken white pizza), pasta dishes, quesadillas, no-carb stir-fries, salads, burgers, and breakfast. Everyone loves the chicken parm, and there's a good selection of beer and wine to wash it all down. Of course, you may bypass all this and make a meal out of one of Chad's eight varieties of cookies, approximately the size of your head, including white-chocolate macadamia-nut and chocolate-chip. ⑤ *Average main: $10* ⊠ *MM 92.3 BS, 92330 Overseas Hwy., Tavernier* ☎ *305/853–5566* ⊕ *www.chadsdeli.com* ⚏ *Reservations not accepted.*

$$$ ✕ **The Fish House.** *Seafood.* Restaurants not on the water
★ have to produce the highest quality food to survive in the Keys. That's how the Fish House has succeeded since the 1980s—so much so that it built the Fish House Encore next door to accommodate fans. The pan-sautéed black grouper will make you moan with pleasure, but it's just one of many headliners in this nautical eatery. On the fin side, the choices include mahimahi, swordfish, tuna, and yellowtail snapper that can be broiled, blackened, baked, or fried. The Matecumbe Catch prepares the day's fresh fish so simply and flavorfully it should be patented—baked with tomatoes, capers, olive oil, and lemon juice. Prefer shellfish? Choose from shrimp, lobster, and (mid-October to mid-May) stone crab. For a sweet ending, try the homemade key lime pie. ⑤ *Average main: $21* ⊠ *MM 102.4 OS, 102341 Overseas Hwy.* ☎ *305/451–4665* ⊕ *www.fishhouse. com* ⚏ *Reservations not accepted* ⊘ *Closed Sept.*

$$$ ✕ **The Fish House Encore.** *Seafood.* To accommodate the crowds that gather at the Fish House, the owners opened this place with similar but more refined cuisine ranging from sushi to steak. It has come into its own as a slightly more formal dining venue than its sister establishment. In the off-season you can get your money's worth with $20 all-you-can-eat specials such as mahimahi, snow crab, and peel 'n' eat shrimp. The favorite, more casual place to dine is on the patio near the trickling fountain. Live piano music entertains Thursday through Sunday. ⑤ *Average main: $23* ⊠ *MM 102.3 OS, 102341 Overseas Hwy.* ☎ *305/451–4665, 305/451–0650* ⊕ *www.fishhouse.com* ⚏ *Reservations not accepted* ⊘ *No lunch. Closed Oct.*

$ ✕ **Harriette's Restaurant.** *American.* If you're looking for comfort food—like melt-in-your-mouth buttermilk biscuits—try this refreshing throwback. The kitchen makes fresh muffins daily, in flavors like mango, chocolate, and key lime. Little has changed over the years in this yellow-and-turquoise eatery. Owner Harriette Mattson often personally greets guests who come for steak and eggs with hash browns or old-fashioned hotcakes with sausage or bacon. Stick to simple dishes; the eggs Benedict are a disappointment. At lunch- and dinnertime, Harriette's shines in the burger department, but there are also hot meals such as chicken-fried steak and a fried shrimp basket. ⑤ *Average main: $8* ✉ *MM 95.7 BS, 95710 Overseas Hwy.* ☎ *305/852–8689* ⚏ *Reservations not accepted* ⊘ *No dinner Fri.–Sun.*

$ ✕ **Key Largo Conch House.** *American.* Tucked into the trees along the Overseas Highway, this Victorian-style home and its true-to-the-Keys style of cooking are worth seeking out—at least the Food Network and the Travel Channel have thought so in the past. Family-owned since 2004, it feels welcoming either indoors around the coffee bar or on the Old South veranda. Raisin pecan French toast and eight varieties of Benedicts, including conch, are reason enough to rise early and get your fresh coffee fix. Lunch and dinner menus cover all bases from conch chowder bread bowl and vegetarian wraps to lobster and conch ceviche, andouille Alfredo, and yellowtail Florentine. ⑤ *Average main: $15* ✉ *Key Largo* ☎ *305/453–4844* ⊕ *www.keylargoconchhouse. com* ⚏ *Reservations essential.*

$ ✕ **Mrs. Mac's Kitchen.** *Seafood.* Townies pack the counters and booths at this tiny eatery, where license plates are stuck on the walls and made into chandeliers. Got a hankering for meat loaf or crab cakes? You'll find them here, along with specials like grilled yellowfin tuna. Bring your appetite for the all-you-can-eat catfish special on Tuesday and all-you-can-eat spaghetti on Thursday. There's also champagne breakfast, an assortment of tasty Angus beef burgers and sandwiches, and its famous chili and key lime freeze (somewhere between a shake and a float). In season, ask about the hogfish special du jour. ⑤ *Average main: $15* ✉ *MM 99.4 BS, 99336 Overseas Hwy.* ☎ *305/451–3722* ⊕ *www.mrsmacskitchen.com* ⚏ *Reservations not accepted* ⊘ *Closed Sun.*

$$$ ✕ **Rib Daddy's Steak & Seafood.** *Seafood.* This comfort-food haven opens for breakfast, lunch, and dinner. Dieters, keep driving. Sunday's brunch buffet has everything the restaurant is famous for with a $14.95 price tag. On the meat side of things, there's Memphis-style barbecue ribs and steaks. Seafood options include crab cakes, seafood pasta, and fresh fish. Try the Hemingway (fried mahimahi and eggs) for breakfast or either the hand-pulled pork sandwich or blackened chicken wrap for lunch. Save room for the key lime pie, creamy mango pie, or coconut cake. Kids love staring at the reef aquarium, the highlight of this rather plain,

open dining room. Ⓢ *Average main: $22* ⊠ *MM 102.2 BS, 102570 Overseas Hwy.* ☎ *305/451–0900* ⊕ *www.ribdaddysrestaurant.com* ⌒ *Reservations not accepted.*

$$ ✕ **Snapper's.** *Seafood.* "You hook 'em, we cook 'em" is the
★ motto here. Alas, "cleanin' 'em" is not part of the bargain. If you bring in your ready-for-the-grill fish, dinner here is $12 for a single, $13 per person family style with a mix of preparations. Otherwise, they'll catch and prepare you a plank-roasted yellowtail snapper, Thai-seared tuna, fish of the day baked with 36 herbs and spices, or a little something from the raw bar. The ceviche of yellowtail, shrimp, and conch (merrily spiced) wins raves, too. The seafood burrito on the sandwich board is a keeper. All this is served up in a lively, mangrove-ringed waterfront setting with live music, an aquarium bar, Sunday brunch (including a Bloody Mary bar), killer rum drinks, and seating alongside the fishing dock. Three-course early-bird dinner specials are available 5–6 for $18.50. Ⓢ *Average main: $15* ⊠ *MM 94.5 OS, 139 Seaside Ave.* ☎ *305/852–5956* ⊕ *www.snapperskeylargo. com* ⌒ *Reservations not accepted.*

$$$ ✕ **Sundowners.** *American.* The name doesn't lie. If it's a clear night and you can snag a reservation, this restaurant will treat you to a sherbet-hue sunset over Florida Bay. If you're here in mild weather—anytime other than the dog days of summer or the rare winter cold snap—the best seats are on the patio. The food is excellent: try the key lime seafood, a happy combo of sautéed shrimp, lobster, and lump crabmeat swimming in a tangy sauce spiked with Tabasco served over penne or rice. Wednesday and Saturday are all about prime rib, and Friday draws the crowds with an all-you-can-eat fish fry ($16). Vegetarian and gluten-free menus are available. Ⓢ *Average main: $22* ⊠ *MM 104 BS, 103900 Overseas Hwy.* ☎ *305/451–4502* ⊕ *sundownerskeylargo.com* ⌒ *Reservations essential.*

WHERE TO STAY

For expanded reviews, facilities, and current deals, visit Fodors.com.

$$$ ⚏ **Amy Slate's Amoray Dive Resort.** *Resort.* The double entendre in its name sums up this hotel's dual charms. **Pros:** top-notch dive operation; free use of kayaks and snorkel equipment. **Cons:** noise from highway. Ⓢ *Rooms from: $159* ⊠ *MM 104.2 BS, 104250 Overseas Hwy.* ☎ *305/451–3595, 800/426–6729* ⊕ *www.amoray.com* ⇌ *23 rooms, 8 apartments* ⓘⓄⓘ *No meals.*

$$$ 🏨 **Azul del Mar.** *B&B/Inn.* The dock points the way to many ★ beautiful sunsets at this adults-only boutique hotel. **Pros:** great garden; good location; sophisticated design. **Cons:** small beach; close to highway; high-priced. Ⓢ *Rooms from: $189 ✉ MM 104.3 BS, 104300 Overseas Hwy. ☎305/451–0337, 888/253–2985 ⊕ www.azulhotels.us ⌁2 studios, 3 1-bedroom suites, 1 2-bedroom suite* ⎮◎⎮ *No meals.*

$$ 🏨 **Coconut Bay Resort & Bay Harbor Lodge.** *Resort.* Some 200 feet of waterfront is the main attraction at this property, a combination of two lodging options. **Pros:** bay front; neatly kept gardens; walking distance to restaurants; complimentary kayak and paddleboat use. **Cons:** a bit dated; small sea-walled sand beach. Ⓢ *Rooms from: $105 ✉ MM 97.7 BS, 97702 Overseas Hwy. ☎305/852–1625, 800/385–0986 ⊕ www.coconutbaykeylargo.com ⌁7 rooms, 5 efficiencies, 2 suites, 1 2-bedroom villa, 6 1-bedroom cottages* ⎮◎⎮ *No meals.*

$$$ 🏨 **Coconut Palm Inn.** *B&B/Inn.* This low-key inn is set in a quiet residential neighborhood of towering gumbo-limbo and buttonwood trees. **Pros:** lovely beach; tranquil location; complimentary use of kayaks and paddleboats. **Cons:** off the beaten path. Ⓢ *Rooms from: $209 ✉ MM 92 BS, 198 Harborview Dr., via Jo-Jean Way off Overseas Hwy., Tavernier ☎305/852–3017 ⊕ www.coconutpalminn.com ⌁13 rooms, 7 suites* ⎮◎⎮ *Breakfast.*

$$$$ 🏨 **Dove Creek Lodge.** *B&B/Inn.* Old-school anglers will likely be scandalized by this 2004 fishing camp's sherbet-hue paint and plantation-style furnishings. **Pros:** great for fishing enthusiasts; luxurious rooms; close to Snapper's restaurant. **Cons:** loud music next door. Ⓢ *Rooms from: $229 ✉ MM 94.5 OS, 147 Seaside Ave. ☎305/852–6200, 800/401–0057 ⊕ www.dovecreeklodge.com ⌁4 room, 10 suites* ⎮◎⎮ *Breakfast.*

$$$ 🏨 **Key Largo Grande Resort & Beach Club.** *Resort.* Nestled within a hardwood hammock (localese for uplands habitat where hardwood trees such as live oak grow) near the southern border of Everglades National Park, this sprawling hotel offers a full slate of amenities in a woodsy setting. **Pros:** nice nature trail on bay side; pretty pools with waterfalls; awesome trees; bicycles available for rent. **Cons:** pools near the highway; $14 per night for parking. Ⓢ *Rooms from: $159 ✉ MM 97 BS, 97000 Overseas Hwy. ☎305/852–5553, 888/871–3437 ⊕ www.keylargogrande.com ⌁190 rooms, 10 suites* ⎮◎⎮ *No meals.*

★ **Fodor's**Choice 🏨 **Kona Kai Resort, Gallery & Botanic Gardens.**
$$$$ *Resort.* Brilliantly colored bougainvilleas, coconut palms, guava trees, and a new botanical garden of rare species

make this 2-acre hideaway one of the prettiest places to stay in the Keys. **Pros:** free custom tours of botanical gardens for guests; free use of sports equipment; knowledgeable staff. **Cons:** expensive; some rooms are very close together. $ *Rooms from: $269* ⊠ *MM 97.8 BS, 97802 Overseas Hwy.* ☎ *305/852–7200, 800/365–7829* ⊕ *www.konakairesort. com* ⇌ *8 suites, 3 rooms* ⊙ *Closed Sept.* |○| *No meals.*

$$$ ⚏ **Largo Lodge.** *B&B/Inn.* When you drive under the dense
★ canopy of foliage at the entrance to Largo Lodge you'll feel like you've escaped Overseas Highway's bustle. **Pros:** lush grounds; great sunset views; affordable rates; boat docking. **Cons:** no pool; some traffic noise outdoors. $ *Rooms from: $175* ⊠ *MM 101.7 BS, 101740 Overseas Hwy.* ☎ *305/451– 0424, 800/468–4378* ⊕ *www.largolodge.com* ⇌ *2 rooms, 6 cottages* |○| *No meals.*

$$ ⚏ **Marriott's Key Largo Bay Beach Resort.** *Resort.* This 17-acre
★ bay-side resort has plenty of diversions, from diving to
☾ parasailing to a day spa. **Pros:** lots of activities; free covered parking; dive shop on property; free Wi-Fi. **Cons:** rooms facing highway can be noisy; thin walls; unspectacular beach. $ *Rooms from: $139* ⊠ *MM 103.8 BS, 103800 Overseas Hwy.* ☎ *305/453–0000, 866/849–3753* ⊕ *www. marriottkeylargo.com* ⇌ *132 rooms, 20 2-bedroom suites, 1 penthouse suite* |○| *No meals.*

$ ⚏ **The Pelican.** *Hotel.* This 1950s throwback is reminiscent of the days when parents packed the kids into the station wagon and headed to no-frills seaside motels, complete with an old-timer fishing off the dock. **Pros:** free use of kayaks and a canoe; well-maintained dock; reasonable rates. **Cons:** some small rooms; basic accommodations and amenities. $ *Rooms from: $60* ⊠ *MM 99.3, 99340 Overseas Hwy.* ☎ *305/451–3576, 877/451–3576* ⊕ *www. hungrypelican.com* ⇌ *13 rooms, 4 efficiencies, 4 suites, 2 trailers* |○| *No meals.*

$$ ⚏ **Popp's Motel.** *Hotel.* Stylized metal herons mark the entrance to this 50-year-old family-run motel. **Pros:** beach; intimate feel; multiple night discounts. **Cons:** limited amenities. $ *Rooms from: $129* ⊠ *95500 Overseas Hwy.(MM 95.5 BS)* ☎ *305/852–5201, 877/852–5201* ⊕ *www.popps. com* ⇌ *9 units* |○| *No meals.*

$ ⚏ **Seafarer Resort.** *Hotel.* It's very basic budget lodging, but the Seafarer Resort is not without its charms. **Pros:** sandy beach; complimentary kayak use; cheap rates. **Cons:** some rooms close to road noise; some complaints about cleanliness; no toiletries of any kind provided. $ *Rooms from: $85* ⊠ *MM 97.6 BS, 97684 Overseas Hwy.* ☎ *305/852–*

5349 ⊕www.seafarerresort.com ⊸8 rooms, 3 studios, 3 1-bedroom cottages, 1 2-bedroom cottage, 2 apartments ᴦ◎ᴵNo meals.

NIGHTLIFE

The semiweekly *Keynoter* (Wednesday and Saturday), weekly *Reporter* (Thursday), and Friday through Sunday editions of the *Miami Herald* are the best sources of information on entertainment and nightlife. Daiquiri bars, tiki huts, and seaside shacks pretty well summarize Key Largo's bar scene.

Breezers Tiki Bar & Grille. Mingle with locals over cocktails and sunsets at Marriott's Key Largo Bay Beach Resort. ⊠*MM 103.8 BS, 103800 Overseas Hwy.* ☎*305/453–0000.*

★ **Caribbean Club.** Walls plastered with Bogart memorabilia remind customers that the classic 1948 Bogart–Bacall flick *Key Largo* has a connection with this club. It draws boaters, curious visitors, and local barfly types, all of whom happily mingle and shoot pool. Postcard-perfect sunsets and live music draw revelers on weekends. ⊠*MM 104 BS, 10404 Overseas Hwy.* ☎*305/451–4466.*

Coconuts. Live music fills both the indoor and outdoor areas of this bar throughout most of the week. Outside around the pool it's a family scene, with food service and a bar. Inside is strictly a thirty- and fortysomething crowd, including a few seasoned townies, playing pool, watching sports TV, and enjoying the music. ⊠*MM 100 OS, Marina Del Mar Resort, 528 Caribbean Dr.* ☎*305/453–9794.*

SPORTS AND THE OUTDOORS

BIKING

Not as big a pursuit as on other islands, biking can be a little dangerous along Key Largo's main drag. Parts of the still-developing Florida Keys Overseas Heritage Trail take you off Highway 1 along Old Highway.

Bubba's. Bubba's organizes custom biking tours through the Keys along the heritage trail. A van accompanies tours to carry luggage and tired riders. Operated by former police officer Bubba Barron, Bubba's hosts an annual one-week ride down the length of the Keys every November. Riders can opt for tent camping ($645) or motel-room accommodations. Meals are included and bike rentals are extra. ☎*321/759–3433 ⊕www.bubbafestbiketours.com.*

BOATING

Everglades Eco-Tours. Captain Sterling operates Everglades and Florida Bay ecology tours ($50 per person) and sunset cruises ($75 per person). ✉ *MM 104 BS, Sundowners Restaurant, 103900 Overseas Hwy.* ☎ *305/853–5161, 888/224–6044* ⊕ *www.captainsterling.com.*

M.V. *Key Largo Princess.* Two-hour glass-bottom-boat trips and sunset cruises on a luxury 75-foot motor yacht with a 280-square-foot glass viewing area (each $30) depart from the Holiday Inn docks three times a day. ✉ *MM 100 OS, 99701 Overseas Hwy.* ☎ *305/451–4655, 877/648–8129* ⊕ *www.keylargoprincess.com.*

CANOEING AND KAYAKING

Sea kayaking continues to gain popularity in the Keys. You can paddle for a few hours or the whole day, on your own or with a guide. Some outfitters even offer overnight trips. The **Florida Keys Overseas Paddling Trail,** part of a statewide system, runs from Key Largo to Key West. You can paddle the entire distance, 110 miles on the Atlantic side, which takes 9 to 10 days. The trail also runs the chain's length on the bay side, which is a longer route.

Coral Reef Park Co. At John Pennekamp Coral Reef State Park, this operator has a fleet of canoes and kayaks for gliding around the 2½-mi mangrove trail or along the coast. It also rents powerboats. ✉ *MM 102.5 OS, 102601 Overseas Hwy.* ☎ *305/451–6300* ⊕ *www.pennekamppark.com.*

Florida Bay Outfitters. Rent canoes or sea kayaks from this company, which sets up self-guided trips on the Florida Keys Overseas Paddling Trail, helps with trip planning, and matches equipment to your skill level. It also runs myriad guided tours around Key Largo. Take a full-moon paddle or a one- to seven-day canoe or kayak tour to the Everglades, Lignumvitae Key, or Indian Key. Trips start at $60 for three hours. ✉ *MM 104 BS, 104050 Overseas Hwy.* ☎ *305/451–3018* ⊕ *www.kayakfloridakeys.com.*

DOLPHIN INTERACTION PROGRAMS

The Keys have the greatest concentration of places where visitors can interact with dolphins. Some people, especially children, love learning about the dolphins and seeing them up close, while others bristle at seeing the animals kept in captivity to serve public whims. If you're among the latter, you'll want to avoid these programs and perhaps opt for a dolphin-spotting tour in the wild (but even these are questioned by some environmentalists if the tour operators do anything to attract the dolphins to the boat). Feeding them is strictly taboo, but some tour operators slap the side of the boat and circle around the spotted dolphin. For listings of businesses that are recognized as dolphin-friendly by the National Oceanic and Atmospheric Administration (NOAA), visit ⊕ *www.dolphinsmart.org.*

Dolphin Cove. This educational program begins at the facility's lagoon with a get-acquainted session from a platform. After that, you slip into the water for some frolicking with your new dolphin pals. The cost is $135 to $185. Spend the day shadowing a dolphin trainer for $630. Admission for nonparticipants is $10 for adults. ⊠ *MM 101.9 BS, 101900 Overseas Hwy.* ☎ *305/451–4020, 877/365–2683* ⊕ *www.dolphinscove.com.*

Dolphins Plus. A sister property to Dolphin Cove, Dolphin Plus offers some of the same programs. Costing $135, the Natural Swim program begins with a one-hour briefing; then you enter the water to become totally immersed in the dolphins' world. In this visual orientation, participants snorkel but are not allowed to touch the dolphins. For tactile interaction (kissing, fin tows, etc.), sign up for the Structured Swim program ($185). The same concept with different critters, the sea lion swim costs $120. ⊠ *MM 99, 31 Corrine Pl.* ☎ *305/451–1993, 866/860–7946* ⊕ *www. dolphinsplus.com.*

FISHING
Private charters and big head boats (so named because they charge "by the head") are great for anglers who don't have their own vessel.

Sailors Choice. Fishing excursions depart twice daily ($40 cash for half-day trips). The 65-foot boat leaves from the Holiday Inn docks. Rods, bait, and license are included. ⊠ *MM 100 OS, Holiday Inn Resort & Marina, 99701 Overseas Hwy.* ☎ *305/451–1802, 305/451–0041* ⊕ *www. sailorschoicefishingboat.com.*

SCUBA DIVING AND SNORKELING
Much of what makes the Upper Keys a singular dive destination is variety. Places like Molasses Reef, which begins 3 feet below the surface and descends to 55 feet, have something for everyone from novice snorkelers to experienced divers. The *Spiegel Grove,* a 510-foot vessel, lies in 130 feet of water, but its upper regions are only 60 feet below

the surface. On rough days, Key Largo Undersea Park's Emerald Lagoon is a popular spot. Expect to pay about $80 to $85 for a two-tank, two-site dive trip with tanks and weights, or $35 to $40 for a two-site snorkel outing. Get big discounts by booking multiple trips.

Amy Slate's Amoray Dive Resort. This outfit makes diving easy. Stroll down to the full-service dive shop (NAUI, PADI, TDI, and BSAC certified), then onto a 45-foot catamaran. The rate for a two-dive trip is $80. ⊠ *MM 104.2 BS, 104250 Overseas Hwy.* ☎ *305/451–3595, 800/426–6729* ⊕ *www.amoray.com.*

★ **Conch Republic Divers.** Book diving instruction as well as scuba and snorkeling tours of all the wrecks and reefs of the Upper Keys. Two-location dives are $85 with tank and weights or $65 without the equipment. ⊠ *MM 90.8 BS, 90800 Overseas Hwy.* ☎ *305/852–1655, 800/274–3483* ⊕ *www.conchrepublicdivers.com.*

Coral Reef Park Co. At John Pennekamp Coral Reef State Park, this company gives 3½-hour scuba ($55) and 2½-hour snorkeling ($30) tours of the park. In addition to the great location and the dependability it's also suited for water adventurers of all levels. ⊠ *MM 102.5 OS, 102601 Overseas Hwy.* ☎ *305/451–6300* ⊕ *www.pennekamppark.com.*

Horizon Divers. The company has customized diving (starting from $80) and snorkeling (starting from $50) trips that depart daily aboard a 45-foot catamaran. ⊠ *100 Ocean Dr. #1* ☎ *305/453–3535, 800/984–3483* ⊕ *www.horizondivers.com.*

Island Ventures. This operator provides daily excursions that take you snorkeling or scuba diving. Scuba trips, offered twice daily, are $80 including tanks and weights; snorkeling trips are $50 each. Ride-alongs pay $40. ⊠ *MM 103.9, 103900 Overseas Hwy., at Sundowner's Restaurant* ☎ *305/451–4957* ⊕ *www.islandventure.com.*

Keys Diver & Snorkel Center. This operator offers snorkel and dive trips that take you to Florida Keys National Marine Sanctuary. Two-tank dives include a weights, tanks, and a restaurant lunch for $80 each; snorkel excursions range $28.95 for one location to $35.95 for three. ⊠ *MM 100 BS, 99696 Overseas Hwy.* ☎ *305/451–1177* ⊕ *www.keysdiver.com.*

Ocean Divers. The PADI five-star facility offers day and night dives, a range of courses, and dive-lodging packages. The cost is $85 for a two-tank reef dive with tank and weight rental. Snorkel trips cost $35 with equipment. ✉ *MM 100 OS, 522 Caribbean Dr.* ☎ *305/451–1113, 800/451–1113* ⊕ *www.oceandivers.com.*

Quiescence Diving Services. This operator sets itself apart in two ways: it limits groups to six to ensure personal attention and offers day and night dives, as well as twilight dives when sea creatures are most active. Two-dive trips start at $69 without equipment. ✉ *MM 103.5 BS, 103680 Overseas Hwy.* ☎ *305/451–2440* ⊕ *www.quiescence.com.*

SHOPPING

For the most part, shopping is sporadic in Key Largo, with a couple of shopping centers and fewer galleries than you find on the other big islands. If you're looking to buy scuba or snorkel equipment, you'll have plenty of choices.

Bluewater Potters. Bluewater Potters creates functional and decorative pieces ranging from signature vases and kitchenware to one-of-a-kind pieces where the owners' creative talent at the wheel blazes. ✉ *MM 102.9 OS, 102991 Overseas Hwy.* ☎ *305/453–1920* ⊕ *www.bluewaterpotters.com.*

Gallery at Kona Kai. Original works by major international artists—including sea captain–turned-painter Dirk Verdoorn, Italian artist Franco Passalaqua, and French sculptor Polles—are shown at this gallery in the Kona Kai Resort. ✉ *MM 97.8 BS, 97802 Overseas Hwy.* ☎ *305/852–7200* ⊕ *www.g-k-k.com.*

Key Lime Products. Go into olfactory overload—you'll find yourself sniffing every single bar of soap and scented candle here. Take home some key lime juice (super-easy pie-making directions are right on the bottle), key lime marmalade, or key lime shampoo. ✉ *MM 95.2 BS, 95231 Overseas Hwy.* ☎ *305/853–0378, 800/870–1780* ⊕ *www.keylimeproducts.com.*

Shell World. You can find lots of shops in the Keys that sell cheesy souvenirs—snow globes, alligator hats, and shell-encrusted anything. This is the granddaddy of them all. This sprawling building in the median of Overseas Highway has clothing, jewelry, and souvenirs from delightfully tacky to tasteful. ✉ *MM 97.5, 97600 Overseas Hwy.* ☎ *305/852–8245, 888/398–6233* ⊕ *www.shellworldflkeys.com.*

ISLAMORADA

Islamorada is between MM 90.5 and 70.

Early settlers named this key after their schooner, *Island Home,* but to make it sound more romantic they translated it into Spanish: *Isla Morada.* The Cchamber of Commerce prefers to use its literal translation "Purple Island," which refers either to a purple-shelled snail that once inhabited these shores or to the brilliantly colored orchids and bougainvilleas.

Early maps show Islamorada as encompassing only Upper Matecumbe Key. But the incorporated "Village of Islands" is made up of a string of islands that the Overseas Highway crosses, including Plantation Key, Windley Key, Upper Matecumbe Key, Lower Matecumbe Key, Craig Key, and Fiesta Key. In addition, two state-park islands accessible only by boat—Indian Key and Lignumvitae Key—belong to the group.

Islamorada (locals pronounce it "*eye*-la-mor-*ah*-da") is one of the world's top fishing destinations. For nearly 100 years seasoned anglers have fished these clear, warm waters teeming with trophy-worthy fish. There are numerous options for those in search of the big ones, including chartering a boat with its own crew or heading out on a vessel rented from one of the plethora of marinas along this 20-mile stretch of the Overseas Highway. More than 150 backcountry guides and 400 offshore captains are at your service.

Islamorada is one of the more affluent resort areas of the Keys. Sophisticated resorts and restaurants meet the needs of those in search of luxury, but there's also plenty for those looking for something more casual and affordable. Art galleries and boutiques make Islamorada's shopping scene the best in the Upper Keys, but if you need groceries, head to Marathon or Key Largo.

GETTING HERE AND AROUND

Most visitors arrive in Islamorada by car. If you're flying in to Miami International Airport or Key West International Airport, you can easily rent a car (reserve in advance) to make the drive.

VISITOR INFORMATION

Contacts Islamorada Chamber of Commerce & Visitors Center ⊠ *MM 83.2 BS, 83224 Overseas Hwy, Upper Matecumbe Key* ☎ *305/664–4503, 800/322–5397* ⊕ *www.islamoradachamber.com.*

EXPLORING

TOP ATTRACTIONS

History of Diving Museum. Adding to the region's reputation for world-class diving, this museum plunges into the history of man's thirst for undersea exploration. Among its 13 galleries of interactive and other interesting displays are a submarine and helmet re-created from the film *20,000 Leagues Under the Sea.* Vintage U.S. Navy equipment, diving helmets from around the world, and early scuba gear explore 4,000 years of diving history. ✉ *MM 83 BS, 82990 Overseas Hwy., Upper Matecumbe Key* ☎ *305/664–9737* ⊕ *www.divingmuseum.org* ⊒ *$12* ⊘ *Daily 10–5.*

★ **Robbie's Marina.** Huge, prehistoric-looking denizens of the
☾ not-so-deep, silver-sided tarpon congregate around the docks at this marina on Lower Matecumbe Key. Children—and lots of adults—pay $3 for a bucket of sardines to feed them and $1 each for dock admission. Spend some time hanging out at this authentic Keys community, where you can grab a bite to eat, do a little shopping at the artisans' booths, or charter a boat. ✉ *MM 77.5 BS, 77522 Overseas Hwy., Lower Matecumbe Key* ☎ *305/664–9814, 877/664–8498* ⊕ *www.robbies.com* ⊒ *Dock access $1* ⊘ *Daily sunrise–sunset.*

☾ **Theater of the Sea.** The second-oldest marine-mammal center in the world doesn't attempt to compete with more modern, more expensive parks. Even so, it's among the better attractions north of Key West, especially if you have kids in tow. Like the pricier parks, there are dolphin, sea lion, and stingray encounters ($55–$185, which includes general admission; reservations required) where you can get up close and personal with underwater creatures. These are popular, so reserve in advance. Ride a "bottomless" boat to see what's below the waves and take a guided tour of the marine-life exhibits. Entertaining educational shows highlight conservation issues. You can stop for lunch at the grill, shop in the boutique, or sunbathe at a lagoon-side beach. This easily could be an all-day attraction. ✉ *MM 84.5 OS, 84721 Overseas Hwy., Windley Key* ☎ *305/664–2431* ⊕ *www.theaterofthesea.com* ⊒ *$26.95* ⊘ *Daily 9:30–5 (last ticket sold at 3:30).*

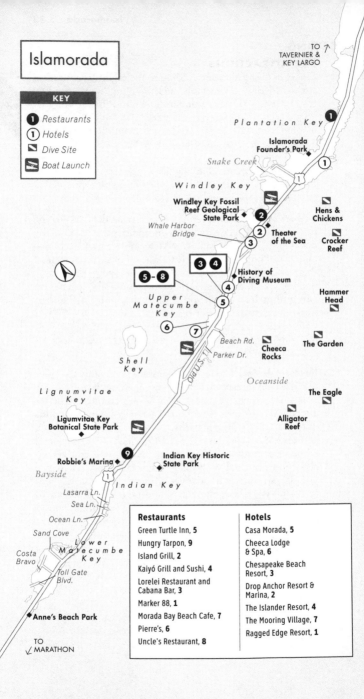

Islamorada

KEY
- 1 Restaurants
- 1 Hotels
- Dive Site
- Boat Launch

TO TAVERNIER & KEY LARGO

Plantation Key

Islamorada Founder's Park

Snake Creek

Windley Key

Windley Key Fossil Reef Geological State Park

Whale Harbor Bridge

Theater of the Sea

Hens & Chickens

Crocker Reef

History of Diving Museum

Hammer Head

Upper Matecumbe Key

Beach Rd.
Parker Dr.

Cheeca Rocks

The Garden

Shell Key

Oceanside

Lignumvitae Key

The Eagle

Ligumvitae Key Botanical State Park

Alligator Reef

Robbie's Marina

Indian Key Historic State Park

Bayside

Indian Key

Lasarra Ln.
Sea Ln.
Ocean Ln.
Sand Cove

Lower Matecumbe Key

Costa Bravo

Toll Gate Blvd.

Anne's Beach Park

TO MARATHON

Restaurants
Green Turtle Inn, 5
Hungry Tarpon, 9
Island Grill, 2
Kaiyó Grill and Sushi, 4
Lorelei Restaurant and Cabana Bar, 3
Marker 88, 1
Morada Bay Beach Cafe, 7
Pierre's, 6
Uncle's Restaurant, 8

Hotels
Casa Morada, 5
Cheeca Lodge & Spa, 6
Chesapeake Beach Resort, 3
Drop Anchor Resort & Marina, 2
The Islander Resort, 4
The Mooring Village, 7
Ragged Edge Resort, 1

WORTH NOTING

Anne's Beach Park. On Lower Matecumbe Key is a popular village park, named for a local environmental activist. Its "beach" (really a typical Keys-style sand flat) is best enjoyed at low tide. The nicest feature here is a ½-mi, elevated, wooden boardwalk that meanders through a natural wetland hammock. Covered picnic areas along the way give you places to linger and enjoy the view. Restrooms are at the north end. Weekends are packed with Miami day-trippers as it's the only public beach until you reach Marathon. ⊠ *MM 73.5 OS, Lower Matecumbe Key* ☎ *305/853–1685.*

Indian Key Historic State Park. Mystery surrounds 10-acre Indian Key, on the ocean side of the Matecumbe islands. Before it became one of the first European settlements outside of Key West, it was inhabited by American Indians for several thousand years. The islet served as a base for 19th-century shipwreck salvagers until an Indian attack wiped out the settlement in 1840. Dr. Henry Perrine, a noted botanist, was killed in the raid. Today his plants grow in the town's ruins. Most people kayak or canoe here from Indian Key Fill or Robbie's Marina (about 20 minutes away by paddle) to tour the nature trails and the town ruins or to snorkel. There are no restrooms or picnic facilities on Indian Key. ☎ *305/664–2540 park, 305/664–8070 boat tour* ⊕ *www.floridastateparks.org/ indiankey* ⊠ *Free* ☉ *Daily 8–5.*

Islamorada Founder's Park. This public park boasts a palm-shaded beach, swimming pool, marina, skate park, tennis, and plenty of other facilities. If you want to rent a boat or learn to sail, businesses here can help you. If you're staying in Islamorada, admission is free. Those staying elsewhere pay $8 to enter the park. Either way, you pay an additional $3 to use the Olympic-size pool. A spiffy amphitheater hosts concerts, plays, and shows. ⊠ *MM 87 BS, 87000 Overseas Hwy., Plantation Key* ☎ *305/853–1685.*

Lignumvitae Key Botanical State Park. On the National Register of Historic Places, this 280-acre bay-side island is the site of a virgin hardwood forest and the 1919 home of chemical magnate William Matheson. His caretaker's cottage serves as the park's visitor center. Access is by boat—your own, a rented vessel, or a tour operated by Robbie's Marina. The tour leaves at 8:30am Friday through Sunday and takes in both Lignumvitae and Indian keys (reservations required).

Paddling here from Indian Key Fill, at MM 78.5, is a popular pastime. The only way to do the trails is by a guided ranger walk, offered at 10 am and 2 pm Friday to Sunday. Wear long sleeves and pants, and bring mosquito repellent. On the first Saturday in December is the Lignumvitae Christmas Celebration, when the historic home is decorated 1930s-style. ☎ *305/664–2540 park, 305/664–8070 boat tours ⊕ www.floridastateparks.org/lignumvitaekey ☜ $1 for ranger tours; $35 for boat tours ☺ Park Thurs.–Mon. 8–5; house tours Fri.–Sun at 10 and 2.*

Upper Matecumbe Key. This was one of the first of the Upper Keys to be permanently settled. Early homesteaders were so successful at growing pineapples in the rocky soil that at one time the island yielded the country's largest annual crop. However, foreign competition and the hurricane of 1935 killed the industry. Today, life centers on fishing and tourism, and the island is filled with bait shops, marinas, and charter-fishing boats. ⊠ *MM 84–79.*

Windley Key. This is the highest point in the Keys, though at 16 feet above sea level it's not likely to give anyone altitude sickness. Originally two islets, this area was first inhabited by American Indians, who left behind a few traces of their dwellings, and then by farmers and fishermen who built their homes here in the mid-1800s. Henry Flagler bought the land from homesteaders in 1908 for his Florida East Coast Railway, filling in the inlet between what were then called the Umbrella Keys. His workers quarried coral rock for the rail bed and bridge approaches—the same rock used in many historic South Florida structures, including Miami's Vizcaya and the Hurricane Monument on Upper Matecumbe. Although the Quarry Station was destroyed by the 1935 hurricane, quarrying continued until the 1960s. Today, there's little really to see here; the island consists of a few resorts and a state park, but it's a good spot for a walk. ⊠ *MM 86–84.*

Windley Key Fossil Reef Geological State Park. The fossilized-coral reef, dating back about 125,000 years, demonstrates that the Florida Keys were once beneath the ocean. Excavation of Windley Key's limestone bed by the Florida East Coast Railway exposed the petrified reef, full of beautifully fossilized brain coral and sea ferns. Visitors can see the fossils along a 300-foot quarry wall when hiking the park's three trails. There are guided (Friday, Saturday, and Sunday only) and self-guided tours along the trails, which lead to the railway's old quarrying equipment and cutting pits, where you can make rubbings of the quarry walls. The **Alison Fahrer Environmental Education Center** holds historic, biological, and geological displays about the area, including videos. The first Saturday in March is Windley Key Day, when the park sells native plants and hosts environmental exhibits. ✉ *MM 84.9 BS, Windley Key* ☎ *305/664-2540* ⊕ *www.floridastateparks.org/windleykey* 💲 *Education center free, $2.50 for park self-tours, $1 for ranger-guided tours* ☉ *Education center Fri.–Sun. 9–5 (tours at 10 and 2).*

WHERE TO EAT

$$$ ✕ **Green Turtle Inn.** *Seafood.* This circa-1928 landmark inn and its vintage neon sign is a slice of Florida Keys history. Period photographs decorate the wood-paneled walls. Breakfast and lunch options include surprises like coconut French toast made with Cuban bread and a yellowtail po' boy. Chef Dan Harris relies heavily on Cajun cuisine with global touches for the dinner menu; think turtle chowder (don't gasp; it's made from farm-raised freshwater turtles), osso bucco, gumbo, and five-spice blackened tuna. Naturally, there's a Turtle Sundae on the dessert menu. 💲 *Average main: $24* ✉ *MM 81.2 OS, 81219 Overseas Hwy., Upper Matecumbe Key* ☎ *305/664-2006* ⊕ *www.greenturtlekeys. com* 💺 *Reservations essential* ☉ *Closed Mon.*

$$ ✕ **Hungry Tarpon.** *Seafood.* As part of the colorful, bustling Old Florida scene at Robbie's Marina, you know that the seafood here is fresh and top-quality. The extensive menu seems as if it's bigger than the dining space, which consists of a few tables and some counter seating indoors, plus a smattering of tables out back, close to where tourists pay dollars to feed the tarpon in the marina. While tarpon are snacking on sardines, diners enjoy such breakfast, lunch, and dinner specialties as biscuits and gravy, grilled ahi tuna nachos, shrimp burrito, lobster thermidor, and mahimahi with brandy lobster cream sauce. 💲 *Average main: $19* ✉ *MM 77.5 BS, 77522 Overseas Hwy., Lower Matecumbe Key* ☎ *305/664–0535* ⊕ *www.hungrytarpon.com* 💺 *Reservations not accepted.*

$ ✕ **Island Grill.** *Seafood.* Don't be fooled by appearances;
★ this shack on the waterfront takes island breakfast, lunch, and dinner cuisine up a notch. The eclectic menu tempts you with such dishes as its famed "original tuna nachos," lobster rolls, and a nice selection of seafood and sand-

wiches. Southern-style shrimp and andouille sausage with grits join island-style specialties such as grilled ribs with guava barbecue sauce on the list of entrées. There's an air-conditioned dining room and bar as well as open seating under a vaulted porch ceiling. The outdoor bar hosts live entertainment Wednesday to Sunday. $ *Average main: $12 ⊠ MM 85.5 OS, 85501 Overseas Hwy., Windley Key* ☎ *305/664–8400* ⊕ *www.keysislandgrill.com* ⚲ *Reservations not accepted.*

$$$ ✕ **Kaiyó Grill & Sushi.** *Japanese.* The decor—an inviting setting that includes colorful abstract mosaics, polished wood floors, and upholstered banquettes—almost steals the show at Kaiyó, but the food is equally interesting. The menu, a fusion of East and West, offers sushi rolls that combine local ingredients with traditional Japanese tastes. A wood grill is used to prepare such dishes as grilled catch-of-the-day and hardwood grilled rack of lamb. The rice paper–wrapped fried banana with warm chocolate ganache and vanilla ice cream exemplifies the collision of Asia and Florida on the dessert menu. $ *Average main: $28 ⊠ MM 81.5 OS, 81701 Overseas Hwy., Upper Matecumbe Key* ☎ *305/664–5556* ⊕ *www.kaiyogrill.com* ☾ *No lunch.*

$ ✕ **Lorelei Restaurant & Cabana Bar.** *American.* Local anglers gather here for breakfast. Lunch and dinner bring a mix of islanders and visitors for straightforward food and yucking good times. Live bands ensure a lively nighttime scene, and the menu staves off inebriation with burgers, barbecued baby back ribs, and Parmesan-crusted snapper. Key lime pie comes frozen with mango sauce. $ *Average main: $15 ⊠ MM 82 BS, 81924 Overseas Hwy., Upper Matecumbe Key* ☎ *305/664–2692* ⊕ *www.loreleicabanabar.com* ⚲ *Reservations not accepted.*

$$$ ✕ **Marker 88.** *Seafood.* A few yards from Florida Bay, this
★ seafood restaurant has been popular since the late '60s. Large picture windows offer great sunset views, but the bay is lovely no matter what time of day you visit. Chef Sal Barrios serves such irresistible entrées as onion-crusted mahi-mahi, crispy yellowtail snapper, and mangrove-honey-and-chipotle–glazed rib eye. In addition, there are a half-dozen burgers and sandwiches, and you can't miss the restaurant's famous key lime baked Alaska dessert. The extensive wine list is an oenophile's delight. $ *Average main: $28 ⊠ MM 88 BS, 88000 Overseas Hwy., Plantation Key* ☎ *305/852–9315* ⊕ *www.marker88.info* ⚲ *Reservations essential.*

$$$ ✕ **Morada Bay Beach Café.** *Eclectic.* This bay-front restau-
★ rant wins high marks for its surprisingly stellar cuisine,
🕒 tables planted in the sand, and tiki torches that bathe the
evening in romance. Entrées feature alluring combinations
like fresh fish of the day sautéed with Meyer lemon but-
ter and whole fried snapper with coconut rice. Seafood
takes center stage, but you can always get roasted organic
chicken or prime rib. Tapas and raw bar menus cater to
smaller appetites or those who can't decide with offerings
like fried calamari, conch fritters, and Wagyu beef sliders.
Lunch adds interesting sandwiches to the mix, plus there's
breakfast Friday through Sunday. Sit in a dining room
outfitted with surfboards, or outdoors on a beach, where
the sunset puts on a mighty show and kids (and your feet)
play in the sand. Ⓢ *Average main: $27* ✉ *MM 81 BS, 81600
Overseas Hwy., Upper Matecumbe Key* ☎ *305/664–0604*
⊕ *www.moradabay-restaurant.com* ⊗ *Closed Tues. No
breakfast Mon.–Thurs.*

★ **Fodor's**Choice ✕ **Pierre's.** *French.* One of the Keys' most elegant
$$$$ restaurants, Pierre's marries colonial style with modern food
trends. Full of interesting architectural artifacts, the place
oozes style, especially the wicker chair–strewn veranda
overlooking the bay. Save your best "tropical chic" duds for
dinner here, so you don't stand out from your surroundings.
The food, drawn from French and Floridian influences, is
multilayered and beautifully presented. Among the season-
ally changing appetizer choices, you might find smoked
hogfish chowder and foie gras sliders with a butternut
squash milk shake. A changing list of entrées might include
hogfish meunière and scallops with pork belly tortellini.
The downstairs bar is a perfect spot for catching sunsets,
sipping martinis, and enjoying light eats. Ⓢ *Average main:
$35* ✉ *MM 81.5 BS, 81600 Overseas Hwy., Upper Mate-
cumbe Key* ☎ *305/664–3225* ⊕ *www.pierres-restaurant.
com* ⌂ *Reservations essential* ⊗ *No lunch.*

$$$ ✕ **Uncle's Restaurant.** *Italian.* Former fishing guide Joe LeP-
ree adds Italian flair to standard seafood dishes. Here you
can have your seafood almandine, Milanese (breaded and
fried), LePree (with artichokes, mushrooms, and lemon-
butter wine sauce), or any of five other different prepara-
tions. For starters, feast on mussels or littleneck clams in a
marinara or garlic sauce. Specials sometimes combine game
(bison, caribou, or elk) with seafood. Portions are huge,
so share dishes or take home a doggie bag. Alternatively
arrive early (between 5 and 7) for the lighter menu, priced
$12.95 to $17.95. Weather permitting, sit outdoors in the

garden; poor acoustics make dining indoors unusually noisy. $ *Average main: $21* ⊠ *MM 81 OS, 80939 Overseas Hwy., Upper Matecumbe Key* ☎ *305/664–4402* ⊕ *www. unclesrestaurant.com* ⊗ *Closed Mon.*

WHERE TO STAY

For expanded reviews, facilities, and current deals, visit Fodors.com.

★ **Fodors**Choice ⊞ **Casa Morada.** *B&B/Inn.* This relic from the
$$$$ 1950s has been restyled into a suave, design-forward, all-suites property with outdoor showers and Jacuzzis in some of the suites. **Pros:** cool design; complimentary snacks and bottled water; complimentary use of bikes, kayaks, and snorkel gear. **Cons:** trailer park across the street; beach is small and inconsequential. $ *Rooms from: $299* ⊠ *MM 82 BS, 136 Madeira Rd., Upper Matecumbe Key* ☎ *305/664–0044, 888/881–3030* ⊕ *www.casamorada.com* ⊅ *16 suites* ⊙| *Breakfast.*

$$$$ ⊞ **Cheeca Lodge & Spa.** *Resort.* In the main lodge, West
★ Indian–style rooms boast luxurious touches like elegant balcony tubs that fill from the ceiling. **Pros:** beautifully landscaped grounds; new designer rooms; dive shop on property. **Cons:** expensive rates; $39 resort fee for activities; busy. $ *Rooms from: $299* ⊠ *MM 82 OS, Box 527, Upper Matecumbe Key* ☎ *305/664–4651, 800/327–2888* ⊕ *www.cheeca.com* ⊅ *60 1-bedroom suites, 64 junior suites* ⊙| *No meals.*

$$$ ⊞ **Chesapeake Beach Resort.** *Resort.* This boutique hotel on the beach mixes modern conveniences with a retro look. High-tech gadgets like flat-screen TVs, CD players, and MP3 players give the place an up-to-date feel. Coral stone and dark wood accent the rooms, each of which has a porch or a balcony. Most units are lined up along the long stretch of sand that all but encircles a lagoon; others overlook the tennis court. **Pros:** oceanfront location; free use of water-sports equipment and Wi-Fi (included in resort fee). **Cons:** dated exterior; mandatory $18 resort fee (per room per night). $ *Rooms from: $179* ⊠ *MM 83.5, 83409 Overseas Hwy., Upper Matecumbe Key* ☎ *305/664–4662, 800/338–3395* ⊕ *www.chesapeake-resort.com* ⊅ *44 rooms, 8 suites, 13 villas* ⊙| *Breakfast.*

$$ ⊞ **Drop Anchor Resort and Marina.** *Hotel.* It's easy to find your
★ cottage here, as they are painted in an array of Crayola colors. **Pros:** bright and colorful; attention to detail; laid-back charm. **Cons:** noise from the highway; beach is better

2

for fishing than swimming. ⑤ *Rooms from: $129* ⊠ *MM 85 OS, 84959 Overseas Hwy., Windley Key* ☎ *305/664–4863, 888/664–4863* ⊕ *www.dropanchorresort.com* ⇨ *18 suites* ⑩ *No meals.*

$$$$ ⛉ **The Islander Resort.** *Resort.* While the general waterfront layout here (including the retro sign) retains a 1950s feel, the decor is modern yet comfortable, with white cottage-style furnishings, elegant fabrics, and sunny yellow bedrooms. **Pros:** spacious rooms; nice kitchens; eye-popping views. **Cons:** pricey for what you get; beach has rough sand; no a/c in the screened gym. ⑤ *Rooms from: $249* ⊠ *MM 82.1 OS, 82200 Overseas Hwy., Upper Matecumbe Key* ☎ *305/664–2031, 800/753–6002* ⊕ *www.islanderflorida-keys.com* ⇨ *114 rooms, 12 suites* ⑩ *Breakfast.*

★ **Fodor'sChoice** ⛉ **The Moorings Village.** *Hotel.* This tropical
$$$$ retreat is everything you imagine when you think of the Keys—from hammocks swaying between towering trees to sugar-white sand (arguably the Keys' best resort beach) lapped by aqua-green waves. **Pros:** romantic setting; good dining options with room-charging privileges; beautiful beach. **Cons:** no room service; extra fee for housekeeping; daily resort fee for activities. ⑤ *Rooms from: $375* ⊠ *MM 81.6 OS, 123 Beach Rd., Upper Matecumbe Key* ☎ *305/664–4708* ⊕ *www.themooringsvillage.com* ⇨ *6 cottages, 12 houses* ⑩ *No meals.*

$ ⛉ **Ragged Edge Resort.** *Hotel.* Tucked away in a residential area at the ocean's edge, this hotel is big on value but short on style. **Pros:** oceanfront location; boat docks and ramp; cheap rates. **Cons:** dated decor; off the beaten path. ⑤ *Rooms from: $100* ⊠ *MM 86.5 OS, 243 Treasure Harbor Rd., Plantation Key* ☎ *305/852–5389, 800/436–2023* ⊕ *www.ragged-edge.com* ⇨ *6 studios, 1 efficiency, 3 2-bedroom suites* ⑩ *No meals.*

NIGHTLIFE

Islamorada is not known for its raging nightlife, but for local fun, Lorelei's is legendary. Others cater to the town's sophisticated clientele and fishing fervor.

Hog Heaven. Situated on sandy oceanfront, Hog Heaven is a lively sports bar with happy hour specials and a reputation for wild theme parties. ⊠ *MM 85.3 OS, 85361 Overseas Hwy.* ☎ *305/664–9669* ⊕ *www.hogheavensportsbar.com.*

Safari Lounge. Locals often refer to Safari Lounge as the Dead Animal Bar, or simply DAB, because of the mounted big-game trophies lining walls and the ceiling. Within eyeshot of the sea, it's a good spot to hoist a few with the island drinking crowd. ✉ *73814 Overseas Hwy., MM 73.5 OS* ☎ *305/664–8142.*

★ **Lorelei Restaurant & Cabana Bar.** Behind a larger-than-life mermaid, this is the kind of place you fantasize about during those long cold winters up north. It's all about good drinks, tasty pub grub, and beautiful sunsets set to live bands playing island tunes and light rock nightly. ✉ *MM 82 BS, 81924 Overseas Hwy., Upper Matecumbe Key* ☎ *305/664–2692* ⊕ *www.loreleicabanabar.com.*

Zane Grey Long Key Lounge. Above the World Wide Sportsman, Zane Grey Long Key Lounge was created to honor writer Zane Grey, one of the most famous members of the Long Key Fishing Club. The lounge displays the author's photographs, books, and memorabilia. Listen to live blues, jazz, and Motown on a wide veranda that invites sunset watching. ✉ *81576 Overseas Hwy., MM 81.5, BS, Upper Matecumbe Key* ☎ *305/664–4615.*

Ziggie & Mad Dog's. The area's glam celebrity hangout, Ziggie & Mad Dog's serves appetizers with its happy-hour drink specials. ✉ *83000 Overseas Hwy., MM 83 BS, Upper Matecumbe Key* ☎ *305/664–3391* ⊕ *www.ziggieandmaddogs.com.*

SPORTS AND THE OUTDOORS

BOATING

Marinas pop up every mile or so in the Islamorada area, so finding a rental or tour is no problem. Robbie's Marina is a prime example of a salty spot where you can find it all—from fishing charters and kayaking rentals to lunch and tarpon feeding.

Bump & Jump. Fishing and deck boats rentals (from 15 to 29 feet) start at $145 per day and $745 per week. ✉ *MM 81.2 OS, 81197 Overseas Hwy., Upper Matecumbe Key* ☎ *305/664–9404, 877/453–9463* ⊕ *www.keysboatrental.com.*

Houseboat Vacations of the Florida Keys. See the islands from the comfort of your own boat (captain's cap optional). The company maintains a fleet of 42- to 55-foot boats that accommodate up to 10 people and come outfitted with everything you need besides food. (You may provision yourself at a nearby grocery store.) The three-day minimum starts at $1,112; one week costs $1,950 and up.

Kayaks, canoes, and skiffs suitable for the ocean are also available. ✉ *MM 85.9 BS, 85944 Overseas Hwy., Plantation Key* ☎ *305/664–4009* ⊕ *www.floridakeys.com/houseboats.*

Nauti-Limo. Captain Joe Fox has converted the design of a 1983 pink Caddy stretch limo into a less-than-luxurious but certainly curious watercraft. One-hour tours start at $60 per couple. The seaworthy hybrid—complete with wheels—can sail with the top down if you're in the mood. Only in the Keys! ✉ *MM 82 BS, Lorelei Restaurant & Yacht Club, Upper Matecumbe Key* ☎ *305/942–3793* ⊕ *www.nautilimo.com.*

Robbie's Boat Rentals & Charters. This full-service company will even give you a crash course on how not to crash your boat. The rental fleet includes an 18-foot skiff with a 60-horsepower outboard for $150 for four hours and $200 for the day to a 23-foot deck boat with a 130-horsepower engine for $185 for a half day and $235 for eight hours. Robbie's also rents fishing and snorkeling gear (there's good snorkeling nearby) and sells bait, drinks and snacks, and gas. Want to hire a guide who knows the local waters and where the fish lurk? Robbie's offers offshore-fishing trips, patch-reef trips, and party-boat fishing. Backcountry flats trips are a specialty. ✉ *MM 77.5 BS, 77522 Overseas Hwy., Lower Matecumbe Key* ☎ *305/664–9814, 877/664–8498* ⊕ *www.robbies.com.*

Treasure Harbor Marine. Captains Pam and Pete Anderson provide everything you'll need for a bareboat sailing vacation at sea. They also give excellent advice on where to find the best anchorages, snorkeling spots, or lobstering sites. Vessels range from a 19-foot Cape Dory to a 41-foot Morgan Out Island. Rates start at $125 a day; $500 a week. Captained sails are $550 a day, $3,250 a week aboard the 41-footer. Marina facilities are basic—water, electric, ice machine, laundry, picnic tables, and restrooms with showers. A store sells snacks, beverages, and sundries. ✉ *MM 86.5 OS, 200 Treasure Harbor Dr., Plantation Key* ☎ *305/852–2458, 800/352–2628* ⊕ *www.treasureharbor.com.*

FISHING

Here in the self-proclaimed "Sportfishing Capital of the World," sailfish is the prime catch in the winter and dolphinfish (mahimahi) in the summer. Buchanan Bank just south of Islamorada is a good spot to try for tarpon in the spring. Blackfin tuna and amberjack are generally plentiful in the area, too. ■TIP→ **The Hump at Islamorada ranks high-**

est among anglers' favorite fishing spots in Florida (declared Florida Monthly magazine's best for seven years in a row) due to the incredible offshore marine life.

Captain Ted Wilson. Go into the backcountry for bonefish, tarpon, redfish, snook, and shark aboard a 17-foot boat that accommodates up to three anglers. For two people, half-day trips run $375, full-day trips $550, two-hour sunset bonefishing $225, and evening excursions $400. There's a $100 charge for an extra person. ⊠ *MM 79.9 OS, 79851 Overseas Hwy., Upper Matecumbe Key* ☎ *305/942–5224, 305/664–9463* ⊕ *www.captaintedwilson.com.*

Florida Keys Outfitters. Long before fly-fishing became popular, Sandy Moret was fishing the Keys for bonefish, tarpon, and redfish. Now he attracts anglers from around the world on a quest for the big catch. Weekend fly-fishing classes, which include classroom instruction, equipment, and daily lunch, cost $695. Add $1,070 for two additional days of fishing. Guided fishing trips cost $395 for a half day, $535 for a full day. Packages combining fishing and accommodations at Islander Resort are available. ⊠ *MM 81.2, Green Turtle, 81219 Overseas Hwy., Upper Matecumbe Key* ☎ *305/664–5423* ⊕ *www.floridakeysoutfitters.com.*

Miss Islamorada. The 65-foot party boat has full-day trips for $60. Bring your lunch or buy one from the dockside deli. ⊠ *Bud n' Mary's Marina, MM 79.8 OS, 79851 Overseas Hwy., Upper Matecumbe Key* ☎ *305/664–2461, 800/742–7945* ⊕ *www.budnmarys.com.*

★ **Hubba Hubba Charters.** Captain Ken Knudsen has fished the Keys waters for more than 40 years. A licensed backcountry guide, he's ranked among Florida's top 10 by national fishing magazines. He offers four-hour sunset trips for tarpon ($425) and two-hour sunset trips for bonefish ($200), as well as half- ($375) and full-day ($550) outings. Prices are for one or two anglers, and tackle and bait are included. ⊠ *MM 79.8 OS, Upper Matecumbe Key* ☎ *305/664–9281.*

Florida Keys Fly Fish. Like other top fly-fishing and light-tackle guides, Captain Geoff Colmes helps his clients land trophy fish in the waters around the Keys ($500–$550). ⊠ *105 Palm La., Upper Matecumbe Key* ☎ *305/853–0741* ⊕ *www.floridakeysflyfish.com.*

SCUBA DIVING AND SNORKELING

About 1¼ nautical miles south of Indian Key is the **San Pedro Underwater Archaeological Preserve State Park,** which includes the wreck of a Spanish treasure-fleet ship that sank in 1733. The state of Florida protects the site for divers; no spearfishing or souvenir collecting is allowed. Resting in only 18 feet of water, its ruins are visible to snorkelers as well as divers, and attract a colorful array of fish.

Florida Keys Dive Center. Dive from John Pennekamp Coral Reef State Park to Alligator Light with this outfitter. The center has two 46-foot Coast Guard–approved dive boats, offers scuba training, and is one of the few Keys dive centers to offer Nitrox and Trimix (mixed gas) diving. Two-tank dives cost $60 with no equipment; two-location snorkeling is $38. ⊠ *MM 90.5 OS, 90451 Overseas Hwy., Plantation Key* ☎ *305/852–4599, 800/433–8946* ⊕ *www. floridakeysdivectr.com.*

Holiday Isle Dive Shop. This one-stop dive shop has a resort, pool, restaurant, lessons, and twice-daily dive and snorkel trips. Rates start at $50 for a two-tank dive or one-tank night dive without equipment. Snorkel trips are $30. ⊠ *MM 84 OS, 84001 Overseas Hwy., Windley Key* ☎ *305/664–3483, 800/327–7070* ⊕ *www.diveholidayisle.com.*

TENNIS

Islamorada Tennis Club. Not all Keys recreation is on the water. Play tennis year-round at a well-run facility with four clay and two hard courts (all lighted), same-day racket stringing, ball machines, private lessons, and a full-service pro shop. Rates are from $25 a day. ⊠ *MM 76.8 BS, 76800 Overseas Hwy., Upper Matecumbe Key* ☎ *305/664–5341* ⊕ *www.islamoradatennisclub.net.*

WATER SPORTS

The Kayak Shack. Rent kayaks for trips to Indian (about 20 min one way) and Lignumvitae (about 45 min one way) keys, two favorite destinations for paddlers. Kayak rental half-day rates (and you'll need plenty of time to explore those mangrove canopies) are $40 for a single kayak and $55 for a double. Pedal kayaks are available for $50 single and $65 double. The company also offers guided three-hour tours, including a snorkel trip to Indian Key ($45). It also rents stand-up paddleboards, at $50 for a half-day including lessons, and canoes. ⊠ *MM 77.5 BS, Robbie's Marina, 77522 Overseas Hwy., Lower Matecumbe Key* ☎ *305/664–4878* ⊕ *www.kayakthefloridakeys.com.*

SHOPPING

Art galleries, upscale gift shops, and the mammoth World Wide Sportsman (if you want to look the part of a local fisherman, you must wear a shirt from here) make up the variety and superior style of Islamorada shopping.

BOOKS

Hooked on Books. Among the best buys in town are the used best sellers at this bookstore, which also sells new titles, audiobooks, and CDs. ⊠ *MM 81.9 OS, 81909 Overseas Hwy., Upper Matecumbe Key* ☎ *305/517–2602* ⊕ *www. hookedonbooksfloridakeys.com.*

GALLERIES

Gallery Morada. The go-to destination for one-of-a-kind gifts beautifully displays blown-glass objects, original sculptures, paintings, lithographs, and jewelry by 200 artists. ⊠ *MM 81.6 OS, 81611 Old Hwy., Upper Matecumbe Key* ☎ *305/664–3650* ⊕ *www.gallerymorada.com.*

Rain Barrel Artisan Village. This is a natural and unhurried shopping showplace. Set in a tropical garden of shady trees, native shrubs, and orchids, the crafts village has shops with works by local and national artists and resident artists in studios, including John Hawver, noted for Florida landscapes and seascapes. The Main Gallery up front showcases the craftsmanship of the resident artisans, who create marine-inspired artwork while you watch. ⊠ *MM 86.7 BS, 86700 Overseas Hwy., Plantation Key* ☎ *305/852–3084.*

Redbone Gallery. One of the largest sportfishing–art galleries in Florida stocks hand-stitched clothing and giftware, in addition to work by wood and bronze sculptors such as Kendall van Sant; watercolorist C.D. Clarke; and painters Daniel Caldwell, David Hall, Steven Left, and Stacie Krupa. Proceeds benefit cystic fibrosis research. ⊠ *MM 81.5 OS, 200 Industrial Dr., Upper Matecumbe Key* ☎ *305/664–2002* ⊕ *www.redbone.org.*

GIFTS

Banyan Tree. A sharp-eyed husband-and-wife team successfully combines antiques and contemporary gifts for the home and garden with plants, pots, and trellises in a stylishly sophisticated indoor–outdoor setting. ⊠ *MM 81.2 OS, 81197 Overseas Hwy., Upper Matecumbe Key* ☎ *305/664–3433* ⊕ *www.banyantreegarden.com.*

Island Silver & Spice. The shop stocks tropical-style furnishings, rugs, and home accessories, as well as women's and men's resort wear and a large jewelry selection with high-end watches and marine-theme pieces. ✉ *MM 82 OS, 81981 Overseas Hwy., Upper Matecumbe Key* ☎ *305/664–2714.*

SPORTING GOODS

World Wide Sportsman. This two-level retail center sells upscale fishing equipment, resort clothing, sportfishing art, and other gifts. When you're tired of shopping, relax at the Zane Grey Long Key Lounge just above World Wide Sportsman. ✉ *MM 81.5 BS, 81576 Overseas Hwy., Upper Matecumbe Key* ☎ *305/664–4615, 800/327–2880.*

LONG KEY

MM 70–65.5.

Long Key isn't a tourist hot spot, making it a favorite destination for those looking to avoid the masses and enjoy some natural history.

EXPLORING

★ **Long Key State Park.** Come here for solitude, hiking, fishing, and camping. On the ocean side, the Golden Orb Trail leads to a boardwalk that cuts through the mangroves (may require some wading) and alongside a lagoon where waterfowl congregate (as do mosquitoes, so be prepared). A 1¼-mi canoe trail leads through a tidal lagoon, and a broad expanse of shallow grass flats is perfect for bonefishing. Bring a mask and snorkel to observe the marine life in the shallow water. The park is particularly popular with campers who long to stake their tent at the campground on a beach. In summer, no-see-ums (biting sand flies) also love the beach, so again—be prepared. The picnic area is on the water, too, but lacks a beach. Canoes rent for $10 per day, and kayak rentals start at $17 for a single for two hours, $21.50 for a double. Rangers lead tours every Wednesday and Thursday at 10 on birding, boating, or beachcombing. ✉ *MM 67.5 OS, 67400 Overseas Hwy.* ☎ *305/664–4815* ⊕ *www.floridastateparks.org/longkey* ✇ *$4.50 for 1 person, $5.50 for 2 people, and 50¢ for each additional person in the group* ☉ *Daily 8–sunset.*

Long Key Viaduct. As you cross Long Key Channel, look beside you at the old viaduct. The second-longest bridge on the former rail line, this 2-mi-long structure has 222 reinforced-concrete arches. The old bridge is popular with cyclists and anglers, who fish off the sides day and night.

WHERE TO STAY

$$ ⬚ **Lime Tree Bay Resort.** *Resort.* Easy on the eye and the wallet, this 2½-acre resort on Florida Bay is far from the hustle and bustle of the larger islands. **Pros:** great views; friendly staff; close to Long Key State Park. **Cons:** no restaurants nearby, shared balconies. ⑤ *Rooms from: $119* ✉ *MM 68.5 BS, 68500 Overseas Hwy., Layton* ☎ *305/664–4740, 800/723–4519* ⊕ *www.limetreebayresort.com* ⇨ *10 rooms, 10 studios, 14 1- and 2-bedroom suites, 5 apartments, 4 efficiencies* ⦿ *No meals.*

The Middle Keys

3

WORD OF MOUTH

"Duck Key has some of the finer residential areas in the Keys. Duck is also the home of Hawks Cay. It is midway between Islamorada and Marathon, maybe 20 minutes either way."

—stumpworks73

Updated
by Chelle
Koster
Walton

MOST OF THE ACTIVITY IN THE MIDDLE KEYS centers around the town of Marathon, the region's third-largest metropolitan area. On either end of it, smaller keys hold resorts, wildlife research and rehab facilities, a historic village, and a state park. The Middle Keys make a fitting transition from the Upper Keys to the Lower Keys not only geographically, but mentally. Crossing Seven Mile Bridge prepares you for the slow pace and don't-give-a-damn attitude you'll find a little farther down the highway. Fishing is one of the main attractions—in fact, the region's commercial fishing industry was founded here in the early 1800s. Diving is another popular pastime. There are also beaches and natural areas to enjoy in the Middle Keys, where mainland stress becomes an ever more distant memory.

ORIENTATION AND PLANNING

GETTING ORIENTED

If you get bridge fever—the heebie-jeebies when driving over long stretches of water—you may need a pair of blinders (or a couple of tranquilizers) before tackling the Middle Keys. Stretching from Conch Key to the far side of the Seven Mile Bridge, this zone is home to the region's two longest bridges: Long Key Viaduct and Seven Mile Bridge, both historic landmarks.

PLANNING

GETTING HERE AND AROUND

To get to the Middle Keys you can fly into either Miami International Airport or Key West International Airport. Key West is closer, but there are far fewer flights coming in and going out. Rental cars are available at both airports. In addition, there is bus service from the Key West airport, $4 one-way with Keys Transit. The SuperShuttle charges $250 for up to 11 passengers from Miami International Airport (MIA) to Big Pine Key. The Keys Shuttle charges $80 per passenger from MIA to Marathon.

U.S. 1 takes you from one end of the region to the other in a direct line that takes in most of the sights, but you'll find some interesting resorts and restaurants off the main drag.

Contacts City of Key West Department of Transportation ☎ *305/809–3910* ⊕ *www.kwtransit.com.* **SuperShuttle** ☎ *305/871–2000* ⊕ *www.supershuttle.com.*

TOP REASONS TO GO

■ **Crane Point.** Visit 63-acre Crane Point Museum, Nature Center & Historic Site in Marathon for a primer on local natural and social history.

■ **A Beach for the Whole Family.** Sun, swim, and play with abandon at Marathon's family-oriented Sombrero Beach.

■ **Pigeon Key.** Step into the era of railroad building with a ferry ride to Pigeon Key's historic village, which was once a residential camp for workers on Henry M. Flagler's Overseas Railroad.

■ **Dolphins.** Kiss a dolphin, and maybe even watch one paint, at Dolphin Research Center, which was begun by the maker of the movie *Flipper.*

■ **Fishing.** Anglers will be happy to hear that the deep-water fishing off Marathon is superb in both the bay and the ocean.

RESTAURANTS

Hope you're not tired of seafood, because the run of fish houses continues in the Middle Keys. In fact, Marathon boasts some of the best. Several are not so easy to find, but worth the search because of their local color and water views. Expect casual and friendly service with a side of sass. Restaurants may close for two to four weeks during the slow season between September and mid-November, so call ahead if you have a particular place in mind.

HOTELS

From quaint old cottages to newly built town-house communities, the Middle Keys have it all, often with prices that are more affordable than at the chain's extremes. Hawks Cay has the region's best selection of lodgings.

HOTEL AND RESTAURANT PRICES

Prices in the restaurant reviews are the average cost of a main course at dinner or, if dinner is not served, at lunch, excluding taxes and service charges. Prices in the hotel reviews are the lowest cost of a standard double room in high season, excluding taxes, service charges, and meal plans (except at all-inclusives). Prices for rentals are the lowest per-night cost for a one-bedroom unit in high season.

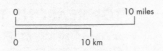

The Middle
Keys

Florida Bay

Seven Mile
Bridge

Marathon see detail map

Marathon Airport

Conch & Duck Keys

Pigeon Key

Vaca Key

Grassy Key

ATLANTIC OCEAN

CONCH AND DUCK KEYS

MM 63–61.

This stretch of islands ranges from rustic fishing village to boating elite. Fishing dominates the economy, and many residents are descendants of immigrants from the mainland South. Across a causeway from the tiny fishing village of Conch Key is Duck Key, home to a more upscale community. There are a few lodging options here for those wanting to explore Marathon but avoid the traffic or take advantage of the water sports on Duck Key.

WHERE TO EAT

$$$ ✕**Alma.** *Latin American.* A refreshing escape from the Mid-
★ dle Keys' same-old menus, Alma serves expertly prepared Florida and Latin-Caribbean dishes in an elegant setting. Nightly changing menus might include a trio of ceviche, ahi tuna with a wonderful garbanzo bean tomato sauce, gnocchi and exotic mushroom ragout, and pan-seared Wagyu steak. Finish your meal with the silky, smooth, passion fruit crème brûlée, which has just the right amount of tartness

to balance the delicate caramelized crust. $ *Average main: $28* ⊠ *Hawks Cay Resort, 61 Hawks Cay Blvd., Duck Cay, Duck Key* ☎ *305/743–7000, 888/432–2242* ⊕ *www. hawkscay.com* ⊗ *No lunch*.

WHERE TO STAY

$$$ ▦ **Conch Key Cottages.** *Hotel.* Pastel-hued cottages, each named for a shell or sea creature, are furnished Bali-style in a secluded setting on a mangrove-framed beach between Marathon and Islamorada. **Pros:** far from the traffic noise, sandy beach; lots of sunny decks. **Cons:** far from restaurants. $ *Rooms from: $159* ⊠ *MM 62.3 OS, 62250 Overseas Hwy., Conch Key* ☎ *305/289–1377, 800/330–1577* ⊕ *www.conchkeycottages.com* ⇆ *9 cottages, 2 villas, 2 rooms* ⏻ *Breakfast*.

★ **Fodor'sChoice** ▦ **Hawks Cay Resort.** *Resort.* The 60-acre, Carib-
$$$$ bean-style retreat has plenty to keep the kids occupied
Ⓒ (and adults happy). **Pros:** huge rooms; restful spa; full-service marina and dive shop. **Cons:** no real beach; far from Marathon's attractions. $ *Rooms from: $240* ⊠ *MM 61 OS, 61 Hawks Cay Blvd., Duck Key* ☎ *305/743–7000, 888/432–2242* ⊕ *www.hawkscay.com* ⇆ *161 rooms, 16 suites, 225 2- and 3-bedroom villas* ⏻ *No meals*.

SPORTS AND THE OUTDOORS

DOLPHIN INTERACTION

Dolphin Connection. Hawk's Cay Resort's Dolphin Connection offers three programs, including Dockside Dolphins, a 30-minute encounter from the dry training docks ($60); Dolphin Discovery, an in-water program that lasts about 45 minutes and lets you kiss, touch, and feed the dolphins ($165); and Trainer for a Day, a three-hour session with the animal training team ($315). ⊠ *MM 61 OS, 61 Hawks Cay Blvd., Duck Key* ☎ *305/743–7000* ⊕ *www.dolphinconnection.com*.

SCUBA AND SNORKELING

Dive Duck Key. Dive Duck Key is a full-service dive shop offering rentals, charters, lessons, and certification courses. Scuba trips are $60 without gear and $75 to $115 with gear. Basic open-water certification courses require four days and cost $525. Day resort courses cost $125. There's also Snuba, a snorkel-scuba hybrid where your tanks float on the surface rather than being attached to your back. Excursions start at $99. ⊠ *Hawks Cay Resort, MM 61 OS, 61 Hawks Cay Blvd., Duck Key, Duck Key* ☎ *305/289–4931, 877/386–3483* ⊕ *www.diveduckkey.com*.

3

WATER SPORTS

Sundance Watersports. Go on a one-hour guided Jet Ski tour ($149 per watercraft), soar on a parasail flight ($79 for single, $139 for tandem), go reef snorkeling ($44 including equipment rentals), or enjoy a sunset cruise ($42 for adults). New in 2011, a JetLev experience shoots you from the water up to 30 feet in the air ($249-$349). ⊠ *MM 61 OS, Hawks Cay Resort, 61 Hawks Cay Blvd., Duck Key, Duck Key* ☎ *305/743–0145* ⊕ *www.sundancewatersports.net.*

GRASSY KEY

MM 60–57.

Local lore has it that this sleepy little key was named not for its vegetation—mostly native trees and shrubs—but for an early settler by the name of Grassy. The key is primarily inhabited by a few families operating small fishing camps and roadside motels. There's no marked definition between it and Marathon, so it feels sort of like a suburb of its much larger neighbor to the south. Grassy Key's sights tend toward the natural, including a worthwhile dolphin attraction and a small state park.

GETTING HERE AND AROUND

Most visitors arriving by air drive to this destination either from Miami International Airport or Key West International Airport. Rental cars are readily available at both, and in the long run, are the most convenient means of transportation for getting here and touring around the Keys.

EXPLORING

Curry Hammock State Park. Looking for a slice of the Keys that's far removed from tiki bars? On the ocean and bay sides of Overseas Highway are 260 acres of upland hammock, wetlands, and mangroves. On the bay side, there's a trail through thick hardwoods to a rocky shoreline. The ocean side is more developed, with a sandy beach, a clean bathhouse, picnic tables, a playground, grills, and a 28-site campground. Locals consider the paddling trails under canopies of arching mangroves one of the best kayaking spots in the Keys. Manatees frequent the area, and it's a great spot for bird-watching. Herons, egrets, ibis, plovers, and sanderlings are commonly spotted. Raptors are often seen in the park, especially during migration periods. ⊠ *MM 57 OS, 56200 Overseas Hwy., Little Crawl Key*

Close Encounters of the Flipper Kind

CLOSE UP

Here in the Florida Keys, where Milton Santini made the 1963 movie *Flipper*, close encounters of the mammalian kind are an everyday occurrence. There are a handful of facilities that allow you to commune with trained dolphins. In-water programs, where you actually swim with these intelligent creatures, are extremely popular, and require advance reservations. All programs begin with a course on dolphin physiology and behavior taught by a marine biologist. Afterward you learn a few important do's and don'ts (for example, don't wave your hands—you might, literally, send the wrong signal). Finally, you take the plunge.

For the in-water programs, the dolphins swim all around you. If you lie on your back with your feet out, they use their snouts to push you around. You can also grab a dorsal fin for an exciting ride. The in-water encounter lasts between 10 and 25 minutes, depending on the program. The entire experience takes about two hours. The best time to go is when it's warm, from March through October. You spend a lot of time in and out of the water, and you can feel your teeth chattering on a chilly day.

There's no need to get completely wet, however. Waterside programs let you feed, shake hands, and do tricks with dolphins from a submerged platform. These are great for people who aren't strong swimmers or for youngsters who don't meet a facility's minimum age requirements for in-water programs.

Possibilities include the Dolphin Connection in Duck Key, Dolphin Cove and Dolphins Plus in Key Largo (FChapter 2, The Upper Keys), and the Dolphin Research Center in Grassy Key.

☎ *305/289–2690* ⊕ *www.floridastateparks.org/curryham-mock* ☞ *$4.50 for 1 person, $6 for 2, 50¢ per additional person* ☉ *Daily 8–sunset.*

★ **Dolphin Research Center.** The 1963 movie *Flipper* popularized the notion of humans interacting with dolphins, and Milton Santini, the film's creator, also opened this center, which is home to a colony of dolphins and sea lions. The nonprofit center has educational sessions and programs that allow you to greet the dolphins from dry land or play with them in their watery habitat. You can even paint a T-shirt with a dolphin—you pick the paint, the dolphin "designs" your shirt ($55 plus admission). The center also offers five-day programs for children and adults with disabilities. ✉ *MM*

59 BS, 58901 Overseas Hwy. ☎*305/289–1121 information, 305/289–0002 reservations* ⊕*www.dolphins.org* ⊜*$20* ⊙*Daily 9–4:30.*

WHERE TO EAT

$$$$ ✕**Hideaway Café.** *American.* The name says it all. Tucked between Grassy Key and Marathon, it's easy to miss if you're barnstorming through the middle islands. When you find it (upstairs at Rainbow Bend Resort), you'll discover a favorite of locals who appreciate a well-planned menu, lovely ocean view, and quiet evening away from the crowds—fancy with white tablecloths, but homey with worn carpeting. For starters, dig into escargots à la Edison (sautéed with vegetables, pepper, cognac, and cream). Then feast on several specialties, such as a rarely found chateaubriand for one, a whole roasted duck, or the seafood medley combining the catch of the day with scallops and shrimp in a savory sauce. ⑤*Average main: $30* ⊠*MM 58 OS, Rainbow Bend Resort, 57784 Overseas Hwy.* ☎*305/289–1554* ⊕*www.hideawaycafe.com* ⊙*No lunch.*

WHERE TO STAY

$$ ⌂**Bonefish Resort.** *B&B/Inn.* Set on a skinny lot bedecked with palm trees, banana trees, and hibiscus plantings, this motel-style hideaway is the best choice among the island's back-to-basics properties. **Pros:** decent price for the location; ocean-side setting. **Cons:** decks are small; simple decor. ⑤*Rooms from: $119* ⊠*MM 58 OS, 58070 Overseas Hwy.* ☎*305/743–7107, 800/274–9949* ⊕*www.bonefishresort. com* ➳*3 rooms, 11 efficiencies* �ﾃ*No meals.*

$$ ⌂**Gulf View Waterfront Resort.** *Resort.* With a flock of 15 caged birds, a tortoise, and an iguana on the property, this homey duplex is part resort, part menagerie. **Pros:** parklike setting; sandy beach area with hammocks; close to restaurants. **Cons:** no elevator to office and second-story accommodations; some traffic noise. ⑤*Rooms from: $123* ⊠*MM 58.7 BS, 58743 Overseas Hwy.* ☎*305/289–1414, 877/289–0111* ⊕*www.gulfviewwaterfrontresort.com* ➳*2 rooms, 3 efficiencies, 3 1-bedroom apartments, 3 2-bedroom apartments* ﾃ*No meals.*

MARATHON

MM 53–47.5.

New Englanders founded this former fishing village in the early 1800s. The community on Vaca Key subsequently served as a base for pirates, salvagers (also known as "wreckers"), spongers, and, later, Bahamian farmers who eked out a living growing cotton and other crops. More Bahamians arrived in the hope of finding work building the railroad. According to local lore, Marathon was renamed when a worker commented that it was a marathon task to position the tracks across the 6-mi-long island.

During the building on the railroad, Marathon developed a reputation for lawlessness that rivaled that of the Old West. It is said that to keep the rowdy workers from descending on Key West for their off-hours endeavors, residents would send boatloads of liquor up to Marathon. Needless to say, things have quieted down considerably since then.

Still, Marathon is a bustling town, at least compared to other communities in the Keys. As it leaves something to be desired in the charm department, Marathon may not be your first choice of places to stay, but water sports types will find plenty to enjoy, and its historic and natural attractions merit a visit. Surprisingly good dining options abound, so you'll definitely want to stop for a bite even if you're just passing through on the way to Key West.

Throughout the year, Marathon hosts fishing tournaments (practically monthly), a huge seafood festival in March, and lighted boat parades around the holidays.

GETTING HERE AND AROUND

The SuperShuttle charges $102 per passenger for trips from Miami International Airport to the Upper Keys. To go farther into the Keys, you must book an entire 11-person van, which costs about $250 to Marathon. For a trip to the airport, place your request 24 hours in advance.

Miami-Dade Transit provides daily bus service from MM 50 in Marathon to the Florida City Wal-Mart Supercenter on the mainland. The bus stops at major shopping centers as well as on-demand anywhere along the route during daily round trips on the hour from 6 am to 10 pm. The cost is $2 one way, exact change required. The Lower Keys Shuttle bus runs from Marathon to Key West ($4 one way), with scheduled stops along the way.

ESSENTIALS

Transportation Contacts Lower Keys Shuttle ☎ *305/809–3910*
⊕ *www.kwtransit.com.* **Miami Dade Transit** ☎ *305/770–3131.*
SuperShuttle ☎ *305/871–2000, 800/258–3826* ⊕ *www.su-*
pershuttle.com.

Visitor Information Greater Marathon Chamber of Com-
merce and Visitor Center ✉ *MM 53.5 BS, 12222 Overseas Hwy.*
☎ *305/743–5417, 800/262–7284* ⊕ *www.floridakeysmarathon.com.*

EXPLORING

Grassy Key segues into Marathon with little more than a
slight increase in traffic and higher concentration of commercial establishments. Marathon's roots are anchored in
fishing and boating, so look for marinas to find local color,
fishing charters, and good restaurants. At its north end,
Key Colony Beach is an old-fashioned island neighborhood
worth a visit for its shops and restaurants. Nature lovers
shouldn't miss the attractions on Crane Point. Other good
places to leave the main road are at Sombrero Beach Road
(MM 50), which leads to the beach, and 35th Street (MM
49), which takes you to a funky little marina and restaurant.
U.S. 1 hightails through Hog Key and Knight Key before
the big leap over Florida Bay and Hawk's Channel via the
Seven Mile Bridge.

★ **Crane Point Museum, Nature Center, and Historic Site.** Tucked
☾ away from the highway behind a stand of trees, Crane
Point—part of a 63-acre tract that contains the last-known
undisturbed thatch-palm hammock—is delightfully undeveloped. This multiuse facility includes the **Museum of**
Natural History of the Florida Keys, which has displays
about local wildlife, a seashell exhibit, and a marine-life
display that makes you feel you're at the bottom of the
sea. Kids love the replica 17th-century galleon and pirate
dress-up room where they can play, and the re-created
Cracker House filled with insects, sea-turtle exhibits, and
children's activities. On the 1-mi indigenous loop trail,
visit the **Laura Quinn Wild Bird Center** and the remnants
of a Bahamian village, site of the restored **George Adderly**
House. It is the oldest surviving example of Bahamian tabby
(a concretelike material created from sand and seashells)
construction outside of Key West. A boardwalk crosses
wetlands, rivers, and mangroves before ending at Adderly
Village. From November to Easter, docent-led tours are
available; bring good walking shoes and bug repellent

Marathon

KEY
- ① Restaurants
- ① Hotels
- ◣ Dive Site
- ◤ Boat Launch

Conch Key
- ◆ Conch Key Cottages

TO ISLAMORADA

Duck Key
- ◆ Hawks Cay Resort & Alma

Dolphin Research Center

Grassy Key
- ◆ Gulf View Waterfront Resort
- ◆ Bonefish Resort
- ◆ Hideaway Café

Bamboo Key

Crawl Key
- ◣ Thunderbolt

Curry Hammock State Park

Greater Marathon Chamber of Commerce

125 St.
117 St.
107 St.
Key Colony Bch.
Coco Plum Dr.

① ◆ Golf Course
Key Colony Beach ②

Marathon

Dolphin Dr.
Marathon Airport

110 St.
100 St.
92 St.
84 St.

③

Crane Point Museum, Nature Center, and Historic Site

④
⑤
The Turtle Hospital

63 St.
Gull Terr.
49 St.
47 St.
Ave.

①

Vaca Key

②
126 St.
111 St.
Boot Key Bridge

⑥

⑦

Sombrero Beach

Boot Key

◣ The American

Old Seven Mile Bridge
◆ Pigeon Key
Seven Mile Bridge

◣ Sombrero Reef

↙ TO LOWER KEYS

Restaurants
Fish Tales Market and Eatery, **1**
Herbie's. **3**
Key Colony Inn, **2**

Keys Fisheries Market & Marina, **4**
Lazy Days South, **6**
The Stuffed Pig, **5**
Sunset Grille and Raw Bar, **7**

Hotels
Crystal Bay Resort & Marina, **1**
Tranquility Bay, **2**

during warm weather. ✉ *MM 50.5 BS, 5550 Overseas Hwy.* ☎ *305/743–9100* ⊕ *www.cranepoint.net* ☜ *$12.50* ⊙ *Mon.–Sat. 9–5, Sun. noon–5; call to arrange trail tours.*

Pigeon Key. There's much to like about this 5-acre island under the Old Seven Mile Bridge. You can reach it via a ferry that departs from the behind the visitors center in an old red railroad car on Knight's Key (MM 47 OS). Once there, tour the island on your own or join a guided tour to explore the buildings that formed the early-20th-century work camp for the Overseas Railroad that linked the mainland to Key West in 1912. Later the island became a fish camp, a state park, and then government-administration headquarters. Exhibits in a small museum recall the history of the Keys, the railroad, and railroad baron Henry M. Flagler. The ferry ride with tour lasts two hours; visitors can self-tour and catch the ferry back in a half hour. ✉ *MM 45 OS, 1 Knights Key Blvd., Pigeon Key* ☎ *305/743–5999* ⊕ *www.pigeonkey.net* ☜ *$12* ⊙ *Daily 9:30–2:30; ferry departures at 10, 11:30, 1, 2:30.*

Seven Mile Bridge. This is one of the most photographed images in the Keys. Actually measuring slightly less than 7 mi, it connects the Middle and Lower Keys and is believed to be the world's longest segmental bridge. It has 39 expansion joints separating its various concrete sections. Each April runners gather in Marathon for the annual Seven Mile Bridge Run. The expanse running parallel to Seven Mile Bridge is what remains of the **Old Seven Mile Bridge,** an engineering and architectural marvel in its day that's now on the National Register of Historic Places. Once proclaimed the Eighth Wonder of the World, it rested on a record 546 concrete piers. No cars are allowed on the old bridge today.

★ **Sombrero Beach.** Here, pleasant, shaded picnic areas over-
☾ look a coconut palm–lined grassy stretch and the Atlantic Ocean. Roped-off areas allow swimmers, boaters, and windsurfers to share the narrow cove. Facilities include barbecue grills, a large playground, a pier, a volleyball court, and a paved, lighted bike path off Overseas Highway. Sunday afternoons draw lots of local families toting coolers. The park is accessible for those with disabilities and allows leashed pets. Turn east at the traffic light in Marathon and follow signs to the end. **Amenities:** showers, toilets. **Best for:** families, swimming, windsurfing. ✉ *MM 50 OS, Sombrero Beach Rd.* ☎ *305/743–0033* ☜ *Free* ⊙ *Daily 8–sunset.*

TURTLE TIME

Five species of threatened and endangered sea turtles frequent the waters of the Florida Keys. The **logger-head**, the most common, is named for the shape of its noggin. It grows to a heft of 300 pounds. It is the only one of the local turtles listed as threatened rather than endangered.

The vegetarian **green turtle** was once hunted for its meat, which has brought populations to their endangered stage. It can reach an impressive 500 pounds.

Named for the shape of its mouth, the **hawksbill turtle** is a relative lightweight at 150 pounds. It prefers rocks and reefs for habitat. The Keys are the only U.S. breeding site for the endangered critter.

The largest reptile alive, the **leatherback turtle** can weigh in at up to 2,000 pounds, attained from a diet of mainly jellyfish.

The rarest of local sea turtles, the **Kemps Ridley** is named after a Key West fisherman. A carnivore, it grows to 100 pounds.

The biggest threats to sea turtle survival include fibro-papilloma tumors, monofilament fishing lines (which can sever their flippers), entanglement in ropes and nets, boat propeller run-ins, swallowing plastic bags (which appear to them as jellyfish), oil spills, and other human and natural impact.

3

☾ **The Turtle Hospital.** More than 100 injured sea turtles check in here every year. The 90-minute guided tours take you into recovery and surgical areas at the world's only state-certified veterinary hospital for sea turtles. In the "hospital bed" tanks, you can see recovering patients and others that are permanent residents due to their injuries. Call ahead—tours are sometime cancelled due to medical emergencies. ⊠ *MM 48.5 BS, 2396 Overseas Hwy.* ☎ *305/743–2552* ⊕ *www.turtlehospital.org* 🖾 *$15* ☉ *Daily 9–5.*

WHERE TO EAT

$ ✕**Fish Tales Market and Eatery.** *Seafood.* This roadside eatery with its own seafood market serves signature dishes such as snapper on grilled rye with coleslaw and melted Muenster cheese and a fried fish burrito. You also can slurp luscious lobster bisque or tomato-based conch chowder. There are burgers, chicken, and dogs for those who don't do seafood. Plan to dine early; it's only open until 6:30 pm.

This is a no-frills kind of place with a loyal local following, unfussy ambiance, a couple of outside picnic tables, and friendly service. ⑤ *Average main: $8 ⊠ MM 52.5 OS, 11711 Overseas Hwy.* ☎ *305/743–9196, 888/662–4822* ⊕ *www.floridalobster.com* ⚑ *Reservations not accepted* ☉ *Closed Sun.*

$ ✕ **Herbie's.** *American.* Since 1972, this has been the go-to spot for quick-and-affordable comfort food from cheeseburgers and fried oysters to shrimp scampi and filet mignon. You'll find all the local staples—conch, lobster tail, and fresh fish—to enjoy at picnic tables in the screened-in porch or inside where it's air-conditioned. Its shack-like appearance gives it an old-Keys feel. ⑤ *Average main: $10 ⊠ MM 50.5, 6350 Overseas Hwy.* ☎ *305/743–6373* ⚑ *Reservations not accepted* ⊟ *No credit cards* ☉ *Closed Sun. and Mon.*

$$ ✕ **Key Colony Inn.** *Italian.* The inviting aroma of an Italian kitchen pervades this family-owned favorite with a supperclub atmosphere. As you'd expect, the service is friendly and attentive. For lunch there are fish and steak entrées served with fries, salad, and bread in addition to Italian specialties. At dinner you can't miss with traditional dishes like veal Oscar and New York strip, or such specialties as seafood *Italiano,* a dish of scallops and shrimp sautéed in garlic butter and served with marinara sauce over a bed of linguine. The place is renowned for its Sunday brunch, served from November to April. ⑤ *Average main: $19 ⊠ MM 54 OS, 700 W. Ocean Dr., Key Colony Beach* ☎ *305/743–0100* ⊕ *www.kcinn.com.*

$$ ✕ **Keys Fisheries Market & Marina.** *Seafood.* From the parking
★ lot, this commercial warehouse flanked by fishing boats and
☺ lobster traps barely hints at the restaurant inside. Order at the window outside, pick up your food, then dine at one of the waterfront picnic tables outfitted with rolls of paper towels. The menu is comprised of fresh seafood and a token hamburger and chicken sandwich. A huge lobster Reuben ($14.95) served on thick slices of toasted bread is the signature dish. Other delights include the shrimp burger, very rich whiskey-peppercorn snapper, and the Keys Kombo (grilled lobster, shrimp, scallops, and mahimahi for $29). There are also sushi and a bar serving beer and wine. Kids like feeding the fish while they wait for their food. ⑤ *Average main: $16 ⊠ MM 49 BS, 3390 Gulfview Ave., at the end of 35th St. (turn right on 35th St. off Gulfview Ave.)* ☎ *305/743–4353, 866/743–4353* ⊕ *www.keysfisheries.com* ⚑ *Reservations not accepted.*

$$$ ✕ **Lazy Days South.** *Seafood.* Tucked into Marathon Marina
★ a half-mile north of the Seven Mile Bridge, this restaurant
offers views just as spectacular as its highly lauded food. A
spin-off of an Islamorada favorite, here you'll find a wide
range of daily offerings from fried or sautéed conch and a
coconut-fried fish du jour sandwich to seafood pastas and
beef tips over rice. Choose a table on the outdoor deck,
or inside underneath paddle fans and surrounded by local
art. ⑤ *Average main: $22* ⊠ *MM 47.3 OS, 725 11th St.*
☎ *305/289–0839* ⊕ *www.keysdining.com/lazydays.*

$ ✕ **The Stuffed Pig.** *American.* With only nine tables and a
counter inside, this breakfast-and-lunch place is always
hopping. When the weather's right, grab a table out back.
The kitchen whips up daily lunch specials like burgers, sea-
food platters, or pulled pork with hand-cut fries, but a quick
glance around the room reveals that the all-day breakfast is
the main draw. You can get the usual breakfast plates, but
most newcomers opt for oddities like the lobster omelet,
alligator tail and eggs, or "grits and grunts" (that's fish,
to the rest of us). ⑤ *Average main: $9* ⊠ *MM 49 BS, 3520
Overseas Hwy.* ☎ *305/743–4059* ⊕ *www.thestuffedpig.com*
⚥ *Reservations not accepted* ▭ *No credit cards* ☉ *No dinner.*

$$ ✕ **Sunset Grille & Raw Bar.** *Seafood.* After a walk or bike
ride along the Old Seven Mile Bridge, treat yourself to a
seafood lunch or dinner at this vaulted tiki hut under the
bridge. For lunch, start with the conch chowder or fritters, and then move on to the Voodoo grouper sandwich
topped with mango-guava mayo, and finish with a tasty
key lime pie. Wear your swimsuit if you want to take a dip
in the pool for a post-lunch swim. Dinner specialties add
a creative twist, like the Brie-stuffed filet mignon, coconut
curry lobster, and Thai peanut shrimp. ⑤ *Average main:
$22* ⊠ *MM 47 OS, 7 Knights Key Blvd.* ☎ *305/396–7235*
⊕ *www.sunsetgrille7milebridge.com.*

WHERE TO STAY

*For expanded reviews, facilities, and current deals, visit
Fodors.com.*

$$$$ ⊡ **Tranquility Bay.** *Resort.* Ralph Lauren could have designed
★ the rooms at this luxurious beach resort. **Pros:** secluded
☾ setting; gorgeous design; lovely crescent beach. **Cons:** a bit
sterile; no real Keys atmosphere; cramped building layout.
⑤ *Rooms from: $399* ⊠ *MM 48.5 BS, 2600 Overseas Hwy.*
☎ *305/289–0888, 866/643–5397* ⊕ *www.tranquilitybay.com*
⚲ *45 2-bedroom suites, 41 3-bedroom suites* ⧈ *No meals.*

SPORTS AND THE OUTDOORS

BIKING

Tooling around on two wheels is a good way to see Marathon. There's easy cycling on a 1-mile off-road path that connects to the 2 miles of the Old Seven Mile Bridge leading to Pigeon Key.

Bike Marathon Bike Rentals. "Have bikes, will deliver" could be the motto of this company, which gets beach cruisers to your hotel door for $35 per week, including a helmet and basket. Note that there's no physical location, but services are available Monday through Saturday 9–4 and Sunday 9–2. ☎ *305/743-3204* ⊕ *www.bikemarathonbikerentals.com.*

Overseas Outfitters. Aluminum cruisers and hybrid bikes are available for rent at this outfitter for $10 to $15 per day. It's open weekdays 9–6 and Saturday 9–3. ✉ *MM 48 BS, 1700 Overseas Hwy.* ☎ *305/289–1670* ⊕ *www.overseasoutfitters.com.*

BOATING

Sail, motor, or paddle: Whatever your choice of modes, boating is what the Keys is all about. Brave the Atlantic waves and reefs or explore the backcountry islands on the Gulf side. If you don't have a lot of boating and chart-reading experience, it's a good idea to tap into local knowledge on a charter.

Captain Pip's. This operator rents 20- to 24-foot outboards, $195–$330 per day, as well as tackle and snorkeling gear. You also can charter a small boat with a guide, $450–$550 for a half day and $700–$800 for a full day. Multi-day packages are also available. ✉ *MM 47.5 BS, 1410 Overseas Hwy.* ☎ *305/743–4403, 800/707–1692* ⊕ *www.captainpips.com.*

Fish 'n Fun. Get out on the water on 19- to 26-foot powerboats starting at $140 for a half day, $190 for a full day. The company offers free delivery in the Middle Keys. You also can rent Jet Skis and kayaks. ✉ *MM 49.5 OS, 4590 Overseas Hwy., at Banana Bay Resort & Marina* ☎ *305/743–2275, 800/471–3440* ⊕ *www.fishnfunrentals.com.*

FISHING

For recreational anglers, the deepwater fishing is superb in both bay and ocean. Marathon West Hump, one good spot, has depths ranging from 500 to more than 1,000 feet. Locals fish from a half-dozen bridges, including Long Key

Bridge, the Old Seven Mile Bridge, and both ends of Tom's Harbor. Barracuda, bonefish, and tarpon all frequent local waters. Party boats and private charters are available.

★ *Marathon Lady.* Morning, afternoon, and night, fish for mahimahi, grouper, and other tasty catch aboard this 73-footer, which departs on half-day ($45) excursions from the Vaca Cut Bridge, north of Marathon. Join the crew for night fishing ($55) from 6:30 to midnight from Memorial Day to Labor Day; it's especially beautiful on a full-moon night. ⊠ *MM 53 OS, at 117th St.* ☎ *305/743–5580* ⊕ *www. fishfloridakeys.com/marathonlady.*

Sea Dog Charters. Captain Jim Purcell, a deep-sea specialist for ESPN's *The American Outdoorsman,* provides one of the best values in Keys fishing. Next to the Seven Mile Grill, his company offers half- and full-day offshore, reef and wreck, and backcountry fishing trips, as well as fishing and snorkeling trips aboard 30- to 37-foot boats. The cost is $60 per person for a half day, regardless of whether your group fills the boat, and includes bait, light tackle, ice, coolers, and fishing licenses. If you prefer an all-day private charter on a 37-foot boat, he offers those, too, for $600 for up to six people. A fuel surcharge may apply. ⊠ *MM 47.5 BS, 1248 Overseas Hwy.* ☎ *305/743–8255* ⊕ *www. seadogcharters.net.*

GOLF

Key Colony Beach Golf & Tennis. This 9-hole course near Marathon charges $13 for the course ($8 for each additional 9 holes), $3 per person for club rental, and $2 for a pull cart. There are no reserved tee times and there's no rush. Play from 7:30 am–dusk. A little pro shop meets basic golf needs. ⊠ *MM 53.5 OS, 460 8th St., Key Colony Beach* ⊕ *www.keycolonybeach.net/recreation.html.*

SCUBA DIVING AND SNORKELING

Local dive operations take you to Sombrero Reef and Lighthouse, the most popular down-under destination in these parts. For a shallow dive and some lobster-nabbing, Coffins Patch, off Key Colony Beach, is a good choice. A number of wrecks such as *Thunderbolt* serve as artificial reefs. Many operations out of this area will also take you to Looe Key Reef.

Hall's Diving Center & Career Institute. The institute has been training divers for more than 40 years. Along with conventional twice-a-day snorkel and two-tank dive trips ($40–

$65) to the reefs at Sombrero Lighthouse and wrecks like the *Thunderbolt,* the company has more unusual offerings like photography and nitrox courses. ✉ *MM 48.5 BS, 1994 Overseas Hwy.* ☎ *305/743–5929, 800/331–4255* ⊕ *www. hallsdiving.com.*

Spirit Snorkeling. Snorkeling excursions to Sombrero Reef and Lighthouse Reef cost $30 a head. ✉ *MM 47.5 BS, 1410 Overseas Hwy., Slip No. 1* ☎ *305/289–0614* ⊕ *www. spiritsnorkeling.net.*

Tildens Scuba Center. Tildens Scuba Center has been providing lessons, tours, gear rental, and daily snorkel and scuba adventures for the past 30 years. Snorkel cruises range from $36 to $46; diving starts at $65. Look for the large moray eel mural on the side of the building. ✉ *MM 49.5 BS, 4650 Overseas Hwy.* ☎ *305/743–7255, 888/728–2235* ⊕ *www. tildensscubacenter.com.*

TOURS

Conch Air. Specializing in romantic sunset flights, this outfitter flies out of Marathon Airport in a 1935 Waco, an open-cockpit biplane for two passengers; scenic rides start at $55 per person for a two-person flight. ✉ *Marathon Airport, 9400 Overseas Hwy.* ☎ *305/395–1117* ⊕ *www. conch-air.com.*

WATER SPORTS

Jerry's Charter Service & Watersport Rentals. For all your watersports-rental needs head to this one-stop place. It rents kayaks, Jet Skis, sailboats, snorkel equipment, fishing rods, and power- and pontoon boats. ✉ *MM 49.5 BS, Banana Bay Resort & Marina, 4590 Overseas Hwy.* ☎ *305/743–7298, 800/775–2646* ⊕ *www.jerryscharters.com.*

The Lower Keys

4

WORD OF MOUTH

"My daughter and I are considering a trip to Miami Beach. Is a day trip to the Keys feasible or would you generally overnight?"

—Nickity

"The activities and stops during the drive are much of the pleasure of a journey through the Keys. I agree with other posters, that making this an overnight is the correct plan. Key West has great character and charm, but racing through the Keys to get to KW is missing much of the best part."

—stumpworks73

www.fodors.com/forums

By Chelle
Koster
Walton

BEGINNING AT BAHIA HONDA KEY, the islands of the Florida Keys become smaller, more clustered, and more numerous, a result of ancient tidal water flowing between the Florida Straits and the gulf. Here you're likely to see more birds and mangroves than other tourists, and more refuges, beaches, and campgrounds than museums, restaurants, and hotels. The islands are made up of two types of limestone, both denser than the highly permeable Key Largo limestone of the Upper Keys. As a result, fresh water forms in pools rather than percolating through the rock, creating watering holes that support alligators, snakes, deer, rabbits, raccoons, and migratory ducks. (Many of these animals can be seen in the National Key Deer Refuge on Big Pine Key.) Nature was generous with her beauty in the Lower Keys, which have both Looe Key Reef, arguably the Keys' most beautiful tract of coral, and Bahia Honda State Park, considered one of the best beaches in the world for its fine sand dunes, clear warm waters, and panoramic vista of bridges, hammocks, and azure sky and sea. Big Pine Key is fishing headquarters for a laid-back community that swells with retirees in the winter. South of it, the dribble of islands can flash by in a blink of an eye if you don't take the time to stop at a roadside eatery or check out tours and charters at the little marinas. They include Little Torch Key, Middle Torch Key, Ramrod Key, Summerland Key, Cudjoe Key, Sugarloaf Keys, and Saddlebunch Key. Lying offshore of Little Torch Key, Little Palm Island once welcomed U.S. presidents and other notables to its secluded fishing camp. It was also the location for the movie *PT 109* about John F. Kennedy's celebrated World War II heroism. Today it still offers respite to the upper class in the form of an exclusive getaway resort accessible only by boat.

ORIENTATION AND PLANNING

GETTING ORIENTED

In truth, the Lower Keys include Key West, but since it's covered in its own section and is as different from the rest of the Lower Keys as peanut butter is from jelly, this section covers just the keys between MM 37 and MM 9. The Seven Mile Bridge drops you into the lap of this homey, quiet part of the Keys.

Heed speed limits in these parts. They may seem incredibly strict, given that the traffic is lightest of anywhere in the

TOP REASONS TO GO

■ **Wildlife-viewing.** The Lower Keys are populated with all kinds of animals. Watch especially for Key deer but also other wildlife at the Blue Hole in National Key Deer Refuge.

■ **Bahia Honda Key State Park.** Explore the beach and trails, then camp for the night at this gorgeous state park.

■ **Kayaking.** Get out in a kayak to spot birds in the Keys' backcountry wildlife refuges.

■ **Snorkeling.** Grab a mask and fin and head to Looe Key Reef to see amazing coral formations and fish so bright and animated they look like cartoons

■ **Fishing.** All kinds of fishing are great in the Lower Keys. Cast from a bridge, boat, or shoreline flats for bonefish, tarpon, and other feisty catches.

Keys, but the purpose is to protect the resident Key deer population, and officers of the law pay strict attention.

PLANNING

GETTING HERE AND AROUND

To get to the Lower Keys, fly into either Miami International Airport or Key West International Airport. Key West is closer, but there are far fewer flights coming in and going out. Rental cars are available at both airports. In addition, there is bus service from the Key West airport; $4 one way with Keys Transit.

ESSENTIALS

Transportation Contacts **City of Key West Department of Transportation** ☎ *305/809–3910* ⊕ *www.kwtransit.com.*

RESTAURANTS

Restaurants are fewer and farther between in the Lower Keys, and you won't find the variety of offerings in eateries closer to Miami and in Key West. Mostly you'll find seafood joints where dinner is fresh off the hook and license plates or dollar bills stuck to the wall count for decor. For a special occasion, hop aboard the ferry at Little Torch Key to experience the globe-trotting cuisine of private Little Palm Island resort. Restaurants may close for a two- to four-week vacation during the slow season—between mid-September and mid-November.

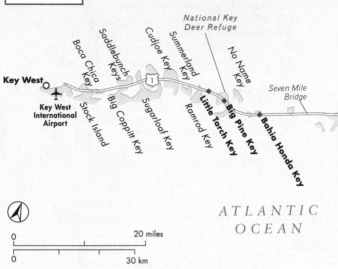

The Lower Keys

Gulf of Mexico

National Key Deer Refuge

Boca Chica Key
Saddlebunch Keys
Cudjoe Key
Summerland Key
No Name Key

Key West

Key West International Airport

Stock Island
Big Coppitt Key
Sugarloaf Key
Ramrod Key
Little Torch Key
Big Pine Key
Bahia Honda Key

Seven Mile Bridge

ATLANTIC OCEAN

0 — 20 miles
0 — 30 km

HOTELS

Fishing lodges, dive resorts, and campgrounds are the most prevalent type of lodging in this part of the Keys. Rates are generally much lower than on other Keys, especially Key West, which makes this a good place to stay if you're on a budget.

HOTEL AND RESTAURANT PRICES

Prices in the restaurant reviews are the average cost of a main course at dinner or, if dinner is not served, at lunch, excluding taxes and service charges. Prices in the hotel reviews are the lowest cost of a standard double room in high season, excluding taxes, service charges, and meal plans (except at all-inclusives). Prices for rentals are the lowest per-night cost for a one-bedroom unit in high season.

BAHIA HONDA KEY

MM 38–36.

All of Bahia Honda Key is devoted to its eponymous state park, which keeps it in a pristine state. Besides the park's outdoor activities, it offers an up-close look of the original railroad bridge.

GETTING HERE AND AROUND

Bahia Honda Key lies a short distance from the southern terminus of the Seven Mile Bridge. A two-lane road travels its 2-mile length. It is 32 miles north of Key West. If you fly into Key West International Airport, you can either rent a car or take the Keys Transit bus to get here.

ESSENTIALS

Transportation Contacts City of Key West Department of Transportation (☎ 305/809–3910 ⊕ www.keywestcity.com).

EXPLORING

★ **Fodor's**Choice **Bahia Honda State Park.** Most first-time visitors ♻ to the region are dismayed by the lack of beaches—but then they discover Bahia Honda Key. The 524-acre park sprawls across both sides of the highway, giving it 2½ mi of fabulous sandy coastline. The snorkeling isn't bad, either; there's underwater life (soft coral, queen conchs, random little fish) just a few hundred feet offshore. Although swimming, kayaking, fishing, and boating are the main reasons to visit, you shouldn't miss biking along the 2½ mi of flat roads or hiking the Silver Palm Trail, with rare West Indian plants and several species found nowhere else in the nation. Along the way you'll be treated to a variety of butterflies. Seasonal ranger-led nature programs take place at or depart from the Sand and Sea Nature Center. There are rental cabins, a campground, snack bar, gift shop, 19-slip marina, nature center, and facilities for renting kayaks and arranging snorkeling tours. Get a panoramic view of the island from what's left of the railroad—the Bahia Honda Bridge. ⊠ MM 37 OS, 36850 Overseas Hwy. ☎ 305/872–2353 ⊕ www.floridastateparks.org/bahiahonda ⊠ $4.50 for 1 person, $9 for 2 people, 50¢ per additional person ☉ Daily 8–sunset.

WHERE TO STAY

For expanded reviews, facilities, and current deals, visit Fodors.com.

★ **Fodor's**Choice 🏨 **Bahia Honda State Park.** *Rental.* Elsewhere $$$ you'd pay big bucks for the wonderful water views available at these cabins on Florida Bay. **Pros:** great bay-front views; beachfront camping; affordable rates. **Cons:** books up fast; area can be buggy. ⑤ *Rooms from: $183* ⊠ *MM 37 OS, 36850 Overseas Hwy.* ☎*305/872-2353, 800/326-3521* ⊕*www.reserveamerica.com* ⌁*80 partial hook-up campsites, 6 cabin units* ⊙*No meals.*

SPORTS AND THE OUTDOORS

BEACHES

Sandspur Beach. Bahia Honda Key State Beach contains three beaches in all—on both the Atlantic Ocean and the Gulf of Mexico. Sandspur Beach, the largest, is regularly declared the best beach in Florida, and you'll be hard-pressed to argue. The sand is baby-powder soft, and the aqua water is warm, clear, and shallow. With their mild currents, the beaches are great for swimming, even with small fry. **Amenities:** food and drink, showers, toilets, water sports. **Best for:** snorkeling, swimming. ⊠ *MM 37 OS, 36850 Overseas Hwy.* ☎*305/872-2353* ⊕*www.floridastateparks.org/bahiahonda* ⌁*$4.50 for 1 person, $9 for 2 people, 50¢ per additional person* ⊙*Daily 8-sunset.*

SCUBA DIVING AND SNORKELING

Bahia Honda Dive Shop. The concessionaire at Bahia Honda State Park manages a 19-slip marina; rents wet suits, snorkel equipment, and corrective masks; and operates twice-a-day offshore-reef snorkel trips ($30 plus $9 for equipment). Park visitors looking for other fun can rent kayaks ($12 per hour for a single, $18 for a double) and beach chairs. ⊠*MM 37 OS, 36850 Overseas Hwy.* ☎*305/872-3210* ⊕*www.bahiahondapark.com.*

BIG PINE KEY

MM 32-30.

Welcome to the Keys' most natural holdout, where wildlife refuges protect rare and endangered animals. Here you have left behind the commercialism of the Upper Keys for an authentic backcountry atmosphere. How could things get more casual than Key Largo, you might wonder? Find out by exiting U.S. 1 to explore the habitat of the charmingly diminutive Key deer or cast a line from No Name Bridge. Tours explore the expansive waters of National Key Deer Refuge and Great White Heron National Wildlife Refuge, one of the first such refuges in the country. Along with Key West National Wildlife Refuge, it encompasses more than 200,000 acres of water and more than 8,000 acres of land on 49 small islands. Besides its namesake bird, the Great

White Heron National Wildlife Refuge provides habitat for uncounted species of birds and three species of sea turtles. It is the only U.S. breeding site for the endangered hawksbill turtle.

GETTING HERE AND AROUND
Most people rent a car to get to Big Pine Key so they can also explore Key West and other parts of the chain.

ESSENTIALS
Visitor Information Big Pine and the Lower Keys Chamber of Commerce ⊠ *MM 31 OS, 31020 Overseas Hwy.* ☎ *305/872–2411, 800/872–3722* ⊕ *www.lowerkeyschamber.com.*

EXPLORING

★ **National Key Deer Refuge.** This 84,824-acre refuge was established in 1957 to protect the dwindling population of the Key deer, one of more than 20 animals and plants classified as endangered or threatened in the Florida Keys. The Key deer, which stands about 30 inches at the shoulders and is a subspecies of the Virginia white-tailed deer, once roamed throughout the Lower and Middle Keys, but hunting, destruction of their habitat, and a growing human population caused their numbers to decline to 27 by 1957. The deer have made a comeback, increasing their numbers to approximately 750. The best place to see Key deer in the refuge is at the end of Key Deer Boulevard and on No Name Key, a sparsely populated island just east of Big Pine Key. Mornings and evenings are the best time to spot them. Deer may turn up along the road at any time of day, so drive slowly. They wander into nearby yards to nibble tender grass and bougainvillea blossom, but locals do not appreciate tourists driving into their neighborhoods after them. Feeding them is against the law and puts them in danger. The refuge also has 21 other listed endangered and threatened species of plants and animals, including five that are found nowhere else.

A quarry left over from railroad days, the **Blue Hole** is the largest body of freshwater in the Keys. From the observation platform and nearby walking trail, you might see the resident alligator, turtles, and other wildlife. There are two well-marked trails, recently revamped: the Jack Watson Nature Trail (.6 mi), named after an environmentalist and the refuge's first warden; and the Fred Mannillo Nature Trail, one of the most wheelchair-accessible places to see an unspoiled pine-rockland forest and wetlands. The visitor center has exhibits on Keys biology and ecology. The refuge also provides information on the Key West National Wildlife Refuge and the Great White Heron National Wildlife Refuge. Accessible only by water, both are popular with kayak outfitters. ⊠ *MM 30.5 BS, Visitor Center–Headquarters, Big Pine Shopping Center, 28950 Watson Blvd.* ☎ *305/872–2239* ⊕ *www.fws.gov/nationalkeydeer* ☜ *Free* ⊙ *Daily sunrise–sunset; headquarters weekdays 8–5.*

WHERE TO EAT

$ ╳**Good Food Conspiracy.** *Vegetarian.* Like good wine, this small natural-foods eatery and market surrenders its pleasures a little at a time. Step inside to the aroma of brewing coffee, and then pick up the scent of fresh strawberries or carrots blending into a smoothie, the green aroma of wheatgrass juice, followed by the earthy odor of hummus. Order raw or cooked vegetarian and vegan dishes, organic soups and salads, and organic coffees and teas. Bountiful sandwiches (available halved) include the popular tuna melt or hummus and avocado. If you can't sit down for a bite in the back courtyard, stock up on healthful snacks like dried fruits, raw nuts, and carob-covered almonds. Ⓢ *Average main: $7* ⊠ *MM 30.2 OS, 30150 Overseas Hwy.* ☎ *305/872–3945* ⊕ *www.goodfoodconspiracy.com* ⌲ *Reservations not accepted* ⊙ *No dinner Sun.*

$ ╳**No Name Pub.** *American.* This no-frills honky-tonk has been around since 1936, delighting inveterate locals and intrepid vacationers who come for the excellent pizza, cold beer, and interesting companionship. The decor, such as it is, amounts to the autographed dollar bills that cover every inch of the place. The full menu printed on place mats includes a tasty conch chowder, a half-pound fried-grouper sandwich, spaghetti and meatballs, and seafood baskets. The lighting is poor, the furnishings are rough, and the music is oldies. This former brothel and bait shop is just before the No Name Key Bridge. It's a bit hard to find, but worth the trouble if you want a singular Keys experience. Ⓢ *Average main: $15* ⊠ *MM 30 BS, turn west on Wilder Rd., left on South St., right on Ave. B, right on Watson Blvd.* ☎ *305/872–9115* ⊕ *www.nonamepub.com* ⌲ *Reservations not accepted.*

WHERE TO STAY

For expanded reviews, facilities, and current deals, visit Fodors.com.

$ ⊡ **Big Pine Key Fishing Lodge.** *Hotel.* There's a congenial atmosphere at this lively family-owned lodge-campground-marina—a happy mix of tent campers (who have the fabulous waterfront real estate), RVers (who look pretty permanent), and motel dwellers (rooms start at $109) who like to mingle at the rooftop pool and challenge each other to a game of poker. **Pros:** local fishing crowd; nice pool; great price. **Cons:** RV park is too close to motel; deer will eat your food if you're camping. Ⓢ *Rooms from: $39* ⊠ *MM 33 OS, 33000 Overseas Hwy.* ☎ *305/872–2351* ⤳ *16 efficiencies, 97 campsites with full hook-ups, 61 campsites without hook-ups* ⋮○⋮ *No meals.*

$$$$ ⊡ **Deer Run Bed & Breakfast.** *B&B/Inn.* Key deer wander the
★ grounds of this beachfront bed-and-breakfast, set on a quiet street lined with buttonwoods and mangroves. **Pros:** quiet location; healthy breakfasts; complimentary bike, kayak, and state park passes use. **Cons:** price is a bit high; hard to find. Ⓢ *Rooms from: $235* ⊠ *MM 33 OS, 1997 Long Beach Dr.* ☎ *305/872–2015* ⊕ *www.deerrunfloridabb.com* ⤳ *4 rooms* ⋮○⋮ *Breakfast.*

SPORTS AND THE OUTDOORS

BIKING

A good 10 miles of paved roads run from MM 30.3 BS, along Wilder Road, across the bridge to No Name Key, and along Key Deer Boulevard into the National Key Deer Refuge. Along the way you might see some Key deer. Stay off the trails that lead into wetlands, where fat tires can damage the environment.

Big Pine Bicycle Center. Owner Marty Baird is an avid cyclist and enjoys sharing his knowledge of great places to ride. He's also skilled at selecting the right bike for the journey, and he knows his repairs, too. His old-fashioned single-speed, fat-tire cruisers rent for $8 per half day and $10 for a full day. Helmets, baskets, and locks are included. ⊠ *MM 30.9 BS, 31 County Rd.* ☎ *305/872–0130.*

FISHING

Cast from No Name Key Bridge or hire a charter to take you into backcountry or deep waters for fishing year-round.

4

Strike Zone Charters. Glass-bottom-boat excursions venture into the backcountry and Atlantic Ocean. The five-hour Island Excursion ($55 plus fuel surcharge) emphasizes nature and Keys history; besides close encounters with birds, sea life, and vegetation, there's a fish cookout on an island. Snorkel and fishing equipment, food, and drinks are included. This is one of the few nature outings in the Keys with wheelchair access. Deep-sea charter rates for up to six people are $650 for a half day, $850 for a full day. It also offers flats fishing in the Gulf of Mexico. Dive excursions head to the wreck of the 110-foot *Adolphus Busch* ($55), and scuba ($45) and snorkel ($35) trips to Looe Key Reef, prime scuba and snorkeling territory, aboard glass-bottom boats. ✉ *MM 29.6 BS, 29675 Overseas Hwy.* ☎ *305/872–9863, 800/654–9560* ⊕ *www.strikezonecharter.com.*

KAYAKING

There's nothing like the vast expanse of pristine waters and mangrove islands preserved by national refuges from here to Key West. The mazelike terrain can be confusing, so it's wise to hire a guide at least the first time out.

★ **Big Pine Kayak Adventures.** There's no excuse to skip a water adventure with this convenient kayak rental service, which delivers them to your lodging or anywhere between Seven Mile Bridge and Stock Island. The company, headed by *The Florida Keys Paddling Guide* author Bill Keogh, will rent you a kayak and then ferry you—called taxi-yakking—to remote islands with clear instructions on how to paddle back on your own. Rentals are by the half day or full day. Group kayak tours ($50 each for three hours) explore the mangrove forests of Great White Heron and Key Deer National Wildlife Refuges. Custom tours ($125 each and up, four hours) transport you to exquisite backcountry areas teeming with wildlife. Kayak fishing charters are also popular. ✉ *MM 30 BS, Old Wooden Bridge Fishing Camp, turn right at traffic light, continue on Wilder Rd. toward No Name Key* ☎ *305/872-7474* ⊕ *www.keyskayaktours.com.*

SCUBA DIVING AND SNORKELING

Close to Looe Key Reef, this is prime scuba and snorkeling territory. Some resorts cater to divers with dive boats that depart from their own dock. Others can make arrangements for you.

LITTLE TORCH KEY

MM 29–10.

Little Torch Key and its neighbor islands, Ramrod Key and Summerland Key, are good jumping-off points for divers headed for Looe Key Reef. The islands also serve as a refuge for those who want to make forays into Key West but not stay in the thick of things.

The undeveloped backcountry at your door makes Little Torch Key an ideal location for fishing and kayaking. Nearby Ramrod Key, which also caters to divers bound for Looe Key, derives its name from a ship that wrecked on nearby reefs in the early 1800s.

Baby's Coffee. The aroma of rich roasting coffee beans arrests you at the door of "the Southernmost Coffee Roaster." Buy it by the pound or by the cup along with sandwiches and sweets. ⊠ *MM 15 OS, 3178 Overseas Hwy.* ☎ *305/744–9866, 800/523–2326* ⊕ *www.babyscoffee.com.*

WHERE TO EAT

$ ✕ **Geiger Key Smokehouse Bar & Grill.** *American.* There's a strong hint of the Old Keys at this oceanside marina restaurant, which came under new management in 2010 by the same folks who own Hogfish Grill on Stock Island. "On the backside of paradise," as the sign says, its tiki structures overlook quiet mangroves at an RV park marina. Locals usually outnumber tourists. For lunch, try a fish sandwich or pulled pork. The all-day menu spans an ambitious array of sandwiches, tacos, and seafood. Local fishermen stop here for breakfast before heading out in search of the big one. Ⓢ *Average main: $12* ⊠ *MM 10, 5 Geiger Key Rd., off Boca Chica Rd., on Geiger Key, Key West* ☎ *305/296–3553, 305/294–1230* ⊕ *www.geigerkeymarina.com.*

$$$$ ✕ **Little Palm Island Restaurant.** *Eclectic.* The oceanfront setting
★ calls to mind St. Barts and the other high-end destinations of the Caribbean. Keep that in mind as you reach for the bill, which can also make you swoon. The restaurant at the exclusive Little Palm Island Resort—its dining room and adjacent outdoor terrace lit by candles and warmed by live music—is one of the most romantic spots in the Keys. The seasonal menu is a melding of French and Caribbean flavors, with exotic little touches. Think shrimp and yellowtail ceviche or coconut lobster bisque as a starter, followed by mahi-mahi with creamy cilantro polenta. The Sunday

brunch buffet, the full-moon dinners with live entertainment, and the Chef's Table Dinner are very popular. The dining room is open to nonguests on a reservations-only basis. ⑤ *Average main: $65* ✉ *MM 28.5 OS, 28500 Overseas Hwy.* ☎ *305/872-2551* ⊕ *www.littlepalmisland.com* ♿ *Reservations essential.*

$$$ ✕ **Square Grouper.** *Contemporary.* Although this restaurant's food draws raves, its name earns snickers. (A "square grouper" is slang for bales of marijuana dropped into the ocean during the drug-running 1970s.) Owner Lynn Bell gives the dishes whimsical touches, making them look as good as they taste. The seared sesame-encrusted tuna is lightly crunchy outside, like butter inside. The square grouper sandwich is a steaming pan-sautéed fillet topped with onion rings and key-lime tartar sauce on a ciabatta roll. In an unassuming strip mall, the dining room is surprisingly suave, with butcher paper-lined tables and a wood-topped zinc bar. ⑤ *Average main: $25* ✉ *MM 22.5 OS, Cudjoe Key* ☎ *305/745-8880* ⊕ *www.squaregrouperbarandgrill.com* ⊘ *Closed Mon. off-season; closed Sept. and several wks in summer.*

$$ ✕ **Zaza Pizzeria Neopolitana.** *Italian.* All that remains of the former Sugarloaf Lodge Restaurant is the pleasant gulf view out the picture windows; ZaZa has a new clean, open look dominated by a blue-tiled wood-fired pizza oven. Besides artisan pizzas such as béchamel with ham, you'll find hand-rolled fried risotto balls filled with ground beef, mozzarella, and peas; risotto infused with fresh lobster; pasta; bruschetta; and fried calzones. There's even pizza for breakfast (or try a frittata with ricotta and spinach or buffalo mozzarella, baby arugula, and prosciutto). Everything's fresh, most of it imported from Italy. ⑤ *Average main: $18* ✉ *MM 17 BS, 17015 Overseas Hwy.* ☎ *305/745-2717.*

WHERE TO STAY

For expanded reviews, facilities, and current deals, visit Fodors.com.

★ **Fodor's**Choice ☷ **Little Palm Island Resort & Spa.** *Resort. Haute*
$$$$ *tropicale* best describes this luxury retreat, and "second mortgage" might explain how some can afford the extravagant prices. **Pros:** secluded setting; heavenly spa; easy wildlife viewing. **Cons:** expensive; might be too quiet for some. ⑤ *Rooms from: $1590* ✉ *MM 28.5 OS, 28500 Overseas Hwy.* ☎ *305/872-2524, 800/343-8567* ⊕ *www.littlepalmisland.com* ⇌ *30 suites* ⧖ *Some meals.*

$ ⌧**Looe Key Reef Resort & Center.** *Hotel.* If your Keys vacation is all about diving, you'll be well served at this scuba-obsessed operation—the closest place to stay to the stellar reef (and affordable to boot). **Pros:** guests get discounts on dive and snorkel trips; fun bar. **Cons:** small rooms; unheated pool; close to road. ⑤ *Rooms from: $75 ⌧ MM 27.5 OS, 27340 Overseas Hwy., Ramrod Key* ☎*305/872–2215, 877/816–3483* ⊕*www.diveflakeys.com* ⇨*23 rooms, 1 suite* ❍*No meals.*

$$ ⌧**Parmer's Resort.** *Hotel.* Almost every room at this budget-friendly option has a view of South Pine Channel, with the lovely curl of Big Pine Key in the foreground. **Pros:** bright rooms; pretty setting; good value. **Cons:** a bit out of the way; housekeeping costs extra; little shade around the pool. ⑤ *Rooms from: $134 ⌧ MM 28.7 BS, 565 Barry Ave.* ☎*305/872–2157* ⊕*www.parmersresort.com* ⇨*18 rooms, 12 efficiencies, 15 apartments, 1 penthouse, 1 2-bedroom cottage* ❍*Breakfast.*

SPORTS AND THE OUTDOORS

BOATING

Dolphin Marina. Dolphin Marina rents 22-foot boats with 150 horsepower for up to eight people by the half day ($200) and full day ($250). ⌧*28530 Overseas Hwy.* ☎*305/872–2685* ⊕*www.dolphinmarina.net.*

SCUBA DIVING AND SNORKELING

This is the closest you can get on land to Looe Key Reef, and that's where local dive operators love to head.

★ **Looe Key Reef.** In 1744 the HMS *Looe,* a British warship, ran aground and sank on one of the most beautiful coral reefs in the Keys. Today the key owes its name to the ill-fated ship. The 5.3-square-nautical-mi reef, part of the **Florida Keys National Marine Sanctuary,** has strands of elkhorn coral on its eastern margin, purple sea fans, and abundant sponges and sea urchins. On its seaward side, it drops almost vertically 50 to 90 feet. In its midst, **Shipwreck Trail** plots the location of nine historic wreck sites in 14 to 120 feet of water. Buoys mark the sites, and underwater signs tell the history of each site and what marine life to expect. Snorkelers and divers will find the sanctuary a quiet place to observe reef life—except in July, when the annual Underwater Music Festival pays homage to Looe Key's beauty and promotes reef awareness with six hours of music broadcast via underwater speakers. Dive shops, charters, and private boats transport about 500 divers and snorkelers to hear the spectacle, which includes classical, jazz, new age, and Caribbean music, as well as a little Jimmy Buffett. There are even underwater Elvis impersonators. ✉ *MM 27.5 OS, 216 Ann St., Key West* ☎ *305/292–0311.*

Looe Key Reef Resort & Dive Center. Rather than the customary morning and afternoon two-tank, two-location trips offered by most dive shops, this center, the closest dive shop to Looe Key Reef, runs a single three-tank, three-location dive ($84 for divers, $44 for snorkelers). The maximum depth is 30 feet, so snorkelers and divers go on the same boat. On Wednesday it runs a trip that visits a wreck and reefs in the area for the same price for either snorkeling or diving. The dive boat, a 45-foot catamaran, is docked at the full-service Looe Key Reef Resort. ✉ *MM 27.5 OS, Looe Key Reef Resort, 27340 Overseas Hwy., Ramrod Key* ☎ *305/872–2215, 877/816–3483* ⊕ *www.diveflakeys.com.*

TOURS

Fantasy Dan's Airplane Rides. Departing from Sugarloaf Key Airport, passengers can spot sharks, stingrays, and other reef life on sightseeing rides starting at $130 for up to three people. ✉ *Sugarloaf Key Airport, MM 17, 16855 Overseas Hwy.* ☎ *305/743–9100* ⊕ *www.floridaairplanetours.com.*

WATER SPORTS

Reelax Charters. For a guided kayak tour, join Captain Andrea Paulson of Reelax Charters, who takes you to remote locations. Charters start at $240 for one to two people and can include snorkeling and beaching on a secluded island in the Keys backcountry. ✉ *MM 17 BS, Sugarloaf Marina, 17015 Overseas Hwy., Sugarloaf Key* ☎ *305/304–1392* ⊕ *www.keyskayaking.com.*

Sugarloaf Marina. Rent a paddle-propelled vehicle for exploring local gulf waters. Rates for one-person kayaks start at $15 for one hour to $35 for a full day. Two-person kayaks are also available. Delivery is free for rentals of three days or more. ✉ *MM 17 BS, 17015 Overseas Hwy., Sugarloaf Key* ☎ *305/745–3135* ⊕ *www.sugarloafkeymarina.com.*

Key West

5

WORD OF MOUTH

"While I do agree that Key West can be a bit risqué at times, it is a place where families can go and have a great family vacation."

—cgenster

"Whether Key West is 'worth it' depends on what kind of vacation towns you like. Do you like funky, lively, outdoor eating, lots of young people in the streets, lots of open bars with loud music, and a Caribbean flavor? If so, you might like Key West. I do."

—montereybob

Updated
by Chelle
Koster
Walton

SITUATED 150 MILES FROM MIAMI, 90 miles from Havana, and an immeasurable distance from sanity, this end-of-the-line community has never been like anywhere else. Even after it was connected to the rest of the country—by the railroad in 1912 and by the highway in 1938—it maintained a strong sense of detachment. The U.S. acquired Key West from Spain in 1821, along with the rest of Florida. The Spanish had named the island Cayo Hueso, or Bone Key, after the Native American skeletons they found on its shores. In 1823 President James Monroe sent Commodore David S. Porter to chase pirates away. For three decades the primary industry in Key West was wrecking—rescuing people and salvaging cargo from ships that foundered on the nearby reefs. According to some reports, when pickings were lean the wreckers hung out lights to lure ships aground. Their business declined after 1849, when the federal government began building lighthouses.

In 1845 the army began construction on Fort Taylor, which kept Key West on the Union side during the Civil War. After the fighting ended, an influx of Cubans unhappy with Spain's rule brought the cigar industry here. Fishing, shrimping, and sponge gathering became important industries, as did pineapple canning. Through much of the 19th century and into the 20th, Key West was Florida's wealthiest city in per-capita terms. But in 1929 the local economy began to unravel. Cigar making moved to Tampa, Hawaii dominated the pineapple industry, and the sponges succumbed to blight. Then the Depression hit, and within a few years half the population was on relief.

Tourism began to revive Key West, but that came to a halt when a hurricane knocked out the railroad bridge in 1935. To help the tourism industry recover from that crushing blow, the government offered incentives for islanders to turn their charming homes—many of them built by shipwrights—into guesthouses and inns. The wise foresight has left the town with more than 100 such lodgings, a hallmark of Key West vacationing today. In the 1950s the discovery of "pink gold" in the Dry Tortugas boosted the economy of the entire region. Catching Key West shrimp required a fleet of up to 500 boats and flooded local restaurants with some of the sweetest shrimp alive. The town's artistic community found inspiration in the colorful fishing boats.

Key West reflects a diverse population: Conchs (natives, many of whom trace their ancestry to the Bahamas), freshwater Conchs (longtime residents who migrated from somewhere else years ago), Hispanics (primarily Cuban immigrants), recent refugees from the urban sprawl of mainland Florida, military personnel, and an assortment of vagabonds, drifters, and dropouts in search of refuge. The island was once a gay vacation hot spot, and it remains a decidedly gay-friendly destination. Some of the once-renowned gay guesthouses, however, no longer cater to an exclusively gay clientele. Key Westers pride themselves on their tolerance of all peoples, all sexual orientations, and even all animals. Most restaurants allow pets, and it's not surprising to see stray cats, dogs, and even chickens roaming freely through the dining rooms. The chicken issue is one that government officials periodically try to bring to an end, but the colorful fowl continue to strut and crow, particularly in the vicinity of Old Town's Bahamian Village.

Although the rest of the Keys are known for outdoor activities, Key West has something of a city feel. Few open spaces remain, as promoters continue to churn out restaurants, galleries, shops, and museums to interpret the city's intriguing past. As a tourist destination, Key West has a lot to sell—an average temperature of 79°F, 19th-century architecture, and a laid-back lifestyle. Yet much has been lost to those eager for a buck. Duval Street looks like a miniature Las Vegas, lined with garish signs for T-shirt shops and tour-company offices. Cruise ships dwarf the town's skyline and fill the streets with day-trippers gawking at the hippies with dogs in their bike baskets, gay couples walking down the street holding hands, and the oddball lot of locals, some of whom bark louder than the dogs.

ORIENTATION AND PLANNING

PLANNING

GETTING HERE AND AROUND

Between mile markers 4 and 0, Key West is the one place in the Keys where you could conceivably do without a car, especially if you plan on staying around Old Town. If you've driven the 106 miles down the chain, you're probably ready to abandon your car in the hotel parking lot anyway. Trolleys, buses, bikes, scooters, and feet are more suitable alternatives. When your feet tire, catch a rickshaw-style pedicab ride, which will run you about $1.50 a minute. To explore the beaches, New Town, and Stock Island, you'll probably need a car.

Greyhound Lines runs a special Keys shuttle two times a day (depending on the day of the week) from Miami International Airport (departing from Concourse E, lower level) and stops throughout the Keys. Fares run about $45 (web fare) to $57 for Key West (3535 S. Roosevelt, Key West International Airport). Keys Shuttle runs scheduled service three times a day in 15-passenger vans between Miami Airport and Key West with stops throughout the Keys for $70 to $90 per person. Key West Express operates air-conditioned ferries between the Key West Terminal (Caroline and Grinnell streets) and Marco Island, and Fort Myers Beach. The trip from Fort Myers Beach takes at least four hours each way and costs $86 one way, $146 round-trip. Ferries depart from Fort Myers Beach at 8:30 am and from Key West at 6 pm. The Miami and Marco Island ferry costs $86 one way and $146 round-trip, and departs at 8:30 am. A photo ID is required for each passenger. Advance reservations are recommended. The SuperShuttle charges $102 per passenger for trips from Miami International Airport to the Upper Keys. To go farther into the Keys, you must book an entire 11-person van, which costs about $350 to Key West. You need to place your request for transportation back to the airport 24 hours in advance.

The City of Key West Department of Transportation has six color-coded bus routes traversing the island from 5:30 am to 11:30 pm. Stops have signs with the international bus symbol. Schedules are available on buses and at hotels, visitor centers, and shops, and online. The fare is $2 one way. Its Lower Keys Shuttle bus runs between Marathon to Key West ($4 one way), with scheduled stops along the way.

ESSENTIALS
Transportation Contacts City of Key West Department of Transportation ☎ *305/809–3910* ⊕ *www.kwtransit.com.* **Greyhound Lines** ☎ *800/410–5397 Local information, 800/231–2222* ⊕ *www. greyhound.com.* **Keys Shuttle** ☎ *305/289–9997, 888/765–9997* ⊕ *www.floridakeysshuttle.com.* **Key West Express** ✉ *100 Grinnell St.* ☎ *888/539–2628* ⊕ *www.seakeywestexpress.com.* **Lower Keys Shuttle** ☎ *305/809–3910* ⊕ *www.kwtransit.com.* **SuperShuttle** ☎ *305/871–2000, 800/258–3826* ⊕ *www.supershuttle.com.*

TOP REASONS TO GO

■ **The Dry Tortugas.** Do a day trip to Dry Tortugas National Park for snorkeling and hiking away from the crowds.

■ **Watching the sunset.** Revel in both the beautiful sunset and the gutsy performers at Mallory Square's nightly celebration.

■ **The Conch Train.** Hop aboard the Conch Train for a narrated tour of the town's tawdry past and rare architectural treasures.

■ **Bar-hopping.** Nightlife rules in Key West. Do the "Duval Crawl," the local version of club-hopping. But first fortify yourself at one of the town's exceptional restaurants.

■ **The Hemingway connection.** Visit Ernest Hemingway's historic home for a page out of Key West's literary past.

Visitor Information Greater Key West Chamber of Commerce ✉ *510 Greene St.* ☎ *305/294–2587, 800/527–8539* ⊕ *www.keywest-chamber.org.* **Gay & Lesbian Community Center** ✉ *513 Truman Ave.* ☎ *305/394–4603* ⊕ *www.gaykeywestfl.com.*

RESTAURANTS

Keys restaurants get their most exotic once you reach Key West, and you can pretty much find anything you want (although bargains are hard to come by). Pricier restaurants serve tantalizing fusion cuisine that reflects the influence of Cuba and other Caribbean islands. Tropical fruits and citrus figure prominently on the menus, and mango, papaya, and passion fruit show up on the lists of beverages. Of course, there are plenty of places that serve local seafood. Key West stays true to island character with a selection of "hole-in-the-wall" places where it doesn't get any more colorful.

HOTELS

Key West's lodgings include historic cottages, restored Conch houses, and large resorts. Quaint guesthouses, the town's trademark, offer a true island experience in residential neighborhoods near Old Town's restaurants, shops, and clubs. A few rooms cost as little as $65 a night in the off-season, but most range from $100 to $300. Some guesthouses and inns do not welcome children under 16, and most do not permit smoking.

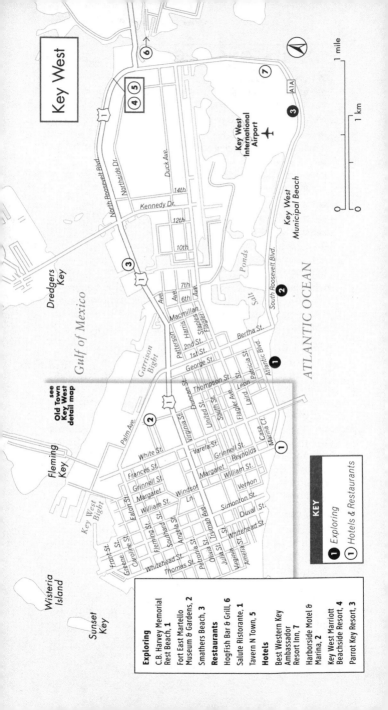

Key West

Gulf of Mexico

Wisteria Island

Sunset Key

Fleming Key

Dredgers Key

Key West Bight

Garrison Bight

Key West International Airport

Key West Municipal Beach

ATLANTIC OCEAN

Salt Ponds

see Old Town Key West detail map

North Roosevelt Blvd.
Northside Dr.
Duck Ave.
Kennedy Dr.
14th
12th
10th
7th Ave.
6th Ave.
South Roosevelt Blvd.
Macmillan
Patterson
Harris
2nd St.
1st St.
Staples
Flagler
George St.
Bertha St.
Atlantic Blvd.
A1A

Palm Ave.
White St.
Frances St.
Grinnell St.
Margaret
William St.
Eaton St.
Fleming St.
Southard St.
Angela St.
Caroline St.
Greene St.
Front St.
Whitehead St.
Thomas St.
Petronia St.
Olivia St.
Julia St.
Truman Ave.
Windsor Ln.
Virginia St.
Duncan St.
United St.
South St.
Varela St.
Grinnell St.
Reynolds
Margaret
William St.
Vernon
Simonton St.
Duval St.
Whitehead St.
Virginia St.
Amelia St.
Thompson St.
Flagler Ave.
Laird
Leon
Patricia St.
Casa Marina Ct.

Exploring
C.B. Harvey Memorial Rest Beach, **1**
Fort East Martello Museum & Gardens, **2**
Smathers Beach, **3**

Restaurants
HogFish Bar & Grill, **6**
Salute Ristorante, **1**
Tavern N Town, **5**

Hotels
Best Western Key Ambassador Resort Inn, **7**
Harborside Motel & Marina, **2**
Key West Marriott Beachside Resort, **4**
Parrot Key Resort, **3**

KEY
1 Exploring
① Hotels & Restaurants

0   1 km
0   1 mile

HOTEL AND RESTAURANT PRICES
Prices in the restaurant reviews are the average cost of a main course at dinner or, if dinner is not served, at lunch, excluding taxes and service charges. Prices in the hotel reviews are the lowest cost of a standard double room in high season, excluding taxes, service charges, and meal plans (except at all-inclusives). Prices for rentals are the lowest per-night cost for a one-bedroom unit in high season.

OLD TOWN

The heart of Key West, the historic Old Town area runs from White Street to the waterfront. Beginning in 1822, wharves, warehouses, chandleries, ship-repair facilities, and eventually in 1891 the U.S. Custom House sprang up around the deep harbor to accommodate the navy's large ships and other sailing vessels. Wreckers, merchants, and sea captains built lavish houses near the bustling waterfront. A remarkable number of these fine Victorian and pre-Victorian structures have been restored to their original grandeur, and now serve as homes, guesthouses, shops, restaurants, and museums. These, along with the dwellings of famous writers, artists, and politicians who've come to Key West over the past 175 years, are among the area's approximately 3,000 historic structures. Old Town also has the city's finest restaurants and hotels, lively street life, and popular nightspots.

TIMING
Allow two full days to see all the Old Town museums and homes, especially with a little shopping thrown in. For a narrated trip on the tour train or trolley, budget an hour to ride the loop without getting off, an entire day if you plan to get off and on at some of the sights and restaurants.

EXPLORING

TOP ATTRACTIONS
Audubon House and Tropical Gardens. If you've ever seen an engraving by ornithologist John James Audubon, you'll understand why his name is synonymous with birds. See his works in this three-story house, which was built in the 1840s for Captain John Geiger and filled with period furniture. It now commemorates Audubon's 1832 stop

A GOOD TOUR

To cover many sights, take the Old Town Trolley, which lets you get off and reboard a later trolley, or the Conch Tour Train. Old Town is also manageable on foot, bicycle, moped, or electric cars. The area is expansive, so you'll want either to pick and choose from the stops on this tour or break it into two or more days. Start on Whitehead Street at the **Ernest Hemingway Home & Museum**, then cross the street and climb to the top of the **Lighthouse Museum** for a spectacular view. Return to Whitehead Street and follow it north to Angela Street, where you'll turn right. At Margaret Street, the **City Cemetery** is worth a look for its above-ground vaults and unusual headstone inscriptions. Head north on Margaret Street, turn left onto Southard Street, then right onto Simonton Street. Halfway up the block, **Nancy Forrester's Secret Garden** occupies Free School Lane. After wandering among the blossoms, return again to Southard Street, turn right, and follow it through Truman Annex to **Fort Zachary Taylor State Park**.

Walk west into Truman Annex to see the **Harry S. Truman Little White House Museum**, President Truman's vacation residence. Return east on Caroline and turn left on Whitehead to visit the **Audubon House and Gardens**, honoring the famed artist and naturalist. Follow Whitehead north to Greene Street and turn left to see the salvaged sea treasures of the **Mel Fisher Maritime Heritage Society Museum**. At Whitehead's northern end are the **Key West Aquarium** and the **Key West Museum of Art and History,** the former historic U.S. Custom House. By late afternoon you should be ready to cool off with a dip or catch a few rays at the beach. From the aquarium, head east two blocks to the end of Simonton Street, where you'll find the appropriately named **Simonton Street Beach**. Like all Key West beaches, it is man-made, with white sand imported from the Bahamas and north Florida. If you've brought your pet, stroll a few blocks east to **Dog Beach**, at the corner of Vernon and Waddell streets. A little farther east is **Higgs Beach–Astro Park**, on Atlantic Boulevard between White and Reynolds streets. As the sun starts to sink, return to the north end of Old Town and follow the crowds to Mallory Square, behind the aquarium, to watch Key West's nightly sunset spectacle. For dinner, head east on Caroline Street to **Historic Seaport at Key West Bight**.

GAY AND PROUD

With its official motto being "One Human Family," Key West has long been a favorite of the gay and lesbian community. In fact, Key West wouldn't be the same without the gay people who renovated many of the ramshackle homes and guesthouses. Following are a couple of the gay-specific activities Key West offers.

Gay & Lesbian Trolley Tour. Decorated with a rainbow, the Gay and Lesbian Trolley Tour rumbles around the town beginning at 4 pm every Saturday afternoon. The 70-minute tour highlighting Key West's gay history costs $25. ⊠ *513 Truman Ave.* ☎ *305/294–4603* ⊕ *www.gaykeywestfl.com.*

in Key West while he was traveling through Florida to study birds. After an introduction by a docent, you can do a self-guided tour of the house and gardens (or just the gardens). An art gallery sells lithographs of the artist's famed portraits. ⊠ *205 Whitehead St.* ☎ *305/294–2116, 877/294–2470* ⊕ *www.audubonhouse.com* ☜ *$7.50 gardens only; $12 house and gardens* ☉ *Daily 9:30–5, last tour starts at 4:30.*

★ **Ernest Hemingway Home and Museum.** Amusing anecdotes spice up the guided tours of Ernest Hemingway's home, built in 1801 by the town's most successful wrecker. While living here between 1931 and 1942, Hemingway wrote about 70% of his life's work, including classics like *For Whom the Bell Tolls*. Few of his belongings remain aside from some books, and there's little about his actual work, but photographs help you visualize his day-to-day life. The supposed six-toed descendants of Hemingway's cats—many named for actors, artists, authors, and even a hurricane— have free rein of the property. Tours begin every 10 minutes and take 30 minutes; then you're free to explore on your own. ⊠ *907 Whitehead St.* ☎ *305/294–1136* ⊕ *www. hemingwayhome.com* ☜ *$12.50* ☉ *Daily 9–5.*

NEED A BREAK? Check out the pretty palm garden next to the Key West Library at 700 Fleming Street, just off Duval. This leafy outdoor reading area, with shaded benches, is the perfect place to escape the frenzy and crowds of downtown Key West. There's free Internet access in the library, too.

Old Town Key West

0 — 1/2 mile
0 — 1/2 km

Fleming Key

Wisteria Island

Sunset Key

Key West Bight

Key West Public Library

ATLANTIC OCEAN

Fort Zachary Taylor Beach

Audubon House and Gardens, 3

City Cemetery, 12

Dog Beach, 17

Eco-Discovery Center, 19

Ernest Hemingway Home & Museum, 1

Fort Zachary Taylor Historic State Park, 20

Harry S Truman Little White House Museum, 5

Higgs Beach—Astro City Playground, 18

Historic Seaport at Key West Bight, 11

Key West Aquarium, 8

Key West Butterfly & Nature Conservatory, 14

Key West Lighthouse Museum, 2

Key West Museum of Art and History, 6

Key West Shipwreck Treasures Museum, 7

Mallory Square & Pier, 9

Mel Fisher Maritime Museum, 4

Simonton Street Beach, 10

South Beach, 16

The Southernmost Point, 15

West Martello Tower, 13

★ **Fort Zachary Taylor Historic State Park.** Construction of the fort began in 1845 but was halted during the Civil War. Even though Florida seceded from the Union, Yankee forces used the fort as a base to block Confederate shipping. More than 1,500 Confederate vessels were detained in Key West's harbor. The fort, finally completed in 1866, was also used in the Spanish-American War. Take a 30-minute guided walking tour of the redbrick fort, a National Historic Landmark, at noon and 2, or self-tour anytime between 8 and 5. In February a celebration called Civil War Heritage Days includes costumed reenactments and demonstrations. From mid-January to mid-April the park serves as an open-air gallery for pieces created for Sculpture Key West. One of its most popular features is its man-made beach, a rest stop for migrating birds in the spring and fall; there are also hiking and biking trails and a kayak launch. ⊠ *Box 6565, end of Southard St., through Truman Annex* ☎ *305/292–6713* ⊕ *www.floridastateparks.org/forttaylor* ☞ *$4.50 for 1 person, $7 for 2 people, 50¢ per additional person* ☉ *Daily 8–sunset.*

Harry S. Truman Little White House Museum. Renovations to this circa-1890 landmark have restored the home and gardens to the Truman era, down to the wallpaper pattern. A free photographic review of visiting dignitaries and presidents—John F. Kennedy, Jimmy Carter, and Bill Clinton are among the chief executives who passed through here—is on display in the back of the gift shop. Engaging 45-minute tours begin every 20 minutes until 4:30. They start with an excellent 10-minute video on the history of the property and Truman's visits. On the grounds of **Truman Annex,** a 103-acre former military parade grounds and barracks, the home served as a winter White House for presidents Truman, Eisenhower, and Kennedy. ■TIP→ **The house tour does require climbing steps. Visitors can do a free self-guided botanical tour of the grounds with a brochure from the museum store.** ⊠ *111 Front St.* ☎ *305/294–9911* ⊕ *www.trumanlittlewhitehouse.com* ☞ *$16* ☉ *Daily 9–5, grounds 7–6.*

☾ **Higgs Beach–Astro City Playground.** This Monroe County park with its groomed pebbly sand is a popular sunbathing spot. A nearby grove of Australian pines provides shade, and the West Martello Tower provides shelter should a storm suddenly sweep in. Kayak and beach-chair rentals are available, as is a volleyball net. The beach also has a marker and cultural exhibit commemorating the gravesite of 295 enslaved Africans who died after being rescued from

5

Hemingway Was Here

In a town where Pulitzer Prize–winning writers are almost as common as coconuts, Ernest Hemingway stands out. Bars and restaurants around the island claim that he ate or drank there.

Hemingway came to Key West in 1928 at the urging of writer John dos Passos, and rented a house with wife number two, Pauline Pfeiffer. They spent winters in the Keys and summers in Europe and Wyoming, occasionally taking African safaris. Along the way they had two sons, Patrick and Gregory. In 1931 Pauline's wealthy uncle Gus gave the couple the house at 907 Whitehead Street. Now known as the Ernest Hemingway Home & Museum, it's Key West's number-one tourist attraction. Renovations included the addition of a pool and a tropical garden.

In 1935, when the visitor bureau included the house in a tourist brochure, Hemingway promptly built the brick wall that surrounds it today. He wrote of the visitor bureau's offense in a 1935 essay for *Esquire,* saying, "The house at present occupied by your correspondent is listed as number eighteen in a compilation of the forty-eight things for a tourist to see in Key West. So there will be no difficulty in a tourist finding it or any other of the sights of the city, a map has been prepared by the local F.E.R.A. authorities to be presented to each arriving visitor. This is all very flattering to the easily bloated ego of your correspondent but very hard on production."

During his time in Key West, Hemingway penned some of his most important works, including *A Farewell to Arms, To Have and Have Not, Green Hills of Africa,* and *Death in the Afternoon.* His rigorous schedule consisted of writing almost every morning in his second-story studio above the pool, then promptly descending the stairs at midday. By afternoon and evening he was ready for drinking, fishing, swimming, boxing, and hanging around with the boys.

One close friend was Joe Russell, a craggy fisherman and owner of the rugged bar Sloppy Joe's, originally at 428 Greene Street but now at 201 Duval Street. Russell was the only one in town who would cash Hemingway's $1,000 royalty check. Russell and Charles Thompson introduced Hemingway to deep-sea fishing, which became fodder for his writing.

Hemingway stayed in Key West for 11 years before leaving Pauline for his third wife. Pauline and the boys stayed on in the house, which sold in 1951 for $80,000, ten times its original cost.

—Jim and Cynthia Tunstall

three South America–bound slave ships in 1860. Across the street, **Astro City Playground** is popular with young children. **Amenities:** parking, toilets, water sports. **Best for:** swimming, snorkeling. ✉ *Atlantic Blvd., between White and Reynolds Sts.* 🎟 *Free* ⊘ *Daily 6 am–11 pm.*

Historic Seaport at Key West Bight. What was once a funky—in some places even seedy—part of town is now an 8½-acre historic restoration of 100 businesses, including waterfront restaurants, open-air bars, museums, clothing stores, bait shops, dive shops, docks, a marina, and watersports concessions. It's all linked by the 2-mi waterfront **Harborwalk,** which runs between Front and Grinnell streets, passing big ships, schooners, sunset cruises, fishing charters, and glass-bottom boats. ✉ *100 Grinnell St.* 🕾 *305/293–8309.*

NEED A BREAK? Coffee Plantation. Get your morning (or afternoon) buzz, and hook up to the Internet in the comfort of a homelike setting in a circa-1890 Conch house. Munch on sandwiches, wraps, and pastries, and sip a hot or cold espresso beverage. ✉ *713 Caroline St.* 🕾 *305/295–9808* ⊕ *www.coffeeplantation-keywest.com.*

★ **Key West Butterfly & Nature Conservatory.** This air-conditioned
☾ refuge for butterflies, birds, and the human spirit gladdens the soul with hundreds of colorful wings—more than 45 species of butterflies alone—in a lovely glass-encased bubble. Waterfalls, artistic benches, paved pathways, birds, and lush, flowering vegetation elevate this above most butterfly attractions. The gift shop and gallery are worth a visit on their own. ✉ *1316 Duval St.* 🕾 *305/296–2988, 800/839–4647* ⊕ *www.keywestbutterfly.com* 🎟 *$12* ⊘ *Daily 9–5, gallery and shop open until 5:30.*

Key West Lighthouse Museum & Keeper's Quarters Museum. For the best view in town, climb the 88 steps to the top of this 1847 lighthouse. The 92-foot structure has a Fresnel lens, which was installed in the 1860s at a cost of $1 million. The keeper lived in the adjacent 1887 clapboard house, which now exhibits vintage photographs, ship models, nautical charts, and lighthouse artifacts from all along the Key reefs. A kids' room is stocked with books and toys. ✉ *938 Whitehead St.* 🕾 *305/295–6616* ⊕ *www.kwahs.com* 🎟 *$10* ⊘ *Daily 9:30–5.*

5

★ Fodor's Choice **Key West Museum of Art & History in the Custom House.** When Key West was designated a U.S. port of entry in the early 1820s, a customhouse was established. Salvaged cargoes from ships wrecked on the reefs were brought here, setting the stage for Key West to become—for a time—the richest city in Florida. The imposing redbrick-and-terracotta Richardsonian Romanesque–style building reopened as a museum and art gallery in 1999. Smaller galleries have long-term and changing exhibits about the history of Key West, including a Hemingway room and a fine collection of folk artist Mario Sanchez's wood paintings. In 2011, to commemorate the 100th anniversary of the railroad's arrival to Key West in 1912, a new permanent Flagler exhibit opened. ⊠ *281 Front St.* ☎ *305/295–6616* ⊕ *www. kwahs.com* ⊡ *$7* ⊘ *Daily 9:30–5.*

Mallory Square and Pier. For cruise-ship passengers, this is the disembarkation point for an attack on Key West. For practically every visitor, it's the requisite venue for a nightly sunset celebration that includes street performers—human statues, sword swallowers, tightrope walkers, musicians, and more—plus craft vendors, conch fritter fryers, and other regulars who defy classification. (Wanna picture with my pet iguana?) With all the activity, don't forget to watch the main show: a dazzling tropical sunset. ⊠ *Mallory Sq.*

The Southernmost Point. Possibly the most photographed site in Key West (even though the actual geographic southernmost point in the continental United States lies across the bay on a naval base, where you see a satellite dish), this is a must-see. Who wouldn't want his picture taken next to the big striped buoy that marks the southernmost point in the continental United States? A plaque next to it honors Cubans who lost their lives trying to escape to America and other signs tell Key West history. ⊠ *Whitehead and South Sts.*

WORTH NOTING

City Cemetery. You can learn almost as much about a town's history through its cemetery as through its historic houses. Key West's celebrated 20-acre burial place may leave you wanting more, with headstone epitaphs such as "I told you I was sick," and, for a wayward husband, "Now I know where he's sleeping at night." Among the interesting plots are a memorial to the sailors killed in the sinking of the battleship USS *Maine,* carved angels and lambs marking graves of children, and grand aboveground crypts that put to shame many of the town's dwellings for the living. There are separate plots for Catholics, Jews, and refugees from Cuba. You're free to walk around the cemetery on your own, but the best way to see it is on a 90-minute tour given by the staff and volunteers of the Historic Florida Keys Foundation. Tours leave from the main gate, and reservations are required. ✉ *Margaret and Angela Sts.* 🕾 *305/292–6718* ⊕ *www.historicfloridakeys.org* 🏷 *Tours $15* ⊙ *Daily sunrise–6 pm; tours Tues. and Thurs. at 9:30 year-round, call for additional times.*

Dog Beach. Next to Louie's Backyard, this tiny beach—the only one in Key West where dogs are allowed unleashed—has a shore that's a mix of sand and rocks. **Amenities:** none. **Best for:** dog owners. ✉ *Vernon and Waddell Sts.* 🏷 *Free* ⊙ *Daily sunrise–sunset.*

⟳ **Eco-Discovery Center.** While visiting Fort Zachary Taylor Historic State Park, stop in at this 6,400-square-foot interactive attraction, which encourages visitors to venture through a variety of Florida Keys habitats from pinelands, beach dunes, and mangroves to the deep sea. Walk through a model of NOAA's (National Oceanic and Atmospheric Administration) Aquarius, a unique underwater ocean laboratory 9 mi off Key Largo, to virtually discover what lurks beneath the sea. Touch-screen computer displays, a dramatic movie, a 2,450-gallon aquarium, and live underwater cameras show off North America's only contiguous barrier coral reef. ✉ *35 E. Quay Rd., at end of Southard St. in Truman Annex* 🕾 *305/809–4750* ⊕ *www.floridakeys. noaa.gov* 🏷 *Free, donations accepted* ⊙ *Tues.–Sat. 9–4.*

⟳ **Key West Aquarium.** Pet a nurse shark and explore the fascinating underwater realm of the Keys without getting wet at this historic aquarium. Hundreds of tropical fish and enormous sea creatures live here. A touch tank enables you to handle starfish, sea cucumbers, horseshoe and hermit crabs, even horse and queen conchs—living totems of the Conch Republic. Built in 1934 by the Works Progress Administration as the world's first open-air aquarium, most of the building has been enclosed for all-weather viewing. Guided tours, included in the admission price, feature shark feedings. ✉ *1 Whitehead St.* 🕾 *305/296–2051* ⊕ *www.key-westaquarium.com* 🏷 *$15.05* ⊙ *Daily 10–8; tours at 11, 1, 2, 4:30, and 6:30.*

5

⟡ **Key West Shipwreck Treasures Museum.** Much of Key West's history, early prosperity, and interesting architecture come from ships that ran aground on its coral reef. Artifacts from the circa-1856 *Isaac Allerton,* which yielded $150,000 worth of wreckage, comprise the museum portion of this multifaceted attraction. Actors and films add a bit of Disneyesque drama. The final highlight is climbing to the top of the 65-foot lookout tower, a reproduction of the 20 or so towers used by Key West wreckers during the town's salvaging heydays. ✉ *1 Whitehead St.* ☎ *305/292–8990* ⊕ *www.shipwreckhistoreum.com* ☜ *$15.05* ⊗ *Daily 9:40–5.*

Mel Fisher Maritime Museum. In 1622 two Spanish galleons laden with riches from South America foundered in a hurricane 40 mi west of the Keys. In 1985 diver Mel Fisher recovered the treasures from the lost ships, the *Nuestra Señora de Atocha* and the *Santa Margarita.* Fisher's incredible adventure tracking these fabled hoards and battling the state of Florida for rights is as amazing as the loot you'll see, touch, and learn about in this museum. Artifacts include a 77.76-carat natural emerald crystal worth almost $250,000. Exhibits on the second floor rotate and might cover slave ships, including the excavated 17th-century *Henrietta Marie,* or the evolution of Florida maritime history. ✉ *200 Greene St.* ☎ *305/294–2633* ⊕ *www.melfisher.org* ☜ *$12.50* ⊗ *Weekdays 8:30–5, weekends 9:30–6.*

South Beach. On the Atlantic, this stretch of sand, also known as City Beach, is popular with travelers staying at nearby motels. It is now part of the new Southernmost Hotel on the Beach resort, but is open to the public with a fun beach bar and grill. There's little parking however, so visitors must walk or bike to the beach. **Amenities:** food and drink, parking, toilets. **Best for:** partiers, sunrise, sunset. ✉ *Duval St. at South St.* ☜ *Free* ⊗ *Daily 7 am–11 pm.*

West Martello Tower. Among the arches and ruins of this redbrick Civil War–era fort, the Key West Garden Club maintains lovely gardens of native and tropical plants, fountains, and sculptures. It also holds art, orchid, and flower shows February through April and leads private garden tours one weekend in March. ✉ *Atlantic Blvd. and White St.* ☎ *305/294–3210* ⊕ *www.keywestgardenclub.com* ☜ *Donation welcome* ⊗ *Daily 9:30–5.*

ALWAYS CELEBRATING. Key West has a growing calendar of festivals and artistic and cultural events—including the Conch Republic Celebration in April and the Halloween Fantasy Fest in October. December brings festivity in the form of a lighted boat parade at the Historic Seaport and New Year's Eve revelry that rivals any in the nation. Few cities of its size—a mere 2 miles by 4 miles—celebrate with the joie de vivre of this one.

NEW TOWN

The Overseas Highway splits as it enters Key West, the two forks rejoining to encircle New Town, the area east of White Street to Cow Key Channel. The southern fork runs along the shore as South Roosevelt Boulevard (Route A1A) and skirts Key West International Airport. Part of New Town was created with dredged fill. The island would have continued growing this way had the Army Corps of Engineers not determined in the early 1970s that it was detrimental to the nearby reef.

TIMING

Allow one to two hours to include brief stops at each attraction. If your interests lie in art, gardens, or Civil War history, you'll need three or four hours. Throw in time at the beach and make it a half-day affair.

A GOOD TOUR. Attractions are few in New Town. The best way to take in the sights is by car or motor scooter. Take South Roosevelt Boulevard from the island's entrance to the historical museum exhibits at **East Martello Tower,** near the airport. Continue past the salt ponds and stop at **Smathers Beach** for a dip, or continue west onto Atlantic Boulevard to **C.B. Harvey Rest Beach.** Between it and Higgs Beach, visit the lovely gardens at **West Martello Tower.**

EXPLORING

C.B. Harvey Memorial Rest Beach. This beach and park were named after Cornelius Bradford Harvey, former Key West mayor and commissioner. Adjacent to Higgs Beach, it has half a dozen picnic areas across the street, dunes, a pier, and a wheelchair and bike path. **Amenities:** none. **Best for:** strolling. ✉ *Atlantic Blvd., east side of White St. Pier* ⊠ *Free* ⊗ *Daily 6 am–11 pm.*

THE CONCH REPUBLIC

Beginning in the 1970s, pot smuggling became a source of income for islanders who knew how to dodge detection in the maze of waterways in the Keys. In 1982 the U.S. Border Patrol threw a roadblock across the Overseas Highway just south of Florida City to catch drug runners and undocumented aliens. Traffic backed up for miles as Border Patrol agents searched vehicles and demanded that the occupants prove U.S. citizenship. Officials in Key West, outraged at being treated like foreigners by the federal government, staged a protest and formed their own "nation," the so-called Conch Republic. They hoisted a flag and distributed mock border passes, visas, and Conch currency. The embarrassed Border Patrol dismantled its roadblock, and now an annual festival recalls the city's victory.

★ **Fort East Martello Museum & Gardens.** This redbrick Civil War fort never saw a lick of action during the war. Today it serves as a museum, with historical exhibits about the 19th and 20th centuries. Among the latter are relics of the USS *Maine,* cigar factory and shipwrecking exhibits, and the citadel tower you can climb to the top. The museum, operated by the Key West Art and Historical Society, also has a collection of Stanley Papio's "junk art" sculptures inside and out, and a gallery of Cuban folk artist Mario Sanchez's chiseled and painted wooden carvings of historic Key West street scenes. ✉ *3501 S. Roosevelt Blvd.* ☎ *305/296–3913* ⊕ *www.kwahs.com* 🎫 *$7* ⊘ *Daily 9:30–4:30.*

Smathers Beach. This wide beach has nearly 1 mi of nice white sand, plus beautiful coconut palms, picnic areas, and volleyball courts, all of which make it popular with the spring-break crowd. Trucks along the road rent rafts, windsurfers, and other beach "toys." **Amenities:** parking, toilets, water sports. **Best for:** partying. ✉ *S. Roosevelt Blvd.* 🎫 *Free* ⊘ *Daily 7 am–11 pm.*

WHERE TO EAT

Bring your appetite, a sense of daring, and a lack of preconceived notions about propriety. A meal in Key West can mean overlooking the crazies along Duval Street, watching roosters and pigeons battle for a scrap of food that may have escaped your fork, relishing the finest in what used to

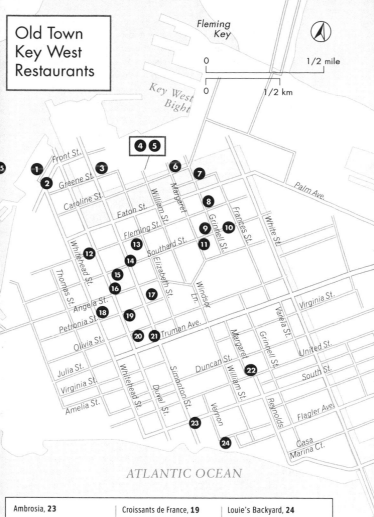

Old Town Key West Restaurants

Fleming Key

Key West Bight

ATLANTIC OCEAN

Ambrosia, 23
Azur Restaurant, 8
Bistro 245, 2
Blue Heaven, 18
B. O.'s Fish Wagon, 6
The Café, 15
Café Marquesa, 13
Café Solé, 10
Conch Republic Seafood Company, 3

Croissants de France, 19
El Meson de Pepe, 1
El Siboney, 22
Finnegan's Wake Irish Pub and Eatery, 7
Half Shell Raw Bar, 5
Jimmy Buffett's Margaritaville Cafe, 12
Latitudes, 25
Lobo's Mixed Grill, 16

Louie's Backyard, 24
Mangia Mangia, 9
Michael's Restaurant, 11
Nine One Five, 20
Pisces, 21
SaraBeth's, 14
Seven Fish, 17
Turtle Kraals, 4

be the dining room of a 19th-century Victorian home, or gazing out at boats jockeying for position in the marina. And that's just the diversity of the setting. Seafood dominates local menus, but the treatment afforded that fish or crustacean can range from Cuban and New World to Asian and continental.

★ **Fodor's**Choice ✕**Ambrosia.** *Japanese.* Ask any savvy local
$$ where to get the best sushi on the island and you'll undoubtedly be pointed to this tiny wood-and-tatami-paneled dining room with indoor waterfall tucked away into a resort near the beach. Grab a seat at the sushi bar and watch owner and head sushi chef Masa prepare an impressive array of superfresh sashimi delicacies. Sushi lovers can't go wrong with the Ambrosia special ($40): miso soup served with a sampler of 15 kinds of sashimi, seven pieces of sushi, and sushi rolls. There's an assortment of lightly fried tempura and teriyaki dishes and a killer bento box at lunch. Enjoy it all with a glass of premium sake or a cold glass of Sapporo beer. ⑤ *Average main: $20* ✉ *Santa Maria Resort, 1401 Simonton St.* ☎ *305/293–0304* ⊕ *keywestambrosia.com* ◷ *No lunch weekends. Closed 2 weeks after Labor Day.*

$$$ ✕**Azur Restaurant.** *Eclectic.* Fuel up on the finest fare at this former gas station, now part of the Eden House complex. In a contemporary setting with indoor and outdoor seating, welcoming staff serves breakfast, lunch, and dinner that stand out from the hordes of Key West restaurants by virtue of originality. For instance, key lime-stuffed French toast and yellowtail snapper Benedict make breakfast a pleasant wake-up call. The fennel-roasted pork sandwich with Fontina cheese, crab cake BLT, and charred marinated octopus command notice on the lunch menu. Four varieties of homemade gnocchi are a dinner-time specialty, along with tasting plates, "almost entrées" like braised lamb ribs over Moroccan-spiced chick peas, and main courses that include seafood risotto with chorizo and grilled sea bass. ⑤ *Average main: $26* ✉ *425 Grinnell St.* ☎ *305/292–2987* ⊕ *www.azurkeywest.com* ⌂ *Reservations essential.*

$ ✕**B.O.'s Fish Wagon.** *Seafood.* What started out as a fish house on wheels appears to have broken down on the corner of Caroline and William streets and is today the cornerstone for one of Key West's junkyard-chic dining institutions. Step up to the wood-plank counter window and order the specialty: a grouper sandwich fried or grilled and topped with key lime sauce. Other choices include fish nuts (don't be scared, they're just fried nuggets), hot dogs, cracked conch sandwich, and shrimp or soft-shell-crab sandwich. Talk sass with your host and find a picnic table or take a seat at the plank. Grab some paper towels off one of the rolls hanging around and busy yourself reading graffiti, license plates, and irreverent signs. It's a must-do Key West experience. ⑤ *Average main: $10* ⊠ *801 Caroline St.* ☎ *305/294–9272* ⊕ *www.bosfishwagon.com* ⊜ *Reservations not accepted* ⊟ *No credit cards.*

$$$ ✕ **Bistro 245.** *Seafood.* The sunset views alone are worth a visit, but the food here is stellar as well. Start upstairs at the bar with a key lime martini and watch the throngs below make Mallory Square a scene. Downstairs, you can choose between the open-air patio or the air-conditioned dining room with picture-window views. For dinner, try the lobster quesadilla or seafood cocktail as an appetizer before moving on to the shrimp and lobster fettuccine with asparagus and chèvre, seared mahi with tangerine butter, or citrus-crusted yellowtail snapper. The breakfast menu features healthy options like fruit smoothies and smoked salmon, tofu, and avocado on a bagel. Creative salads and sandwiches make lunch an intriguing affair. ⑤ *Average main: $25* ⊠ *Westin Key West Resort, 245 Front St.* ☎ *305/294–4000* ⊕ *www.westin.com/keywest.*

$$$ ✕ **Blue Heaven.** *Caribbean.* The outdoor dining area here is ★ often referred to as "the quintessential Keys experience," and it's hard to argue. There's much to like about this historic restaurant where Hemingway refereed boxing matches and customers cheered for cockfights. Although these events are no more, the free-roaming chickens and cats add that "what-a-hoot" factor. Nightly specials include black bean soup, Caribbean BBQ shrimp, bison strip steak with blackberry salad, and jerk chicken. Desserts and breads are baked on the premises; the banana bread and lobster Benedict with key lime hollandaise are hits during breakfast, the signature meal here. ⑤ *Average main: $24* ⊠ *729 Thomas St.* ☎ *305/296–8666* ⊕ *www. blueheavenkw.com* ⊜ *Reservations not accepted* ⊗ *Closed after Labor Day for 6 weeks.*

$ ✕ **The Café.** *Vegetarian.* You don't have to be a vegetarian to love this new-age café decorated with bright artwork and a corrugated tin–fronted counter. Local favorites include homemade soup, veggie sandwiches and burgers (order them with a side of sweet potato fries), grilled portobello mushroom salad, seafood, vegan specialties, stir-fry dinners, and grilled Gorgonzola pizza. There's also a nice selection of draft beer and wines by the glass, plus daily desserts (including vegan selections). $ *Average main: $11* ✉ *509 Southard St.* ☎ *305/296–5515* ⌾ *Reservations not accepted.*

★ **Fodor's**Choice ✕ **Café Marquesa.** *European.* Chef Susan Ferry
$$$ presents seven or more inspired entrées on her changing menu each night; delicious dishes can include yellowtail snapper with pear, ricotta pasta purses with caponata, and Australian rack of lamb crusted with goat cheese and a port-fig sauce. End your meal on a sweet note with key lime napoleon with tropical fruits and berries. There's also a fine selection of wines and custom martinis such as the key limetini and the Irish martini. Adjoining the intimate Marquesa Hotel, the dining room is equally relaxed and elegant. $ *Average main: $29* ✉ *600 Fleming St.* ☎ *305/292–1244* ⊕ *www.marquesa.com* ⌾ *Reservations essential* ⊗ *No lunch.*

$$$ ✕ **Café Solé.** *French.* This little corner of France hides behind a high wall in a residential neighborhood. Inside, French training intertwines with local ingredients, creating delicious takes on classics, including a must-try conch Carpaccio, yellowtail snapper with mango salsa, and some of the best bouillabaisse that you'll find outside of Marseilles. Hog snapper, a.k.a. hogfish, is a house specialty here, prepared several ways by Chef John Correa, including with beurre blanc or red pepper custard sauce. From the land, there is filet mignon with a wild-mushroom demi-glace. $ *Average main: $27* ✉ *1029 Southard St.* ☎ *305/294–0230* ⊕ *www. cafesole.com* ⌾ *Reservations essential* ⊗ *No lunch.*

$$$ ✕ **Conch Republic Seafood Company.** *Seafood.* Because of its location where the fast ferry docks, Conch Republic does a brisk business. It's huge, open-air, and on the water, so the place is hard to miss. The menu is ambitious, offering more than just standard seafood fare. The baked oysters *callaloo* (a spinachlike green), for instance, are a Caribbean-style twist on oysters Rockefeller. The grilled or fried shrimp basket comes with a trio of sauces, including the house mixture. Paella, plantain-crusted mahi, seafood stir-fry, and steaks are some other options. Live music adds to the decibel level. $ *Average main: $25* ✉ *631 Greene St., at Elizabeth St.* ☎ *305/294–4403* ⊕ *www.conchrepublicseafood.com* ⌾ *Reservations not accepted.*

$ ✕ **Croissants de France.** *French.* Pop into the bakery for something sinfully sweet or spend some time people-watching at the sidewalk café next door. Try the eggs brioche with mustard sauce for breakfast. Quiche and savory crêpes (shrimp and brie, for instance) are the standouts at lunch and dinner, but they also have delicious burgers and paninis. Finish off your meal with a dessert crêpe or chocolate Grand Marnier mousse. $ *Average main: $14* ⊠ *816 Duval St.* ☎ *305/294–2624* ⊕ *www.croissantsdefrance.com* ⊙ *Closed Wed. Easter to Thanksgiving.*

$$ ✕ **El Meson de Pepe.** *Cuban.* If you want to get a taste of the island's Cuban heritage, this is the place. Perfect for after watching a Mallory Square sunset, you can dine alfresco or in the dining room on refined versions of Cuban classics. Begin with a megasized mojito while you enjoy the basket of bread and savory sauces. The expansive menu offers *tostones rellenos* (green plantains with different traditional fillings), *ceviche* (raw fish "cooked" in lemon juice), and more. Choose from Cuban specialties such as roasted pork in a cumin mojo sauce and *ropa vieja* (shredded beef stew). At lunch, the local Cuban population and cruise-ship passengers enjoy Cuban sandwiches and smaller versions of dinner's most popular entrées. A Latin band performs outside at the bar during sunset celebration. $ *Average main: $19* ⊠ *Mallory Sq., 410 Wall St.* ☎ *305/295–2620* ⊕ *www. elmesondepepe.com.*

$ ✕ **El Siboney.** *Cuban.* Dining at this family-style restaurant is like going to Mom's for Sunday dinner—if your mother is Cuban. The dining room is noisy, and the food is traditional *cubano.* There are well-seasoned black beans, a memorable paella, traditional ropa vieja, and local seafood served grilled, stuffed, and breaded. Dishes come with plantains and beans and rice or salad and fries. To make a good thing even better, the prices are very reasonable. $ *Average main: $10* ⊠ *900 Catherine St.* ☎ *305/296–4184* ⊕ *www. elsiboneyrestaurant.com* ⚭ *Reservations not accepted.*

$ ✕ **Finnegan's Wake Irish Pub and Eatery.** *Irish.* "Come for the beer. Stay for the food. Leave with the staff," is the slogan of this popular pub. The pictures of Beckett, Shaw, Yeats, and Wilde on the walls and the creaky wood floors underfoot exude Irish country warmth. Traditional fare includes bangers and mash, chicken potpie, and colcannonballs— rich mashed potatoes with scallions, cabbage, and cheese sauce. Irish bread pudding topped with whiskey sauce and custard is a true treat. Live music on weekends and daily happy hours from 4 to 7 and midnight to 2 featuring more than 30 beers on tap make it popular with the spring break and sometimes-noisy drinking crowd, but you can find quieter spots in the back room and on the porch. $ *Average main: $13* ⊠ *320 Grinnell St.* ☎ *305/293–0222* ⊕ *www. keywestirish.com* ⚭ *Reservations not accepted.*

5

$$ ✕**Half Shell Raw Bar.** *Seafood.* Smack-dab on the docks, this legendary institution gets its name from the oysters, clams, and peel-and-eat shrimp that are a departure point for its seafood-based diet. It's not clever recipes or fine dining (or even air-conditioning) that packs 'em in; it's fried fish, po'boy sandwiches, and seafood combos. For a break from the deep fryer, try the fresh and light conch ceviche "cooked" with lime juice. The potato salad is flavored with dill, and the "PamaRita" is a new twist in Margaritaville. ⑤ *Average main: $16* ✉ *Lands End Village at Historic Seaport, 231 Margaret St.* ☎ *305/294–7496* ⊕ *www.halfshellrawbar.com* ⚓ *Reservations not accepted.*

$ ✕**Hogfish Bar & Grill.** *Seafood.* It's worth a drive to Stock ★ Island, a couple of islands up from Key West, to sit along one of Florida's last surviving working waterfronts, watch the shrimpers and fishermen unloading their catch, and indulge in the freshness you're witnessing at this down-to-earth spot. Hogfish is of course the specialty. The "Killer Hogfish Sandwich" comes on Cuban Bread (you can also have it as a breakfast Benedict); sprinkle it with one of the house hot sauces. Other favorites include lobster BLT, pulled pork sandwich, hogfish tacos, gator bites, lobster potpie, and barbeque ribs. ⑤ *Average main: $13* ✉ *6810 Front St., Stock Island* ☎ *305/293–4041* ⊕ *www.hogfishbar.com.*

$$ ✕**Jimmy Buffett's Margaritaville Cafe.** *American.* If you must have your cheeseburger in paradise, it may as well be here, where you can chew along with the songs playing on the sound system, TV monitors, and movie screen. The first of Buffett's line of chain eateries, it belongs here more than anywhere else, but quite frankly it's more about the name, music, and attitude (and margaritas) than the food. The menu has a Cajun-Caribbean flair, with such offerings as conch chowder (good and spicy!), blackened hot dog, grilled andouille sausage with red beans and rice, grilled mahi with pineapple-mango salsa, and barbecued ribs. Live bands pack the place come dinner and into the wee hours. ⑤ *Average main: $16* ✉ *500 Duval St.* ☎ *305/292–1435* ⊕ *www.margaritaville.com* ⚓ *Reservations not accepted.*

$$$ ✕**Latitudes.** *Eclectic.* For a special treat, take the short boat ★ ride to lovely Sunset Key for lunch or dinner on the beach. Creativity and quality ingredients combine for dishes that are bound to impress as much as the setting. For lunch, the fish tacos with chipotle aioli and salsa are a fine example of the chef's use of local foods. At dinner, start with the crispy lobster-crab cakes or seared yellowfin tuna stacked

with mango, then move on to one of the delightful entrées, such as yellowtail snapper with coconut-lime sauce, sweet potato–crusted grouper, or Wagyu skirt steak with mocha demi-glace. Choose a table inside looking out over the gulf or on the patio. The restaurant also serves breakfast. $ Average main: $28 ⊠ Sunset Village, 245 Front St. ☎ 305/292–5300, 888/477–7786 ⊕ www.sunsetkeyisland. com ⚠ Reservations essential.

$ ✕ **Lobo's Mixed Grill.** *American.* Famous for its selection of wrap sandwiches, Lobo's has a reputation among locals for its 8-ounce, charcoal-grilled ground chuck burger—thick and juicy and served with lettuce, tomato, and pickle on a toasted bun. Mix it up with toppings like Brie, blue cheese, or portobello mushroom. The menu of 30 wraps includes rib eye, oyster, grouper, Cuban, and chicken Caesar. The menu includes salads and quesadillas, as well as a fried-shrimp-and-oyster combo. Beer and wine are served. This courtyard food stand closes around 5, so eat early. Most of Lobo's business is takeout (it has a half-dozen outdoor picnic tables), and it offers free delivery within Old Town. $ Average main: $9 ⊠ 5 Key Lime Sq., east of intersection of Southard and Duval Sts. ☎ 305/296–5303 ⊕ www. lobosmixedgrill.com ⚠ Reservations not accepted ⊗ Closed Sun. Apr.–early Dec.

$$$$ ✕ **Louie's Backyard.** *Eclectic.* Feast your eyes on a steal-your-breath-away view and beautifully presented dishes prepared by executive chef Doug Shook. Once you get over sticker shock on the seasonally changing menu (appetizers cost around $9–$18; entrées can hover around the $36 mark), settle in on the outside deck and enjoy dishes like grilled scallops with portobello relish, grilled king salmon with fried risotto, and mint-rubbed pork chop with salsa verde. A more affordable option upstairs is the Upper Deck, which serves tapas such as flaming ouzo shrimp, roasted olives with onion and feta, and Gruyère and duck confit pizza. If you come for lunch, the menu is less expensive but the view is just as fantastic. For night owls, the tin-roofed Afterdeck Bar serves cocktails on the water until the wee hours. $ Average main: $36 ⊠ 700 Waddell Ave. ☎ 305/294–1061 ⊕ www.louiesbackyard.com ⚠ Reservations essential ⊗ Closed Labor Day to mid-Sept. Upper Deck closed Sun. and Mon. No lunch at Upper Deck.

$$ ✕ **Mangia Mangia.** *Italian.* This longtime favorite serves large portions of homemade pastas that can be matched with any of their homemade sauces. Tables are arranged in a brick garden hung with twinkling lights and in a cozy,

Everything's Fishy in the Keys

CLOSE UP

Fish. It's what's for dinner (and lunch—and sometimes even breakfast!) in the Florida Keys. The Keys' runway between the Gulf of Mexico or Florida Bay and Atlantic warm waters means fish of many fin. Restaurants take full advantage by serving it fresh, whether you caught it or a local fisherman did.

Menus at a number of colorful waterfront shacks such as **Snapper's** (⊠ 139 Seaside Ave., Key Largo ☎ 305/852–5956) in Key Largo and **Half Shell Raw Bar** (⊠ 231 Margaret St., Key West ☎ 305/294–7496) range from basic raw, steamed, broiled, grilled, or blackened fish to some Bahamian and New Orleans–style interpretations. Other seafood houses dress up their tables in linens and their fish in creative haute-cuisine styles, such as **Pierre's** (⊠ MM 81.5 BS, Islamorada ☎ 305/664–3225) hogfish meunière. And if you're looking for that seafood breakfast

Keys-style, try the "grits and grunts"—fried fish and grits—at **The Stuffed Pig** (⊠ 3520 Overseas Hwy., Marathon ☎ 305/743–4059).

You know it's fresh when you see a fish market as soon as you open the door to the restaurant where you're dining. It happens all the time in the Keys. You can even study the seafood showcases and pick the fish fillet or lobster tail you want.

Many of the Keys' best restaurants are found in marina complexes, where the commercial fishermen bring their catches straight from the sea. Some, however, such as **Hogfish Bar & Grill** on Stock Island, one island north of Key West (⊠ 6810 Front St., Stock Island ☎ 305/293–4041 ⊕ www.hogfishbar.com), and **Keys Fisheries Market & Marina** (⊠ End of 35th St., Marathon, MM 49 BS ☎ 305/743–4353 or 866/743–4353), take some finding.

casual dining room in an old house. Everything out of the open kitchen is outstanding, including the *bollito misto di mare* (fresh seafood sautéed with garlic, shallots, white wine, and pasta) or the memorable spaghettini "schmappellini," homemade pasta with asparagus, tomatoes, pine nuts, and Parmesan. The wine list—with more than 350 offerings—includes old and rare vintages, and also has a good by-the-glass selection. ⑤ *Average main: $16* ⊠ *900 Southard St.* ☎ *305/294–2469* ⊕ *www.mangia-mangia.com* ⊰ *Reservations not accepted* ⊗ *No lunch*.

$$$ ✕**Michaels Restaurant.** *American.* White tablecloths, subdued lighting, and romantic music give Michaels the feel of an urban eatery. Garden seating reminds you that you are in the Keys. Chef–owner Michael Wilson flies in prime rib, cowboy steaks, and rib eyes from Allen Brothers in Chicago, which has supplied top-ranked steak houses for more than a century. Also on the menu is a melt-in-your-mouth grouper stuffed with jumbo lump crab, Kobe and tenderloin meat loaf, veal saltimbocca, and a variety of made-to-order fondue dishes (try the pesto pot, spiked with hot pepper and basil). To lighten up, smaller portions of many of the favorites are available until 7:30 Sunday through Thursday. The Hemingway (mojito-style) and the Third Degree (raspberry vodka and white crème de cacao) top the cocktail menu. Ⓢ*Average main: $25* ✉*532 Margaret St.* ☎*305/295–1300* ⊕*www.michaelskeywest. com* ♨*Reservations essential* ⊗*No lunch.*

$$$ ✕**Nine One Five.** *Eclectic.* Twinkling lights draped along the lower- and upper-level outdoor porches of a 100-year-old Victorian mansion set an elegant—though unstuffy—stage here. If you like to sample and sip, you'll appreciate the variety of smaller plate selections and wines by the glass. Starters include a cheese platter, crispy duck confit, a tapas platter, and the signature "tuna dome" with fresh crab, lemon-miso dressing, and an ahi tuna–sashimi wrapping. There are also larger plates if you're craving something like seafood soup or steak au poivre frites. Dine outdoors and people-watch along upper Duval, or sit at a table inside while listening to light jazz. Ⓢ*Average main: $28* ✉*915 Duval St.* ☎*305/296–0669* ⊕*www.915duval.com* ♨*Reservations essential* ⊗*No lunch.*

$$$$ ✕**Pisces.** *European.* In a circa-1892 former store and home, ★ chef William Arnel and staff create a contemporary setting with a stylish granite bar, Andy Warhol originals, and glass oil lamps. Favorites include "lobster tango mango," flambéed in cognac and served with saffron butter sauce and sliced mangoes; Pisces Aphrodite (seafood in puff pastry); fillet *au poivre*; and black grouper braised in champagne. Ⓢ*Average main: $35* ✉*1007 Simonton St.* ☎*305/294–7100* ⊕*www.pisceskeywest.com* ♨*Reservations essential* ⊗*No lunch.*

$$ ✕**Salute Ristorante at the Beach.** *Italian.* This colorful restaurant sits on Higgs Beach, giving it one of the island's best lunch views—and a bit of sand and salt spray on a windy day. Owners of the popular Blue Heaven restaurant took it over and have designed an intriguing dinner menu that

includes linguine with mussels, lasagna, and white bean soup. At lunch the gazpacho refreshes with great flavor and texture, and the calamari marinara, antipasti sandwich, pasta primavera, and yellowtail sandwich do not disappoint. Plans are under way to expand the kitchen and serve breakfast. $ *Average main: $20 ⊠ 1000 Atlantic Blvd., Higgs Beach ☎ 305/292–1117 ⊕ saluteonthebeach. com ⚓ Reservations not accepted.*

$$ ✕ **Sarabeth's.** *American.* Named for the award-winning
★ jam-maker and pastry chef Sarabeth Levine, who runs the kitchen, it naturally is proclaimed for its all-morning, all-afternoon breakfast, best enjoyed in the picket-fenced front yard of this sweet circa-1870 cottage. Lemon ricotta pancakes, pumpkin waffles, omelets, and homemade jams make the meal. Lunch offerings range from a griddled smoked mozzarella sandwich to poached salmon "Cobb" salad. Start dinner with the signature velvety cream of tomato soup, or roasted red beets and Gorgonzola salad. The daily special augments the short entrée listing that includes meatloaf, green chile pepper macaroni with three cheeses, and grilled mahimahi with tomatillo sauce. In the mood for dessert? The warm orange-apricot bread pudding takes its cues from Sarabeth's most popular flavor of jam. $ *Average main: $20 ⊠ 530 Simonton St. ☎ 305/293–8181 ⊕ www.sarabethskeywest.com ⚓ Reservations not accepted ⊘ Closed Mon. Easter through Christmas, no dinner Mon. Christmas through Easter, closed Tues.*

$$$ ✕ **Seven Fish.** *Seafood.* A local hot spot, this intimate, off-the-
★ beaten-track eatery is good for an eclectic mix of dishes like tropical shrimp salsa, wild-mushroom quesadilla, seafood marinara, and old-fashioned meat loaf with real mashed potatoes. For dessert, the sweet potato pie provides an added measure of down-home comfort. Those in the know reserve for dinner early to snag one of the 20 or so tables clustered in the bare-bones dining room. $ *Average main: $21 ⊠ 632 Olivia St. ☎ 305/296–2777 ⊕ www.7fish.com ⚓ Reservations essential ⊘ Closed Tues. No lunch.*

$$$ ✕ **Tavern N Town.** *Eclectic.* This handsome and warm restaurant has an open kitchen that adds lovely aromas from the wood-fired oven. The dinner menu offers a variety of options such as small plates of shrimp cocktail and Wagyu beef sliders and small pizzas for starters. For an entree, try the coffee-crusted pork tenderloin with pine chutney or the prime rib. Breakfast is served buffet-style or à la carte (try the homemade corned beef hash). $ *Average main: $29 ⊠ Key West Marriott Beachside Resort, 3841 N. Roosevelt*

Blvd. ☎*305/296–8100, 800/546–0885* ⊕*www.beachside-keywest.com* ⊗*No lunch.*

$$ ✕**Turtle Kraals.** *Seafood.* Named for the kraals, or corrals, ♧ where sea turtles were once kept until they went to the cannery, this place calls to mind the island's history. The lunch–dinner menu offers an assortment of marine cuisine that includes seafood enchiladas, mesquite-grilled fish of the day, and mango crab cakes. The slow-cook wood smoker results in wonderfully tender ribs, brisket, mesquite-grilled oysters with Parmesan and cilantro, and mesquite-grilled chicken sandwich. The open restaurant overlooks the marina at the Historic Seaport. Turtle races entertain during happy hour on Monday and Friday at 6 pm. ⑤*Average main: $16* ⊠*231 Margaret St.* ☎*305/294–2640* ⊕*www.turtlekraals. com* ⩘*Reservations not accepted.*

WHERE TO STAY

Historic cottages, restored century-old Conch houses, and large resorts are among the offerings in Key West, the majority charging between $100 and $300 a night. In high season, Christmas through Easter, you'll be hard pressed to find a decent room for less than $200, and most places raise prices considerably during holidays and festivals. Many guesthouses and inns do not welcome children under 16, and most do not permit smoking indoors. Most tariffs include an expanded continental breakfast and, often, afternoon wine or snack.

LODGING ALTERNATIVES

The Key West Innkeepers Association is an umbrella organization for dozens of local properties. Vacation Rentals Key West lists historic cottages, homes, and condominiums for rent. Rent Key West Vacations specializes in renting vacation homes and condos for a week or longer. Vacation Key West lists all kinds of properties throughout Key West.

Key West Innkeepers Association ⑤*Rooms from: $16* ⊠*316A Simonton St.* ☎*305/295–1334, 800/492–1911* ⊕*www. keywestinns.com.*

Vacation Rentals Key West ⑤*Rooms from: $16* ⊠*1511 Truman Ave.* ☎*305/292–7997, 888/775–3993* ⊕*www.key-westvacations.com.*

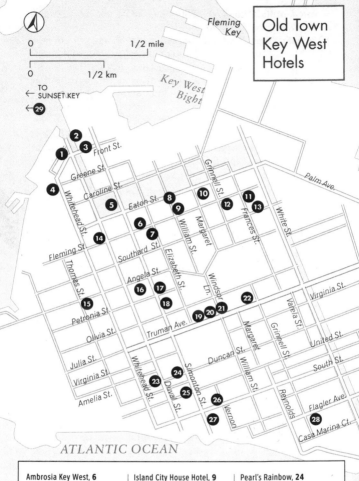

Old Town Key West Hotels

Ambrosia Key West, 6
Angelina Guest House, 15
Azul Key West, 22
Casa Marina Resort, 28
Courtney's Place, 17
Crown Plaza Key West–La Concha, 14
Eden House, 12
The Gardens Hotel, 16
Heron House Court, 11
Hyatt Key West Resort & Spa, 3

Island City House Hotel, 9
Island House, 13
Key Lime Inn, 19
Key West B&B/The Popular House, 8
La Pensione, 21
Marquesa Hotel, 7
Merlin Guesthouse, 18
Mermaid & the Alligator, 20
Ocean Breeze Inn, 26
Ocean Key Resort & Spa, 1

Pearl's Rainbow, 24
Pier House Resort & Caribbean Spa, 2
The Reach Resort, 27
Simonton Court, 5
Southernmost Hotel, 25
Speakeasy Inn, 23
Sunset Key, 29
Westin Key West Resort & Marina, 4
Westwinds Inn, 10

Rent Key West Vacations ⓢ *Rooms from: $16* ✉ *1075 Duval St., Ste. C11* ☎ *305/294–0990, 800/833–7368* ⊕ *www.rent-keywest.com.*

Vacation Key West ⓢ *Rooms from: $16* ✉ *100 Grinnell St.* ☎ *305/295–9500, 800/595–5397* ⊕ *www.vacationkw.com.*

RECOMMENDED INNS AND HOTELS

For expanded reviews, facilities, and current deals, visit Fodors.com.

$$$$ ⊞ **Ambrosia Key West.** *B&B/Inn.* If you desire personal atten-
★ tion, a casual atmosphere, and a dollop of style, stay at
these twin inns spread out on nearly 2 acres. **Pros:** spacious rooms; poolside breakfast; friendly staff. **Cons:** on-
street parking can be tough to come by; a little too spread
out. ⓢ *Rooms from: $319* ✉ *615, 618, 622 Fleming St.*
☎ *305/296–9838, 800/535–9838* ⊕ *www.ambrosiakey-
west.com* ⇆ *6 rooms, 3 town houses, 1 cottage, 10 suites*
⏸ *Breakfast.*

$$ ⊞ **Angelina Guest House.** *B&B/Inn.* In the heart of Old Town,
this home away from home offers simple, clean, attractively
priced accommodations. **Pros:** good value; nice garden;
friendly staff. **Cons:** thin walls; basic rooms; shared balcony.
ⓢ *Rooms from: $109* ✉ *302 Angela St.* ☎ *305/294–4480,
888/303–4480* ⊕ *www.angelinaguesthouse.com* ⇆ *13 rooms*
⏸ *Breakfast.*

$$$$ ⊞ **Azul Key West.** *B&B/Inn.* The ultramodern—nearly mini-
malistic—redo of this classic circa-1903 Queen Anne man-
sion is a break from the sensory overload of Key West's
other abundant Victorian guesthouses. **Pros:** lovely build-
ing; marble-floored baths; luxurious linens. **Cons:** on a busy
street. ⓢ *Rooms from: $239* ✉ *907 Truman Ave.* ☎ *305/296–
5152, 888/253–2985* ⊕ *www.azulhotels.us* ⇆ *11 rooms, 1
suite* ⏸ *Breakfast.*

$$$ ⊞ **Best Western Key Ambassador Resort Inn.** *Hotel.* You know
what to expect from this chain hotel: well-maintained
rooms, predictable service, and competitive prices. **Pros:** big
pool area; popular tiki bar. **Cons:** airport noise; lacks per-
sonality. ⓢ *Rooms from: $200* ✉ *3755 S. Roosevelt Blvd.,
New Town* ☎ *305/296–3500, 800/432–4315* ⊕ *www.key-
ambassador.com* ⇆ *101 rooms* ⏸ *Breakfast.*

$$$ ⊞ **Casa Marina Resort & Beach Club.** *Resort.* At any moment,
★ you expect the landed gentry to walk across the oceanfront
☾ lawn, just as they did when this 13-acre resort was built
back in the 1920s. **Pros:** nice beach; historic setting; away

from the crowds. **Cons:** long walk to central Old Town; $25 resort fee. ⑤ *Rooms from: $159* ✉ *1500 Reynolds St.* ☎ *305/296–3535, 866/203–6392* ⊕ *www.casamarinaresort. com* ⌁ *241 rooms, 70 suites* ⧉ *No meals.*

$$$$ ⌷ **Courtney's Place.** *B&B/Inn.* If you like kids, cats, and dogs, you'll feel right at home in this collection of accommodations ranging from cigar-maker cottages to shotgun houses. **Pros:** near Duval Street; fairly priced. **Cons:** small parking lot; small pool, minimum stay requirements. ⑤ *Rooms from: $229* ✉ *720 Whitmarsh Ln., off Petronia St.* ☎ *305/294–3480, 800/869–4639* ⊕ *www.courtneysplacekeywest.com* ⌁ *6 rooms, 2 suites, 2 efficiencies, 8 cottages* ⧉ *Breakfast.*

$$$ ⌷ **Crowne Plaza Key West–La Concha.** *Hotel.* History and franchises can mix, as this 1920s-vintage hotel proves with its handsome faux-palm atrium lobby and sleep-conducive rooms. **Pros:** restaurant and Starbucks in-house; close to downtown attractions; free Wi-Fi. **Cons:** high-traffic area; confusing layout; $20/night valet-only parking. **TripAdvisor:** "amazing experience," "rooms are beautiful," "courteous staff." ⑤ *Rooms from: $199* ✉ *430 Duval St.* ☎ *305/296–2991* ⊕ *www.laconchakeywest.com* ⌁ *160 rooms, 8 rooms with balconies, 10 suites.*

$$$ ⌷ **Eden House.** *Hotel.* From the vintage metal rockers on the ★ street-side porch to the old neon hotel sign in the lobby, this 1920s rambling Key West mainstay hotel is high on character, low on gloss. **Pros:** free parking; hot tub is actually hot; daily happy hour around the pool; discount at excellent Azur restaurant. **Cons:** pricey; a bit of a musty smell in some rooms; no TV in some rooms. ⑤ *Rooms from: $200* ✉ *1015 Fleming St.* ☎ *305/296–6868, 800/533–5397* ⊕ *www.edenhouse.com* ⌁ *36 rooms, 8 suites* ⧉ *No meals.*

★ **Fodor's**Choice ⌷ **The Gardens Hotel.** *Hotel.* Built in 1875, this **$$$$** gloriously shaded property covers a third of a city block in Old Town, among orchids, ponytail palms, black bamboo, walks, fountains, and earthen pots imported from Cuba. **Pros:** luxurious bathrooms; secluded garden seating; free phone calls. **Cons:** hard to get reservations; expensive; $20 per night parking fee. ⑤ *Rooms from: $385* ✉ *526 Angela St.* ☎ *305/294–2661, 800/526–2664* ⊕ *www.gardenshotel. com* ⌁ *17 rooms* ⧉ *Breakfast.*

$$$ ⌷ **Harborside Motel & Marina.** *Hotel.* This little motel neatly packages three appealing characteristics—affordability, safety, and a pleasant location between Old Town and New Town at Garrison Bight. **Pros:** grills for cookouts; friendly fishing atmosphere; boat slips. **Cons:** more than a mile from

Duval Street; $10 cash key deposit. $ *Rooms from: $139* ✉ *903 Eisenhower Dr.* ☎ *305/294–2780, 800/501–7823* ⊕ *www.keywestharborside.com* ⌁ *7 rooms, 5 efficiencies, 4 houseboats.*

$$$$ ⚏ **Heron House Court.** *B&B/Inn.* Conch-style architecture harks back to this property's circa-1900 origins as a boardinghouse and cigar-maker cottages. **Pros:** charming; fluffy bathrobes. **Cons:** faces noisy Eaton Street; owner's suite smells musty. $ *Rooms from: $219* ✉ *412 Frances St.* ☎ *305/296–4719, 888/265–2395* ⊕ *www.heronhousecourt. com* ⌁ *3 suites, 12 rooms* ⍥ *Breakfast.*

$$$$ ⚏ **Hyatt Key West Resort and Spa.** *Resort.* With its own manmade beach, the Hyatt Key West is one of few resorts where you can dig your toes in the sand, then walk a short distance away to the streets of Old Town. **Pros:** a little bit away from the bustle of Old Town; plenty of activities. **Cons:** beach is small; cramped-feeling property. $ *Rooms from: $290* ✉ *601 Front St.* ☎ *305/809–1234* ⊕ *www.keywest.hyatt. com* ⌁ *118 rooms* ⍥ *No meals.*

$$$$ ⚏ **Island City House Hotel.** *B&B/Inn.* A private garden with brick walkways, tropical plants, and a canopy of palms sets this convivial guesthouse apart from the pack. **Pros:** lush gardens; knowledgeable staff. **Cons:** spotty Wi-Fi service; no front-desk staff at night; some rooms are small. $ *Rooms from: $230* ✉ *411 William St.* ☎ *305/294–5702, 800/634–8230* ⊕ *www.islandcityhouse.com* ⌁ *24 suites* ⍥ *Breakfast.*

$$$ ⚏ **Island House.** *Hotel.* Geared specifically toward gay men, this hotel features a health club, a video lounge, a café and bar, and rooms in historic digs. Clothing is optional everywhere but in the gym. **Pros:** lots of privacy; just the place to get that all-over tan; free happy hour for guests. **Cons:** no women allowed; some shared baths. $ *Rooms from: $189* ✉ *1129 Fleming St.* ☎ *305/294–6284, 800/890–6284* ⊕ *www.islandhousekeywest.com* ⌁ *371 rooms, 3 with shared bath.*

$$$ ⚏ **Key Lime Inn.** *B&B/Inn.* This 1854 Grand Bahama–style house on the National Register of Historic Places succeeds by offering amiable service, a great location, and simple rooms with natural-wood furnishings. **Pros:** free parking; some rooms have private outdoor spaces. **Cons:** standard rooms are pricey; pool faces a busy street; mulch-covered paths. $ *Rooms from: $179* ✉ *725 Truman Ave.* ☎ *305/294–5229, 800/549–4430* ⊕ *www.keylimeinn.com* ⌁ *37 rooms* ⍥ *Breakfast.*

5

$ ▣ **Key West Bed and Breakfast/The Popular House.** *B&B/Inn.*
★ There are accommodations for every budget, but the owners reason that budget travelers deserve as pleasant an experience (and lavish a tropical Continental breakfast) as their well-heeled counterparts. **Pros:** lots of art; tiled outdoor shower; hot tub and sauna area is a welcome hangout. **Cons:** some rooms are small. ⑤ *Rooms from: $99 ⊠415 William St.* ☎305/296–7274, 800/438–6155 ⊕*www.keywestbandb.com* ➹10 *rooms, 6 with private bath* ⏏*Breakfast.*

$$$$ ▣ **Key West Marriott Beachside Hotel.** *Hotel.* This new hotel vies for convention business with one of the biggest ballrooms in Key West, but it also appeals to families with its spacious condo units decorated with impeccable good taste. **Pros:** private beach; poolside cabanas. **Cons:** small beach; long walk to Old Town; cookie-cutter facade. ⑤ *Rooms from: $228 ⊠3841 N. Roosevelt Blvd., New Town* ☎305/296–8100, 800/546–0885 ⊕*www.keywestmarriottbeachside.com* ➹93 *rooms, 93 1-bedroom suites, 10 2-bedroom suites, 26 3-bedroom suites* ⏏*No meals.*

$$$ ▣ **La Pensione.** *B&B/Inn.* Hospitality and period furnishings make this 1891 home, once owned by a cigar executive, a wonderful glimpse into Key West life in the late 19th century. **Pros:** pine-paneled walls; off-street parking; some rooms have wraparound porches. **Cons:** street-facing rooms are noisy; baths need updating. ⑤ *Rooms from: $168 ⊠809 Truman Ave.* ☎305/292–9923, 800/893–1193 ⊕*www.lapensione.com* ➹9 *rooms* ⏏*Breakfast.*

★ **Fodor's**Choice ▣ **Marquesa Hotel.** *Hotel.* In a town that prides
$$$$ itself on its laid-back luxury, this complex of four restored 1884 houses stands out. **Pros:** elegant setting; romantic atmosphere; turndown service. **Cons:** street-facing rooms can be noisy; expensive rates. ⑤ *Rooms from: $330 ⊠600 Fleming St.* ☎305/292–1919, 800/869–4631 ⊕*www.marquesa.com* ➹27 *rooms* ⏏*No meals.*

$$$$ ▣ **Merlin Guesthouse.** *B&B/Inn.* Key West guesthouses don't
★ usually welcome families, but this laid-back jumble of rooms and suites is an exception. **Pros:** good location near Duval Street; good rates. **Cons:** neighbor noise; street parking. ⑤ *Rooms from: $279 ⊠811 Simonton St.* ☎305/296–3336, 800/642–4753 ⊕*www.merlinguesthouse.com* ➹10 *rooms, 6 suites, 4 cottages* ⏏*Breakfast.*

$$$$ ▣ **Mermaid & the Alligator.** *B&B/Inn.* An enchanting com-
★ bination of flora and fauna makes this 1904 Victorian house a welcoming retreat. **Pros:** hot plunge pool; massage pavilion; island-getaway feel. **Cons:** minimum stay

required (length depends on season); dark public areas; plastic lawn chairs. ⑤ *Rooms from: $248* ⊠ *729 Truman Ave.* ☎ *305/294–1894, 800/773–1894* ⊕ *www.kwmermaid. com* ⟿ *9 rooms* ⑩ *Breakfast.*

$$$ ⊡ **Ocean Breeze Inn.** *B&B/Inn.* What this simple South Beach area motel lacks in style it makes up for in value. Rooms, with peachy floral colors and wicker furniture, are clustered around a tiny pool in one-story cement-block strips. **Pros:** early (2 pm) check-in; clean and spacious rooms; staff remembers your name. **Cons:** bland decor; small pool; no staff after 6 pm. ⑤ *Rooms from: $169* ⊠ *625 South St.* ☎ *305/296–2829, 877/879–2362* ⊕ *www.oceanbreezeinn. com* ⟿ *15 rooms* ⑩ *Breakfast.*

$$$$ ⊡ **Ocean Key Resort & Spa.** *Resort.* A pool and lively open-air bar and restaurant sit on Sunset Pier, a popular place
★ to watch the sun sink into the horizon. **Pros:** well-trained staff; lively pool scene; best spa on the island. **Cons:** $20 per night valet parking; too bustling for some; noise from plumbing and bar. ⑤ *Rooms from: $348* ⊠ *Zero Duval St.* ☎ *305/296–7701, 800/328–9815* ⊕ *www.oceankey.com* ⟿ *64 rooms, 36 suites* ⑩ *No meals.*

$$$ ⊡ **Parrot Key Resort.** *Hotel.* This revamped destination resort
★ feels like an old-fashioned beach community with picket fences and rocking-chair porches. **Pros:** four pools; finely appointed units; access to marina and other facilities at three sister properties in Marathon. **Cons:** outside of walking distance to Old Town; no transportation provided; hefty resort fee. ⑤ *Rooms from: $199* ⊠ *2801 N. Roosevelt Blvd., New Town* ☎ *305/809–2200* ⊕ *www.parrotkeyresort.com* ⟿ *74 rooms, 74 suites, 3 3-bedroom cottages* ⑩ *No meals.*

$$$ ⊡ **Pearl's Rainbow.** *B&B/Inn.* This guesthouse—which once catered only to lesbians and gay-friendly women—is now open to everyone. **Pros:** full breakfast; plenty of privacy. **Cons:** bar attracts late-night partiers. ⑤ *Rooms from: $189* ⊠ *525 United St.* ☎ *305/292–1450, 800/749–6696* ⊕ *www. pearlsrainbow.com* ⟿ *32 rooms, 2 efficiencies, 4 suites* ⑩ *Breakfast.*

$$$$ ⊡ **Pier House Resort and Caribbean Spa.** *Resort.* The location—
★ on a quiet stretch of beach at the foot of Duval—is ideal as a buffer from and gateway to the action. **Pros:** beautiful beach; good location; nice spa. **Cons:** lots of conventions; poolside rooms are small; minimum stays during busy times. ⑤ *Rooms from: $339* ⊠ *1 Duval St.* ☎ *305/296–4600, 800/327–8340* ⊕ *www.pierhouse.com* ⟿ *116 rooms, 26 suites* ⑩ *No meals.*

THE HOLIDAYS KEY WEST STYLE

On New Year's Eve, Key West celebrates the turning of the calendar page with three separate ceremonies that parody New York's dropping-of-the-ball drama. Here they let fall a 6-foot conch shell from Sloppy Joe's Bar, a pirate wench from the towering mast of a tall ship at the Historic Seaport, and a drag queen (elegantly decked out in a ball gown and riding an oversize red high-heel shoe) at Bourbon Street Pub. You wouldn't expect any less from America's most outrageous city.

Key West is one of the nation's biggest party towns, so the celebrations here take on a colorful hue. In keeping with Key West's rich maritime heritage, its month-long Bight Before Christmas begins Thanksgiving Eve at Key West Bight. The Lighted Boat Parade creates a quintessential Florida spectacle with live music and decorated vessels of all shapes and sizes.

Some years, Tennessee Williams Theatre hosts a Key West version of the Nutcracker. In this unorthodox retelling, the heroine sails to a coral reef and is submerged in a diving bell. (What? No sugarplum fairies?) Between Christmas and New Year's Day, the Holiday House and Garden Tour is another yuletide tradition.

$$$$ ☎ **The Reach Resort.** *Resort.* Embracing Key West's only
★ natural beach, this recently reinvented and reopened full-service resort has its roots in the 1980s when locals rallied against the loss of the topless beach it displaced. **Pros:** removed from Duval hubbub; great sunrise views; pullout sofas in most rooms. **Cons:** $25 per day per room resort fee; expensive. ⑤ *Rooms from: $279* ✉ *1435 Simonton St.* ☎ *305/296–5000, 888/318–4316* ⊕ *www.reachresort.com* ↪ *72 rooms, 78 suites* ⑴⑴ *No meals.*

$$$$ ☎ **Simonton Court.** *B&B/Inn.* A small world all of its own,
★ this lodging makes you feel deliciously sequestered from Key West's crasser side, but close enough to get there on foot. **Pros:** lots of privacy; well-appointed accommodations; friendly staff. **Cons:** minimum stays required in high season. ⑤ *Rooms from: $260* ✉ *320 Simonton St.* ☎ *305/294–6386, 800/944–2687* ⊕ *www.simontoncourt.com* ↪ *17 rooms, 6 suites, 6 cottages* ⑴⑴ *Breakfast.*

$$$ ☎ **Southernmost Hotel.** *Hotel.* This hotel's location on the quiet end of Duval means you don't have to deal with the hustle and bustle of downtown unless you want to—

it's within a 20-minute walk (but around sunset, this end of town gets its share of car and foot traffic). **Pros:** pool attracts a lively crowd; access to nearby properties and beach; free parking. **Cons:** can get crowded around the pool and public areas. ⑤ *Rooms from: $209* ⊠ *1319 Duval St.* ☎ *305/296–6577, 800/354–4455* ⊕ *www.southernmostresorts.com* ⇆ *125 rooms* ⦿ *No meals.*

$$$ ⊞ **Speakeasy Inn.** *B&B/Inn.* During Prohibition, Raul Vasquez made this place popular by smuggling in rum from Cuba. **Pros:** good location; reasonable rates; kitchenettes. **Cons:** no pool; on busy Duval. ⑤ *Rooms from: $149* ⊠ *1117 Duval St.* ☎ *305/296–2680* ⊕ *www.speakeasyinn. com* ⇆ *4 suites* ⦿ *Breakfast.*

★ **Fodor's**Choice ⊞ **Sunset Key.** *Resort.* This private island retreat
$$$$ feels completely cut off from the world, yet you're just minutes away from the action. **Pros:** peace and quiet; roomy verandas; free 24-hour shuttle; free Wi-Fi. **Cons:** luxury doesn't come cheap. ⑤ *Rooms from: $695* ⊠ *245 Front St.* ☎ *305/292–5300, 888/477–7786* ⊕ *www.westinsunsetkeycottages.com* ⇆ *40 cottages* ⦿ *Breakfast.*

$$$$ ⊞ **Westin Key West Resort & Marina.** *Resort.* This waterfront resort's two three-story, Keys-style buildings huddle around its 37-slip marina in the middle of Old Town. **Pros:** good location; bar and restaurant overlook Mallory Square; access to Sunset Key; free Wi-Fi. **Cons:** feels too big for Key West; often crowded; conference clientele. ⑤ *Rooms from: $399* ⊠ *245 Front St.* ☎ *305/294–4000* ⊕ *www.westin.com/ keywest* ⇆ *146 rooms, 32 suites.*

$$$ ⊞ **Westwinds Inn.** *B&B/Inn.* This cluster of historic gingerbread-trimmed houses has individually decorated rooms that make you feel right at home. **Pros:** away from Old Town's bustle; lots of character; affordable rates. **Cons:** small lobby; confusing layout; a long walk from Duval Street. ⑤ *Rooms from: $190* ⊠ *914 Eaton St.* ☎ *305/296–4440, 800/788–4150* ⊕ *www.westwindskeywest.com* ⇆ *21 rooms, 4 suites* ⦿ *Breakfast.*

NIGHTLIFE AND THE ARTS

NIGHTLIFE

Rest up: Much of what happens in Key West does so after dark. Open your mind and take a stroll. Scruffy street performers strum next to dogs in sunglasses. Characters wearing parrots or iguanas try to sell you your photo with their pet. Brawls tumble out the doors of Sloppy Joe's. Drag queens strut across stages in Joan Rivers garb. Tattooed men lick whipped cream off women's body parts. And margaritas flow like a Jimmy Buffett tune.

BEST OF THE BARS. Southernmost Scavenger Hunt's "Best of the Bars" challenge has teams of two to five touring the bars of Key West for clues, libations, and prizes. It hosts the event at 7 pm most Fridays, Saturdays, and Sundays, starting at Sloppy Joe's. The cost is $20 per person. For information, call ☎ 305/292–9994 or visit ⊕ www.keywesthunt.com.

BARS AND LOUNGES

Capt. Tony's Saloon. When it was the original Sloppy Joe's in the mid-1930s Hemingway was a regular. Later, a young Jimmy Buffett sang here and made this watering hole famous in his song "Last Mango in Paris." Bands play nightly while regulars play pool. ✉ *428 Greene St.* ☎ *305/294–1838.*

Cowboy Bill's Honky Tonk Saloon. Ride the mechanical bucking bull, listen to live bands croon cry-in-your-beer tunes, and grab some pretty decent chow at the indoor-outdoor spread known as Cowboy Bill's Honky Tonk Saloon. Wednesday brings—we kid you not—Sexy Bull Riding. ✉ *610½ Duval St.* ☎ *305/295–8219* ⊕ *www.cowboybillskw.com.*

Durty Harry's. The megasize entertainment complex has live music in a variety of indoor-outdoor bars including Rick's Dance Club Wine & Martini Bar and the tiny Red Garter strip club. ✉ *208 Duval St.* ☎ *305/296–5513.*

The Garden of Eden. Perhaps one of Duval's more unusual and intriguing watering holes, The Garden of Eden sits atop the Bull & Whistle saloon and has a clothing-optional policy. Most drinkers are looky-lous, but some actually bare it all. ✉ *224 Duval St.* ☎ *305/396–4565* ⊕ *www.bullkeywest.com.*

Green Parrot Bar. Pause for a libation in the open-air. Built in 1890, the bar is said to be Key West's oldest. The sometimes-rowdy saloon has locals outnumbering out-of-towners, especially on nights when bands play. ✉ *601 Whitehead St., at Southard St.* ☎ *305/294–6133* ⊕ *www. greenparrot.com.*

Hog's Breath Saloon. Belly up to the bar for a cold mug of the signature Hog's Breath Lager at this infamous joint, a must-stop on the Key West bar crawl. Live bands play daily 1 pm–2 am (except when the game's on TV). ✉ *400 Front St.* ☎ *305/296–4222* ⊕ *www.hogsbreath.com.*

Margaritaville Café. A youngish, touristy crowd mixes with aging Parrot Heads. It's owned by former Key West resident and recording star Jimmy Buffett, who has been known to perform here. The drink of choice is, of course, a margarita, made with Jimmy's own brand of Margaritaville tequila. There's live music nightly, as well as lunch and dinner. ✉ *500 Duval St.* ☎ *305/292–1435* ⊕ *www.margaritaville.com.*

Pier House. The party here begins with a steel-drum band to celebrate the sunset on the beach (on select Thursdays and Fridays), then moves indoors to the Wine Galley piano bar for live jazz. ✉ *1 Duval St.* ☎ *305/296–4600, 800/327–8340* ⊕ *www.pierhouse.com.*

Schooner Wharf Bar. An open-air waterfront bar and grill in the historic seaport district retains its funky Key West charm and hosts live entertainment daily. Its margarita ranks among Key West's best. ✉ *202 William St.* ☎ *305/292–3302* ⊕ *www.schoonerwharf.com.*

Sloppy Joe's. There's history and good times at the successor to a famous 1937 speakeasy named for its founder, Captain Joe Russell. Decorated with Hemingway memorabilia and marine flags, the bar is popular with travelers and is full and noisy all the time. A Sloppy Joe's T-shirt is a de rigueur Key West souvenir, and the gift shop sells them like crazy. ✉ *201 Duval St.* ☎ *305/294–5717* ⊕ *www.sloppyjoes.com.*

The Top. On the seventh floor of the Crowne Plaza Key West La Concha, this is one of the best places in town to view the sunset and enjoy live entertainment on Friday and Saturday nights. ✉ *430 Duval St.* ☎ *305/296–2991* ⊕ *www. laconchakeywest.com.*

Two Friends Patio Lounge. Love karaoke? Get it out of your system at Two Friends Patio Lounge, where your performance gets a live Internet feed via the bar's Karaoke Cam. The singing starts at 8:30 pm most nights. ✉ *512 Front St.* ☎ *305/296–3124* ⊕ *www.twofriendskeywest.com.*

Virgilio's. In the best traditions of a 1950s cocktail lounge, this bar serves chilled martinis to the soothing tempo of live jazz and blues nightly. ✉ *524 Duval St.* ☎ *305/296–8118* ⊕ *www.virgilioskeywest.com.*

5

CLOSE UP Margarita Madness

Mojitos, martinis, and caipirinhas may be the popular drinks in Miami's South Beach, but in Key West the margarita Jimmy Buffett crooned about is still alive and well.

Every bar and club serves them, either the classic version or in dozens of variations. Every bartender claims to make the best. Here are some that rank tops in their category. At the **Half Shell Raw Bar**, the Raw Bar Rita, made with 1800 Sauza Silver Tequila and a splash of Patrón Citronge, has a funky green glow but good tartness. The Pama Rita, which the menu claims is "for the health nut," is much prettier, dyed and flavored with a splash of red Pama liqueur, and also fueled with Sauza Silver. It scores best in the novelty category.

Although **El Meson de Pepe** brags about its mojitos, its Gold Margarita, made with El Jimador Reposado, is no slouch. It goes especially well with a basket of Cuban bread served with addictive red and green dipping sauces, so it rates tops for its ability to play well with food.

At Bagatelle's **Toucan Bar** the Patrón's Margarita, named for its brand of top-shelf tequila, gets points for being smooth, almost creamy. It's the perfect balance of tart and sweet. The view of Duval Street adds to the enjoyment.

At **Mangoes**, the Mangorita is naturally the signature drink. Very tropical, but made with Cuervo and Marie Brizard, it ranks in the "tourist drink" category.

The Conch-a-Rita at **Conch Republic Seafood Company** pours on the Herradura tequila with a splash of Cointreau. This is a strong contender in the classic category.

At Jimmy Buffett's **Margaritaville** one would expect high competition. Buffett on the stereo makes a margarita go down just right, with or without a shaker of salt. Jimmy's own brand of gold Margaritaville tequila goes into the potent Uptown Margarita, topped with a float of Gran Gala.

Schooner Wharf's Schoonerita takes top rating in the classic class. The bartender shakes the cocktail and squeezes in a healthy dose of real lime juice at the end. Made with Sauza tequila, it comes served in a proper glass birdbath–shaped vessel, although this one has a stem in the shape of a cactus. (South-of-the-border kitsch and margaritas go well together.)

—Chelle Koster Walton

GAY AND LESBIAN BARS

Aqua. Key West's largest gay bar, Aqua hosts drag shows, karaoke contests, dancing, and live entertainment at three bars, including one outside on the patio. ✉ *711 Duval St.* ☎ *305/294–0555* ⊕ *www.aquakeywest.com.*

Bourbon Street Complex. Pick your entertainment at the Bourbon Street Complex, a club within an all-male guesthouse. There are 10 video screens along with dancers grooving to the latest music spun by DJs at the Bourbon Street Pub. ✉ *724 Duval St.* ☎ *305/293–9800* ⊕ *www.bourbonstpub.com.*

Island House Café + Bar. Part of a men's resort, Island House Café + Bar serves frozen and other cocktails along with creative cuisine in tropical gardens with a pool where clothing is optional. It is open 24 hours. ✉ *Island House, 1129 Fleming St.* ☎ *305/294–6284, 800/890–6284* ⊕ *www.islandhousekeywest.com.*

LaTeDa Hotel and Bar. This venue hosts female impersonators (catch Christopher Peterson when he's on stage) and riotously funny cabaret shows nightly in the Crystal Room Cabaret Lounge. There is also live entertainment nightly, including the popular local singer Lenore Troia in the Terrace Garden Bar and smooth jazz and pricey martinis in the ultracool piano bar. ✉ *1125 Duval St.* ☎ *305/296–6706* ⊕ *www.lateda.com.*

Pearl's Patio. Part of the Pearl's Key West guesthouse, this bar features a full range of drinks, a menu of light dishes, and nightly activities. ✉ *Pearl's Rainbow, 525 United St., between Duval and Simonton Sts.* ☎ *305/293–9805, 800/749–6696* ⊕ *www.pearlsrainbow.com.*

THE ARTS

Tropic Cinema. Catch the classics and the latest art, independent, and foreign films shown daily in this four-screen theater. A newly upgraded cafe enhances the complex. ✉ *416 Eaton St.* ☎ *305/295–9493, 877/761–3456* ⊕ *www.tropiccinema.com.*

Red Barn Theatre. With more than 30 years' experience, the Red Barn Theatre, a small professional theater, performs dramas, comedies, and musicals, including works by new playwrights. ✉ *319 Duval St.* ☎ *305/296–9911, 866/870–9911* ⊕ *www.redbarntheatre.com.*

Tennessee Williams Fine Arts Center. On Stock Island, the Tennessee Williams Fine Arts Center presents chamber music, dance, jazz concerts, and dramatic and musical plays with major stars, as well as other performing arts events. ⊠ *Florida Keys Community College, 5901 College Rd.* ☏ *305/296–1520 administration, 305/295–7676 box office* ⊕ *www.tennesseewilliamstheatre.com.*

Waterfront Playhouse. Home to the Key West Players, the community-run Waterfront Playhouse is an1880s ice warehouse that was converted into a 180-seat regional theater presenting comedy and drama from December to May. The troupe first banded together in 1940, counting Tennessee Williams among its members. ⊠ *Mallory Sq.* ☏ *305/294–5015* ⊕ *www.waterfrontplayhouse.org.*

SCULPTURE KEY WEST. Key West bursts with art, especially every year between January and April, when artists unveil their latest works at two exhibitions in Fort Zachary Taylor State Park and West Martello Tower. More than 30 artists from around the country are selected to bring their contemporary sculpture for outdoor exhibitions. In years past, sculptures have ranged from a dinosaur surfacing in a pond and a giant Key West chicken to heads floating in the water and abstract formations suggesting sea and seaside vegetation.

SPORTS AND THE OUTDOORS

Unlike the rest of the region, Key West isn't known primarily for outdoor pursuits. But everyone should devote at least half a day to relaxing on a boat tour, heading out on a fishing expedition, or pursuing some other adventure at sea. The ultimate excursion is a boat or seaplane trip to Dry Tortugas National Park for snorkeling and exploring Fort Jefferson. Other excursions cater to nature lovers, scuba divers, and snorkelers, and folks who just want to get out in the water and enjoy the scenery and sunset. For those who prefer land-based recreation, biking is the way to go. Hiking is limited, but walking the streets of Old Town provides plenty of exercise.

BIKING

Key West was practically made for bicycles, but don't let that lull you into a false sense of security. Narrow and one-way streets along with car traffic result in several bike accidents a year. Some hotels rent or lend bikes to guests; others will refer you to a nearby shop and reserve a bike for you. Rentals usually start at about $12 a day, but some places also rent by the half-day. ■TIP➔ **Lock up; bikes—and porch chairs!—are favorite targets for local thieves.**

A&M Rentals. Rent beach cruisers with large baskets for $15 a day. Rates for scooters start at $30 for four hours. Look for the huge American flag on the roof, or call for free airport, ferry, or cruise ship pick-up. ⊠ *523 Truman Ave.* ☎ *305/294–0399* ⊕ *www.amscooterskeywest.com.*

Eaton Bikes. Tandem, three-wheel, and children's bikes are available in addition to the standard beach cruisers ($18 for first day) and hybrid bikes ($25). Delivery is free for all Key West rentals. ⊠ *830 Eaton St.* ☎ *305/294–8188* ⊕ *www.eatonbikes.com.*

Moped Hospital. This outfit supplies balloon-tire bikes with yellow safety baskets for adults and kids ($12 for the first day, $8 for extra days), as well as scooters ($35) and double-seater scooters ($55). ⊠ *601 Truman Ave.* ☎ *305/296–3344, 866/296–1625* ⊕ *www.mopedhospital.com.*

BOATING

Key West is surrounded by marinas, so it's easy to find what you're looking for, whether it's sailing with dolphins or paddling in the mangroves.

Key West Eco-Tours. Key West is surrounded by marinas, so it's easy to find what you're looking for, whether it's sailing with dolphins or paddling in the mangroves. These sail-kayak-snorkel excursions take you into backcountry flats and mangrove forests. The 4½-hour trip costs $95 per person and includes lunch. Sunset sails ($295 or $65 per person) and private charters ($495) are also available. ⊠ *Historic Seaport, 100 Grinnell St.* ☎ *305/294–7245* ⊕ *www.javacatcharters.com.*

Sunset Culinaire Tours. This tour operator serves a full menu of gourmet meals with fine wine and beer aboard a sleek cruising yacht every evening at sunset. The cost is $85 per person; you must have a group of six or more. ⊠ *5555 College Rd.* ☎ *305/296–0982* ⊕ *www.sunsetculinaire.com.*

FISHING

Any number of local fishing guides can take you to where the big ones are biting, either in the backcountry for snapper and snook or to the deep water for the marlins and shark that lured Hemingway here.

Key West Bait & Tackle. Prepare to catch a big one with the live bait, frozen bait, and fishing equipment provided here. This outfitter also has the Live Bait Lounge, where you can sip ice-cold beer while telling fish tales. ⊠ *241 Margaret St.* ☎ *305/292–1961* ⊕ *www.keywestbaitandtackle.com.*

Key West Pro Guides. Trips include flats and backcountry fishing ($400–$450 for a half day) and reef and offshore fishing (starting at $550 for a half day). ⊠ *G-31 Miriam St.* ☎ *866/259–4205* ⊕ *www.keywestproguides.com.*

GOLFING

Not in the least a golfing destination, Key West does have one course on Stock Island. Make your tee times early in season.

Key West Golf Club. Key West isn't a major golf destination, but there is one course on Stock Island. This 18-hole, par 70 course has $50–$95 greens fees. Book your tee time early in the season. ⊠ *6450 E. College Rd.* ☎ *305/294–5232* ⊕ *www.keywestgolf.com.*

KAYAKING

Key West Eco-Tours. The sail-kayak-snorkel excursions here take you into backcountry flats and mangrove forests. The 4½-hour trip costs $95 per person and includes lunch. Sunset sails and private charters are also available. ⊠ *Historic Seaport, 100 Grinnell St.* ☎ *305/294–7245* ⊕ *keywestecotours.co.*

Lazy Dog Kayak Guides. Take a two- or four-hour guided sea kayak–snorkel tour around the mangrove islands just east of Key West. The $35 or $60 charge, respectively, covers transportation, bottled water, a snack, and supplies, including snorkeling gear. Paddleboard tours are $40. Rentals for self-touring are also available. ⊠ *5114 Overseas Hwy.* ☎ *305/295–9898* ⊕ *www.lazydog.com.*

SUP Key West. The latest Florida hybrid water sport involves a surfboard and a paddle, a Hawaii transplant known as stand-up paddleboarding. SUP Key West does lessons and tours of the estuaries for $40–$60. Call ahead to make arrangements. ✉ *110 Grinnell St.* ☏ *305/240–1426* ⊕ *www.supkeywest.com.*

SCUBA DIVING AND SNORKELING

The Florida Keys National Marine Sanctuary extends along Key West and beyond to the Dry Tortugas. Key West National Wildlife Refuge further protects the pristine waters. Most divers don't make it this far out in the Keys, but if you're looking for a day of diving as a break from the nonstop party in Old Town, expect to pay about $65 and upward for a two-tank dive. Serious divers can book dive trips to the Dry Tortugas. The USS *Vandenberg* is another popular dive spot, known for its world's first underwater transformative art exhibit on an artificial reef.

Captain's Corner. This PADI–certified dive shop has classes in several languages and twice-daily snorkel and dive trips ($40–$65) to reefs and wrecks aboard the 60-foot dive boat *Sea Eagle.* Use of weights, belts, masks, and fins is included. ✉ *125 Ann St.* ☏ *305/296–8865* ⊕ *www.captainscorner.com.*

Dive Key West. Operating nearly 40 years, Dive Key West is a full-service dive center that has charters, instruction, gear rental, sales, and repair. Snorkel excursions are $49; scuba trips start at $69. ✉ *3128 N. Roosevelt Blvd.* ☏ *305/296–3823* ⊕ *www.divekeywest.com.*

Eco Scuba Key West. Eco Scuba Key West offers daily eco-tours plus tech diving, lobstering, snorkel, and scuba diving packages. Snorkel trips start at $89; scuba from $129. ✉ *5130 Overseas Hwy.* ☏ *305/851–1899.*

Snuba of Key West. Safely dive the coral reefs without getting a scuba certification. Ride out to the reef on a catamaran, then follow your guide underwater for a one-hour tour of the coral reefs. You wear a regulator with a breathing hose that is attached to a floating air tank on the surface. No prior diving or snorkeling experience is necessary, but you must know how to swim. The $99 price includes beverages. ✉ *Garrison Bight Marina, Palm Ave., between Eaton St. and N. Roosevelt Blvd.* ☏ *305/292–4616* ⊕ *www.snubakeywest.com.*

TOURING

BIKE TOURS

Lloyd's Original Tropical Bike Tour. Explore the natural, non-commercial side of Key West at a leisurely pace, stopping on backstreets and in backyards of private homes to sample native fruits and view indigenous plants and trees with a 30-year Key West veteran. The behind-the-scenes tours run two hours and cost $39, including bike rental. ⊠ *Truman Ave. and Simonton St.* ☎ *305/304–4700, 305/294–1882* ⊕ *www.lloydstropicalbiketour.com.*

BOAT TOURS

Dancing Dolphin Spirit Charters. Victoria Impallomeni, a 34-year wilderness guide and marine scientist, invites up to six nature lovers—especially children—aboard the *Imp II,* a 25-foot Aquasport, for four-hour ($500) and seven-hour ($700) ecotours that frequently include encounters with wild dolphins. While island-hopping, you visit underwater gardens, natural shoreline, and mangrove habitats. For her Dolphin Day for Humans tour, Impallomeni pulls you through the water, equipped with mask and snorkel, on a specially designed "dolphin water massage board" that simulates dolphin swimming motions. Sometimes dolphins follow the boat and swim among participants. All equipment is supplied. ⊠ *MM 5 OS, Murray's Marina, 5710 Overseas Hwy.* ☎ *305/304–7562, 888/822–7366* ⊕ *www.captainvictoria.com.*

White Knuckle Thrill Boat Ride. For something with an adrenaline boost, book with this speedboat. It holds up to 10 people and does 360s, fishtails, and other water stunts in the gulf. Cost is $69 each, and includes pickup shuttle. ⊠ *Sunset Marina, 555 College Rd.* ☎ *305/797–0459* ⊕ *www.whiteknucklethrillboatride.com.*

BUS TOURS

City View Trolley Tours. In 2010, City View Trolley Tours began service, offering a little competition to the Conch Train and Old Town Trolley, which are owned by the same company. Its rates are more affordable at $19 per adult. Tours depart every 30 minutes from 9:30 to 4:30. Passengers can board and disembark at any of nine stops, and can reboard at will. ☎ *305/294–0644* ⊕ *www.cityviewtrolleys.com.*

Conch Tour Train. The Conch Tour Train is a 90-minute narrated tour of Key West, traveling 14 mi through Old

Town and around the island. Board at Mallory Square or Angela Street and Duval Street depot every half-hour (9–4:30 from Mallory Square). The cost is $29 (go online for discounted tickets). ☎305/294–5161, 888/916–8687 ⊕ www.conchtourtrain.com.

Gay & Lesbian Trolley Tour. Decorated with a rainbow, the Gay and Lesbian Trolley Tour rumbles around the town beginning at 4 pm every Saturday afternoon. The 70-minute tour highlighting Key West's gay history costs $25. ✉ 513 Truman Ave. ☎305/294–4603 ⊕ www.gaykeywestfl.com.

Old Town Trolley. Old Town Trolley operates trolley-style buses, departing from the Mallory Square every 30 minutes from 9 to 4:30, for 90-minute narrated tours of Key West. The smaller trolleys go places the larger Conch Tour Train won't fit. You may disembark at any of 12 stops and reboard a later trolley. The cost is $29, but you can save a little by booking online. It also offers package deals with Old Town attractions. ✉ 201 Front St. ☎305/296–6688, 888/910–8687 ⊕ www.trolleytours.com.

WALKING TOURS
Historic Florida Keys Foundation. In addition to publishing several good guides on Key West, the foundation conducts tours of the City Cemetery Tuesday and Thursday at 9:30. ✉ 510 Greene St., Old City Hall ☎305/292–6718 ⊕ www. historicfloridakeys.org.

SHOPPING

On these streets you'll find colorful local art of widely varying quality, key limes made into everything imaginable, and the raunchiest T-shirts in the civilized world. Browsing the boutiques—with frequent pub stops along the way—makes for an entertaining stroll down Duval Street. Cocktails certainly help the appreciation of some goods, such as the figurine of a naked man blowing bubbles out his backside or the swashbuckling pirate costumes that are not just for Halloween anymore.

ARTS AND CRAFTS

Key West is filled with art galleries, and the variety is truly amazing. Most of them congregate around the south end of Duval Street. Much is locally produced by the town's large artist community, but many galleries carry international artists from as close as Haiti and as far away as France.

Local artists do a great job of preserving the island's architecture and spirit.

Alan S. Maltz Gallery. The owner, declared the state's official wildlife photographer by the Wildlife Foundation of Florida, captures the state's nature and character in stunning portraits. Spend four figures for large-format images on canvas or save on small prints and closeouts. ✉ *1210 Duval St.* ☎ *305/294–0005* ⊕ *www.alanmaltz.com.*

Art@830. This gallery carries a little bit of everything, from pottery to paintings. Most outstanding is its selection of glass art, particularly the jellyfish lamps. ✉ *830 Caroline St., Historic Seaport* ☎ *305/295–9595* ⊕ *www.art830.com.*

Cuba, Cuba!. Check out this shop's stock of cigars, coffee, and paintings, sculptures, pottery, and photos by Cuban artists and artisans. ✉ *814 Duval St.* ☎ *305/295–9442, 800/621–3596* ⊕ *www.cubacubastore.com.*

Gallery on Greene. Showcasing politically incorrect art by Jeff MacNelly and three-dimensional paintings by Mario Sanchez, this is the largest gallery–exhibition space in Key West. ✉ *606 Greene St.* ☎ *305/294–1669.*

Gingerbread Square Gallery. The oldest private art gallery in Key West represents local and internationally acclaimed artists on an annually changing basis, in mediums ranging from graphics to art glass. ✉ *1207 Duval St.* ☎ *305/296–8900* ⊕ *www.gingerbreadsquaregallery.com.*

Glass Reunions. Find a collection of wild and impressive fine-art glass here. It's worth a stop in just to see the imaginative and over-the-top glass chandeliers, jewelry, dishes, and platters. ✉ *825 Duval St.* ☎ *305/294–1720* ⊕ *www. glassreunions.com.*

Haitian Art Company. Haitian-art connoisseurs will love the bright colors in the paintings, the bead-and-sequin work in the handicrafts, and fine metal sculptures. ✉ *605 Simonton St.* ☎ *305/735–4664* ⊕ *www.haitian-art-co.com.*

KW Light Gallery. Historian, photographer, and painter Sharon Wells opened this gallery to showcase her own fine-art photography and painted tiles and canvases, as well as the works of other national artists. You can find historic photos here as well. ✉ *1203 Duval St.* ☎ *305/294–0566* ⊕ *www. keywestlightgallery.com.*

Lucky Street Gallery. High-end contemporary paintings are the focus here. There are also a few pieces of jewelry by internationally recognized Key West–based artists. Changing exhibits, artist receptions, and special events make this a lively venue. ✉ *1130 Duval St.* ☎ *305/294–3973* ⊕ *www.luckystreetgallery.com.*

Pelican Poop Shoppe. Caribbean art sells in a historic building (with Hemingway connections, of course). For a $2 admission or a $10 purchase, you can stroll the tropical courtyard garden. The owners buy directly from the artisans every year, so the prices are very attractive. ✉ *314 Simonton St.* ☎ *305/292–9955* ⊕ *www.pelicanpoopshoppe.com.*

Whitehead St. Pottery. Potters Charles Pearson and Tim Roeder display their porcelain stoneware and raku-fired vessels. The setting, around two koi ponds with a burbling fountain, is as sublime as the art. ✉ *322 Julia St.* ☎ *305/294–5067* ⊕ *www.whiteheadstreetpottery.com.*

BOOKS

Key West Island Bookstore. This home away from home for the large Key West writers' community carries new, used, and rare titles. It specializes in Hemingway, Tennessee Williams, and South Florida mystery writers. ✉ *513 Fleming St.* ☎ *305/294–2904.*

CIGARS

Conch Republic Cigar Factory. At Conch Republic Cigar Factory a cigar roller demonstrates hand-rolling techniques. The shop sells flavored and unflavored varieties. ✉ *540 Greene St.* ☎ *305/295–9036, 800/317–2167* ⊕ *www.conchcigars.com.*

CLOTHING AND FABRICS

Fairvilla Megastore. Don't leave town without a browse through the legendary shop, where you'll find an astonishing array of fantasy wear, outlandish costumes (check out the pirate section), and other "adult" toys. ✉ *520 Front St.* ☎ *305/292–0448* ⊕ *www.fairvilla.com.*

Kino Sandals. A pair of Kino Sandals was once a public declaration that you'd been to Key West. The attraction? You can watch these inexpensive items being made. The factory has been churning out several styles since 1966.

Walk up to the counter, grab a pair, try them on, and lay down some cash. It's that simple. ✉ *107 Fitzpatrick St.* ☎ *305/294–5044* ⊕ *www.kinosandalfactory.com* ☉ *Closed Sun. in off-season.*

Seam Shoppe. Take home a shopping bag full of scarlet hibiscus, fuchsia heliconias, blue parrot fish, and even pink flamingo fabric, selected from the city's widest selection of tropical-print fabrics. ✉ *1114 Truman Ave.* ☎ *305/296–9830* ⊕ *www.tropicalfabricsonline.com.*

Towels of Key West. Get beach ready with colorful towels from Towels of Key West. There are more than 60 unique towel designs, some you'd expect, others more whimsical. All are hand-sewn on the island. ✉ *806 Duval St.* ☎ *305/292–1120, 800/927–0316* ⊕ *www.towelsofkeywest.net.*

FOOD AND DRINK

Fausto's Food Palace. Since 1926 Fausto's has been the spot to catch up on the week's gossip and to chill out in summer—it has groceries, organic foods, marvelous wines, a sushi chef on duty 8 am–3 pm, and box lunches to go. ✉ *522 Fleming St.* ☎ *305/296–5663* ⊕ *www.faustos.com* ✉ *1105 White St.* ☎ *305/294–5221.*

★ **Kermit's Key West Lime Shoppe.** You'll see Kermit himself standing on the corner every time a trolley passes, pie in hand. Besides pie, his shop carries a multitude of key lime products from barbecue sauce to jellybeans. His prefrozen pies, dressed with a special long-lasting whipped cream instead of meringue, travels well. ✉ *200 Elizabeth St., Historic Seaport* ☎ *305/296–0806, 800/376–0806* ⊕ *www.keylimeshop.com.*

Key West Winery. You'll be pleasantly surprised with the fruit wines sold here. Display crates hold bottles of wines made from blueberries, blackberries, pineapples, cherries, mangoes, watermelons, passion fruit, and, of course, key limes. Stop in for a free tasting. ✉ *103 Simonton St.* ☎ *305/292–1717, 866/880–1717* ⊕ *www.thekeywestwinery.com.*

Peppers of Key West. If you like it hot, you'll love this collection of hundreds of sauces, salsas, and sweets guaranteed to light your fire. ✉ *602 Greene St.* ☎ *305/295–9333, 800/597–2823* ⊕ *www.peppersofkeywest.com.*

GIFTS AND SOUVENIRS

Cayo Hueso y Habana. Part museum, part shopping center, this circa-1879 warehouse includes a hand-rolled cigar shop, one-of-a-kind souvenirs, a Cuban restaurant, and exhibits that tell of the island's Cuban heritage. Outside, a memorial garden pays homage to the island's Cuban ancestors. ⊠ *410 Wall St., Mallory Sq.* ☎ *305/293–7260.*

★ **Montage.** For that unique (but slightly overpriced) souvenir of your trip to Key West head here, where you'll discover hundreds of handcrafted signs of popular Key West guesthouses, inns, hotels, restaurants, bars, and streets. If you can't find what you're looking for, they'll make it for you. ⊠ *291 Front St.* ☎ *305/395–9101, 877/396–4278* ⊕ *www. montagekeywest.com.*

HEALTH AND BEAUTY

Key West Aloe. This shop produces hundreds of soap, candle, sunscreen, and skin-care products for men and women. ⊠ *540 Greene St., at Simonton St.* ☎ *305/293–1885, 800/445–2563* ⊕ *www.keywestaloe.com.*

SHOPPING CENTERS

Bahama Village. Where to start your shopping adventure? This cluster of spruced-up shops, restaurants, and vendors is responsible for the restoration of the colorful historic district where Bahamians settled in the 19th century. The village lies roughly between Whitehead and Fort streets and Angela and Catherine streets. Hemingway frequented the bars, restaurants, and boxing rings in this part of town. ⊠ *Between Whitehead and Fort Sts. and Angela and Catherine Sts.*

EXCURSION TO DRY TORTUGAS NATIONAL PARK

70 mi southwest of Key West.

The Dry Tortugas lies in the Central Time Zone. Key West Seaplane pilots like to tell their passengers that they land 15 minutes before they take off.

GETTING HERE AND AROUND
For now, the ferry boat *Yankee Freedom III* departs from a marina in Old Town and does day trips to Garden Key.

Key West Seaplane Adventures has half- and full-day trips to the Dry Tortugas, where you can explore Fort Jefferson, built in 1846, and snorkel on the beautiful protected reef. Departing from the Key West airport, the flights include soft drinks and snorkel equipment for $265 half-day, $465 full-day, plus there's a $5 park fee (cash only). If you want to explore the park's other keys, look into renting a boat or hiring a private charter. In September 2012, the Dry Tortugas National Park and Fort Jefferson Interpretive Center at 240 Margaret Street was scheduled to open.

Key West Seaplane Adventures. The 35- to 40-minute trip to the Dry Tortugas skims above the trademark windowpane-clear waters of the Florida Keys. The seaplane perspective provides an awesome experience that could result in a stiff neck from craning to look out the window and down from 500 feet above. In the Flats that edge Key West, you can spot stingrays, sea turtles, and sharks in the shallow water. In the area dubbed The Quicksands, water plunges to 30-foot depths and sand undulates in dune-like formations. Shipwrecks also festoon these waters; here's where Mel Fisher harvested treasure from the *Atocha* and *Margarita.* His 70-foot work ship, the *Arbutus,* deteriorated and eventually sank at the northern edge of the treasure sites. With its mast poking out above water, it's easy to spot and fun to photograph. From there, the water deepens from emerald hues to shades of deep blue as depths reach 70 feet. Seaplanes of Key West's most popular trip is the half-day option, where you spend about 2½ hours on Garden Key. The seaplanes leave during your stay, so be prepared to carry all of your possessions with you. The half-day tour costs $265 per person. The morning trip beats the ferries to the island, so you'll have it to yourself until the others arrive. Snorkeling equipment, soft drinks, and birding lists are supplied. ⊠ *Key West International Airport, 3471 S. Roosevelt Blvd., Key West* ☎ *305/293–9300* ⊕ *www.key-westseaplanecharters.com.*

Yankee Freedom II. The fast, sleek, 100-foot catamaran *Yankee Freedom II* travels to the Dry Tortugas in 2¼ hours. The time passes quickly on the roomy vessel equipped with three restrooms, two freshwater showers, and two bars. Stretch out on two decks: one an air-conditioned salon with cushioned seating, the other an open sundeck with sunny and shaded seating. Continental breakfast and lunch are included. On arrival, a naturalist leads a 40-minute guided tour, which is followed by lunch and a free afternoon for swimming, snorkeling (gear included), and exploring. The vessel is ADA–certified for visitors using wheelchairs. ■ TIP➜ **The Dry Tortugas lies in the central time zone.** ⊠ *Lands End Marina, 240 Margaret St., Key West* ☎ *305/294–7009, 800/634–0939* ⊕ *www.yankeefreedom.com* ☎ *$169, parking $5* ⊙ *Trips daily at 8 am; check in 7:15 am.*

VISITOR INFORMATION
Contacts Dry Tortugas National Park ☎ *305/242–7700* ⊕ *www.nps.gov/drto.*

EXPLORING

Dry Tortugas National Park. This park, 70 mi off the shores of Key West, consists of seven small islands. Tour the fort; then lay out your blanket on the sunny beach for a picnic before you head out to snorkel on the protected reef. Many people like to camp here ($3 per person per night, eight sites plus group site and overflow area; first come, first served), but note that there's no freshwater supply and you must carry off whatever you bring onto the island.

The typical visitor from Key West, however, makes it no farther than the waters of Garden Key. Home to 19th-century Fort Jefferson, it is the destination for seaplane and fast ferry tours out of Key West. With 2½ to 6½ hours to spend on the island, visitors have time to tour the mammoth fort-come-prison and then cool off with mask and snorkel along the fort's moat wall.

History buffs might remember long-deactivated Fort Jefferson, the largest brick building in the western hemisphere, as the prison that held Dr. Samuel Mudd, who unwittingly set John Wilkes Booth's leg after the assassination of Abraham Lincoln. Three other men were also held there for complicity in the assassination. Original construction on the fort began in 1846 and continued for 30 years, but was never completed because the invention of the rifled cannon made it obsolete. That's when it became a Civil War prison and later a wildlife refuge. In 1935 President Franklin Roosevelt declared it a national monument for its historic and natural value.

The brick fort acts as a gigantic, almost 16-acre reef. Around its moat walls, coral grows and schools of snapper, grouper, and wrasses hang out. To reach the offshore coral heads requires about 15 minutes of swimming over sea-grass beds. The reef formations blaze with the color and majesty of brain coral, swaying sea fans, and flitting tropical fish. It takes a bit of energy to swim the distance, but the water depth pretty much measures under 7 feet all the way, allowing for sandy spots to stop and rest. (Standing in sea-grass meadows and on coral is detrimental to marine life.)

Serious snorkelers and divers head out farther offshore to epic formations, including Palmata Patch, one of the few surviving concentrations of elkhorn coral in the Keys. Day-trippers congregate on the sandy beach to relax in the sun and enjoy picnics. Overnight tent campers have use of restroom facilities and achieve a total getaway from noise, lights, and civilization in general. Remember that no matter how you get here, the park's $5 admission fee must be paid in cash.

The park has set up with signage a self-guided tour that takes about 45 minutes. You should budget more time if you're into photography, because the scenic shots are hard to pass up. Ranger-guided tours are also available at certain times. Check in at the visitor center for a schedule. The small office also shows an orientation video, sells books and other educational materials, and, most importantly, provides a blast of air-conditioning on hot days.

Birders in the know bring binoculars to watch some 100,000 nesting sooty terns at their only U.S. nesting site, Bush Key, adjacent to Garden Key. Noddy terns also nest in the spring. During winter migrations, birds fill the airspace so thickly they literally fall from the sky to make their pit stops, birders say. Nearly 300 species have been spotted in the park's seven islands, including frigatebirds, boobies, cormorants, and broad-winged hawks. Bush Key is closed to foot traffic during nesting season, January through September. ☎ *305/242–7700* ⊕ *www.nps.gov/drto* ✆ *$5.*

Gateways to the Keys

WORD OF MOUTH

"The Keys are definitely a get out on the water type place instead of a driving up and down U.S. 1 kind of place. Bars and restaurants open early and close early. Get out over the water. That is where the most amazing things in the Keys are."

—GoTravel

6

ALTHOUGH IT'S POSSIBLE TO FLY INTO KEY WEST, many people don't because of the expense and because of the limited number of flights. Furthermore, if you are visiting the Upper or Middle Keys, there is a drive regardless of which airport you fly into. This means that many visitors flying into Florida to visit the Keys will pass through Miami. In some cases, people choose to stay a while to absorb some of the new luxe hotels, hot nightlife, and stylish restaurants, not to mention the expansive beaches, of which the Keys do not have an abundance. Travelers on more of a budget may want to look a bit farther afield to either Homestead or Florida City, both south of Miami, the two major gateways to both the Keys and the Everglades.

PLANNING

See ⇨ **Travel Smart Florida Keys** for information on flights and car rentals in Miami.

RESTAURANTS

Miami has a vibrant dining scene, with prices to match, but you can still find reasonably priced local restaurants and chains, mostly outside the trendy South Beach area. Most restaurants south of Miami are small mom-and-pop establishments serving homestyle food or local specialties such as alligator, fish, stone crab, frogs' legs, and fresh Florida lobster from the Keys. There are plenty of chain restaurants and fast-food establishments, especially in the Homestead and Florida City areas.

HOTELS

If you are looking for the hot spots, then you need look no farther than Miami's South Beach, which is awash with both new high-rises and restored Art Deco gems. The choices in Homestead and Florida City are more pedestrian, but also more friendly to the wallet and the budget and closer to the Keys. And given the driving distance, if you arrive late in Miami, you may just want to sleep before getting an early start to drive down to the Keys; in that case, a basic room may be just what the travel agent ordered.

HOTEL AND RESTAURANT PRICES

Prices in the restaurant reviews are the average cost of a main course at dinner or, if dinner is not served, at lunch, excluding taxes and service charges. Prices in the hotel reviews are the lowest cost of a standard double room in high season, excluding taxes, service charges, and meal

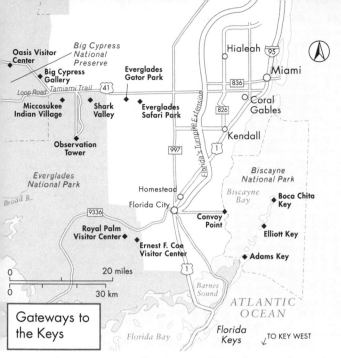

Gateways to the Keys

plans (except at all-inclusives). Prices for rentals are the lowest per-night cost for a one-bedroom unit in high season.

MIAMI

Updated by Paul Rubio

In the 1950s Miami was best known for alligator wrestlers and you-pick strawberry fields or citrus groves. Well, things have changed. Miami on the mainland is South Florida's commercial hub, while its sultry sister, Miami Beach (America's Riviera), encompasses 17 islands in Biscayne Bay. Seducing winter refugees with its sunshine, beaches, palms, and nightlife, Miami Beach is what most people envision when they think of Miami. Exploring the city will require a car if you intend to go beyond South Beach.

EXPLORING

TOP ATTRACTIONS

★ Fodor's Choice **Fairchild Tropical Botanic Garden.** With 83 acres of lakes, sunken gardens, a 560-foot vine pergola, orchids, bellflowers, coral trees, bougainvillea, rare palms, and flowering trees, Fairchild is the largest tropical botanical garden in the continental United States. The tram tour highlights the best of South Florida's flora; then you can set off exploring on your own. A 2-acre rain-forest exhibit showcases tropical plants from around the world complete with a waterfall and stream. The conservatory, Windows to the Tropics, is home to rare tropical plants, including the Titan Arum (*Amorphophallus titanum*), a fast-growing variety that attracted thousands of visitors when it bloomed in 1998. (It was only the sixth documented bloom in this country in the 20th century.) The Keys Coastal Habitat, created in a marsh and mangrove area in 1995 with assistance from the Tropical Audubon Society, provides food and shelter to resident and migratory birds. Check out the Montgomery Botanical Center, a research facility devoted to palms and cycads. Spicing up Fairchild's calendar are plant sales, afternoon teas, and genuinely special events year-round, such as the International Mango Festival the second weekend in July. The excellent bookstore–gift shop carries books on gardening and horticulture, and the Garden Café serves sandwiches and, seasonally, smoothies made from the garden's own crop of tropical fruits. ✉ *10901 Old Cutler Rd., Coral Gables* ☎ *305/667–1651* ⊕ *www. fairchildgarden.org* ⬛ *$25* ☉ *Daily 9:30–4:30.*

☾ **Jungle Island.** Originally located deep in south Miami and known as Parrot Jungle, South Florida's original tourist attraction opened in 1936 and moved closer to Miami Beach in 2003. Located on Watson Island, a small stretch of land off of I–395 between Downtown Miami and South Beach, Jungle Island is far more than a park where cockatoos ride tricycles; this interactive zoological park is home to just about every unusual and endangered species you would want to see, including a rare albino alligator, a liger (lion and tiger mix), and myriad exotic birds. The most intriguing offerings are the VIP animal tours, including the Lemur Experience ($45 for 45 minutes), in which the highly social primates make themselves at home on your lap or shoulders. Jungle Island offers complimentary shuttle service to most Downtown Miami and South Beach hotels. ✉ *1111 Parrot Jungle Trail, off MacArthur Causeway (I–395), Downtown* ☎ *305/400–7000* ⊕ *www. jungleisland.com* ⬛ *$32.95, plus $8 parking* ☉ *Weekdays 10–5, weekends 10–6.*

★ **Fodor's** Choice **Lincoln Road Mall.** This open-air pedestrian mall ☾ flaunts some of Miami's best people-watching. The eclectic interiors of myriad fabulous restaurants, colorful boutiques,

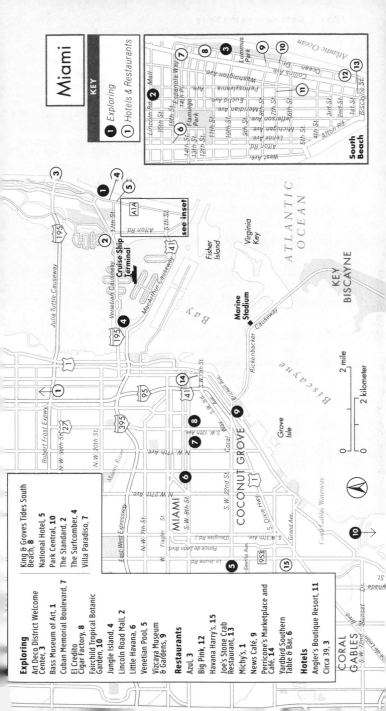

Miami

KEY
- **1** Exploring
- **①** Hotels & Restaurants

Exploring
Art Deco District Welcome Center, **3**
Bass Museum of Art, **1**
Cuban Memorial Boulevard, **7**
El Credito Cigar Factory, **8**
Fairchild Tropical Botanic Garden, **10**
Jungle Island, **4**
Lincoln Road Mall, **2**
Little Havana, **6**
Venetian Pool, **5**
Vizcaya Museum & Gardens, **9**

King & Groves Tides South Beach, **8**
National Hotel, **5**
Park Central, **10**
The Standard, **2**
The Surfcomber, **4**
Villa Paradiso, **7**

Restaurants
Azul, **3**
Big Pink, **12**
Havana Harry's, **15**
Joe's Stone Crab Restaurant, **13**
Michy's, **1**
News Café, **9**
Perricone's Marketplace and Café, **14**
Yardbird Southern Table & Bar, **6**

Hotels
Angler's Boutique Resort, **11**
Circa 39, **3**

art galleries, lounges, and cafés are often upstaged by the bustling outdoor scene. It's here among the prolific alfresco dining enclaves that you can pass the hours easily beholding the beautiful people. Indeed, outdoor restaurant and café seating take center stage along this wide pedestrian road adorned with towering date palms, linear pools, and colorful broken-tile mosaics. Some of the shops on Lincoln Road are owner-operated boutiques carrying a smart variety of clothing, furnishings, jewelry, and decorative elements. You'll also find typical upscale chain stores—French Connection, Banana Republic, and so on. Lincoln Road is fun, lively, and friendly for people–old, young, gay, and straight—and their dogs.

Two landmarks worth checking out at the eastern end of Lincoln Road are the massive 1940s keystone building at 420 Lincoln Road, which has a 1945 Leo Birchanky mural in the lobby, and the 1921 Mission-style Miami Beach Community Church, at Drexel Avenue. The Lincoln Theatre (No. 541–545), at Pennsylvania Avenue, is a classical four-story art deco gem with friezes. At Euclid Avenue there's a monument to Morris Lapidus, the brains behind Lincoln Road Mall, who in his 90s watched the renaissance of his whimsical South Beach creation. At Lenox Avenue, a black-and-white art deco movie house with a Mediterranean barrel-tile roof is now the Colony Theater (1040 Lincoln Rd.), where live theater and experimental films are presented. ⊠ *Lincoln Rd. between Washington Ave. and Alton Rd., South Beach, Miami Beach ⊕ www. lincolnroad.org.*

★ **Venetian Pool.** Sculpted from a rock quarry in 1923 and fed
Ⓒ by artesian wells, this 820,000-gallon municipal pool had a major face-lift in 2010. It remains quite popular because of its themed architecture—a fantasy version of a waterfront Italian village—created by Denman Fink. The pool has earned a place on the National Register of Historic Places and showcases a nice collection of vintage photos depicting 1920s beauty pageants and swank soirees held long ago. Paul Whiteman played here, Johnny Weissmuller and Esther Williams swam here, and you should, too (but no kids under 3). A snack bar, lockers, and showers make this must-see user-friendly as well. ⊠ *2701 De Soto Blvd., at Toledo St., Coral Gables* ☎ *305/460–5306 ⊕ www.gablesrecreation.com* ⓐ *$11; free parking across De Soto Blvd.* ⊙ *Usually open Tues.–Sun. 11–4:30, but best to call ahead.*

★ **Fodor's** Choice **Vizcaya Museum and Gardens.** Of the 10,000 people living in Miami between 1912 and 1916, about 1,000 of them were gainfully employed by Chicago industrialist James Deering to build this European-inspired residence. Once comprising 180 acres, this National Historic Landmark now occupies a 30-acre tract that includes a rockland hammock (native forest) and more than 10 acres of formal gardens with fountains overlooking Biscayne Bay. The house, open to the public, contains 70 rooms, 34 of which are filled with paintings, sculpture, antique furniture, and other fine and decorative arts. The collection spans 2,000 years and represents the Renaissance, baroque, rococo, and neoclassical periods. The 90-minute self-guided Discover Vizcaya Audio Tour is available in multiple languages for an additional $5. Guided tours are also available in English, Wednesday through Monday at 11:30, 12:30, 1:30, and 2:30. Moonlight tours, offered on evenings that are nearest the full moon, provide a magical look at the gardens; call for reservations. ⊠ *3251 S. Miami Ave., Coconut Grove* ☎ *305/250–9133* ⊕ *www.vizcayamuseum.org* ⊠ *$15* ⊗ *Wed.–Mon. 9:30–4:30.*

WORTH NOTING

Art Deco District Welcome Center. Run by the Miami Design Preservation League, the center provides information about the buildings in the district. An improved gift shop sells 1930s–50s art deco memorabilia, posters, and books on Miami's history. Several tours—covering Lincoln Road, Española Way, North Beach, and the entire Art Deco District, among others—start here. You can choose from a self-guided iPod audio tour or join one of the regular morning walking tours at 10:30 am, every day except Thursday when the tour takes place at 6:30 pm. Arrive at the center 15 minutes beforehand. All of the options provide detailed histories of the art deco hotels as well as an introduction to the art deco, Mediterranean revival, and Miami Modern (MiMo) styles found within the Miami Beach Architectural Historic District. Don't miss the special boat tours during Art Deco Weekend, in early January. *(⇨ For a map of the Art Deco District and info on some of the sites there, see the "A Stroll Down Deco Lane" in-focus feature.)* ⊠ *1001 Ocean Dr., at Ocean Dr., South Beach, Miami Beach* ☎ *305/672–2014* ⊕ *www.mdpl.org* ⊠ *Tours $20* ⊗ *Daily 9:30–7.*

Bass Museum of Art. Special exhibitions join a diverse collection of European art at this museum whose original building is constructed of keystone and has unique Maya-inspired carvings. An expansion designed by Japanese architect Arata Isozaki houses another wing and an outdoor sculpture garden. Works on permanent display include *The Holy Family,* a painting by Peter Paul Rubens; *The Tournament,* one of several 16th-century Flemish tapestries; and works by Albrecht Dürer and Henri de Toulouse-Lautrec. Docent tours are by appointment but free with entry. ✉*2100 Collins Ave., South Beach, Miami Beach* ☎*305/673-7530* ⊕*www. bassmuseum.org* ✍*$8* ⊙ *Wed.–Sun. noon–5.*

Cuban Memorial Boulevard. Two blocks in the heart of Little Havana are filled with monuments to Cuba's freedom fighters. Among the memorials are the *Eternal Torch of the Brigade 2506,* commemorating those who were killed in the failed Bay of Pigs invasion of 1961; a bust of 19th-century hero Antonio Maceo; and a bas-relief map of Cuba depicting each of its *municipios.* There's also a bronze statue in honor of Tony Izquierdo, who participated in the Bay of Pigs invasion, served in Nicaragua's Somozan forces, and was also on the CIA payroll. Nearby on the southeast corner of SW 15th Avenue and SW 8th Street at Maximo Gomez Park, also known as Domino Park, Cuban elders gather daily for domino matches. ✉*S.W. 13th Ave., between S.W. 15th and S.W. 16th Sts., Little Havana.*

BEACHES

Almost every east–west side street in Miami Beach dead-ends at the ocean. Sandy shores also stretch along the southern side of the Rickenbacker Causeway to Key Biscayne, where you'll find more popular beaches. Greater Miami is best known for its ocean beaches, but there's freshwater swimming here, too, in pools and lakes. Below are the highlights for the get-wet set.

CORAL GABLES

☺ **Matheson Hammock Park Beach.** Kids love the gentle waves and warm water of this beach in Coral Gables suburbia, near Fairchild Tropical Botanic Garden. But the beach is only part of the draw—the park includes a boardwalk trail, a playground, and a golf course. The man-made lagoon, or "atoll pool," is perfect for inexperienced swimmers, and it's one of the best places in mainland Miami for a picnic. But the water can be a bit murky, and with the emphasis on families, it's not the best place for singles. **Amenities:** parking (fee); toilets. **Best for:** swimming. ✉*9610 Old Cutler Rd.* ☎*305/665-5475.*

KEY BISCAYNE

★ **Fodor's**Choice **Bill Baggs Cape Florida State Park.** Thanks to inviting beaches, sunsets, and a tranquil lighthouse, this park at Key Biscayne's southern tip is worth the drive. In fact, the 1-mile stretch of pure beachfront has been named several times in Dr. Beach's revered America's Top 10 Beaches list. It has 18 picnic pavilions available as daily rentals, two cafés that serve light lunches (Lighthouse Café, overlooking the Atlantic Ocean, and the Boater's Grill, on Biscayne Bay), and plenty of space to enjoy the umbrella and chair rentals. A stroll or ride along walking and bicycle paths provides wonderful views of Miami's dramatic skyline. From the southern end of the park you can see a handful of houses rising over the bay on wooden stilts, the remnants of Stiltsville, built in the 1940s and now protected by the Stiltsville Trust. The nonprofit group was established in 2003 to preserve the structures, because they showcase the park's rich history. Bill Baggs has bicycle rentals, a playground, fishing piers, and guided tours of the **Cape Florida Lighthouse,** South Florida's oldest structure. The lighthouse was erected in 1845 to replace an earlier one damaged in an 1836 Seminole attack, in which the keeper's helper was killed. Free tours are offered at the restored cottage and lighthouse at 10 am and 1 pm Thursday to Monday. Be there a half hour beforehand. **Amenities:** food and drink, lifeguards, parking, showers, toilets. **Best for:** solitude, sunsets, walking. ✉ *1200 S. Crandon Blvd., Key Biscayne* ☎ *305/361–5811* ⊕ *www.floridastateparks.org/capeflorida* 🖃 *$8 per vehicle; $2 per person on bicycle, bus, motorcycle, or foot* ☉ *Daily 8–dusk.*

SOUTH BEACH

★ **Fodor's**Choice **South Beach.** A 10-block stretch of white sandy beach hugging the turquoise waters along Ocean Drive— from 5th to 15th streets—is one of the most popular in America, known for drawing unabashedly modelesque sunbathers and posers. With the influx of new luxe hotels and hot spots from 16th to 25th streets, the South Beach stand-and-pose scene is now bigger than ever. The beaches crowd quickly on the weekends with a blend of European tourists, young hipsters, and sun-drenched locals offering Latin flavor. Separating the sand from the traffic of Ocean Drive is palm-fringed **Lummus Park,** with its volleyball nets and chickee huts (huts made of palmetto thatch over a cypress frame) for shade. The beach at **12th Street** is popular with gays, in a section often marked with rainbow flags. Locals hang out on 3rd Street Beach, in an area called **SoFi** (South of Fifth), where they watch fit Brazilians play foot volley, a variation of volleyball that uses everything but the hands. Because much of South Beach leans toward skimpy sunning—women are often in G-strings and casually topless—many families prefer the tamer sections of Mid- and North Beach. Metered parking spots next to the ocean are a rare find. Instead, opt for a public garage a few blocks away and enjoy the people-watching as you walk to find your perfect spot on the sand. **Amenities:** food and drink; lifeguards; parking (fee); showers; toilets. **Best for:** partiers; sunrise; swimming; walking. ⊠ *Ocean Dr. from 5th to 15th Sts., then Collins Ave. to 25th St., South Beach, Miami Beach* ☎ *305/673–7714.*

WHERE TO EAT

Because Miami dining is a part of the trendy nightlife scene, most dinners don't start until 8 or 9 pm, and may go well into the night. To avoid a long wait among the late-night partyers at hot spots, arrive before 7 or make reservations. Attire is usually casual-chic, but patrons like to dress to impress. When you get your bill, check whether a gratuity is already included; most restaurants add between 15% and 20% (ostensibly for the convenience of, and protection from, the many Latin American and European tourists who are used to this practice in their homelands), but supplement it depending on your opinion of the service.

★ **Fodor'sChoice** ✕ **Azul.** *Eclectic.* A restaurant known for producing celebrity chefs and delivering dining fantasies of Food
$$$$ Network proportions, Azul is a Miami foodie insitution. With its award-winning team, Azul offers a haute-cuisine experience on par with a two- or three-Michelin-star restaurant. Chefs fuse disparate ingredients, merging as decadent, gastronomic art. Headliners include almond gazpacho with foie gras "snow," Moroccan argan oil, orange essence, and golden-raisin pudding, and the "silver and gold egg" with American caviar, 63-degree quail egg, caramelized onions, and potato *espuma* (a foaming technique). Dine here and you'll undoubtedly experience bold new taste sensations while enjoying one of the finest wine lists in the city and an incomparable skyline view. Ⓢ *Average main: $48* ⊠ *Mandarin Oriental, Miami, 500 Brickell Key Dr., Downtown* ☎ *305/913–8358* ⊕ *www.mandarinoriental.com/miami* ⚑ *Reservations essential* ⊗ *Closed Sun. No lunch.*

$$ ✕**Big Pink.** *American.* The decor in this innovative, super-popular diner may remind you of a roller-skating rink—everything is pink Lucite, stainless steel, and campy (think sports lockers as decorative touches)—and the menu is 3 feet tall, complete with a table of contents. Food is solidly all-American, with dozens of tasty sandwiches, pizzas, turkey or beef burgers, and side dishes, each and every one composed with gourmet flair. Big Pink also makes a great spot for brunch. ⑤ *Average main: $14* ⊠ *157 Collins Ave., South Beach, Miami Beach* ☎ *305/532–4700* ⊕ *www.mylesrestaurantgroup.com.*

$$ ✕**Havana Harry's.** *Cuban.* When Cuban families want an affordable home-cooked meal but don't want to cook it themselves or go supercheap at the Cuban fast-food joint, Pollo Tropical, they come to this big, unassuming restaurant. In fact, you're likely to see whole families here representing multiple generations. The fare is traditional Cuban: the long thin steaks known as *bistec palomilla* (a panfried steak), roast chicken with citrus marinade, and fried pork chunks; contemporary flourishes—mango sauce and guava-painted pork roast—are kept to a minimum. Most dishes come with white rice, black beans, and a choice of ripe or green plantains. The sweet ripe ones offer a good contrast to the savory dishes. Start with the $5.25 *mariquitas* (plantain chips) with mojo. Finish with the acclaimed flan. ⑤ *Average main: $12* ⊠ *4612 Le Jeune Rd.* ☎ *305/661–2622* ⊕ *www.havanaharrys.net.*

★ **Fodor's**Choice ✕**Joe's Stone Crab Restaurant.** *Seafood.* In South $$$$ Beach's decidedly new-money scene, the stately Joe's Stone Crab is an old-school testament to good food and good service. South Beach's most storied restaurant started as a turn-of-the-century eating house when Joseph Weiss discovered succulent stone crabs off the Florida coast. Almost a century later, the restaurant stretches a city block and serves 2,000 dinners a day to local politicians and moneyed patriarchs. Stone crabs, served with legendary mustard sauce, crispy hash browns, and creamed spinach, remain the staple. Though stone-crab season runs from October 15 to May 15, Joe's remains open year-round (albeit with a limited schedule) serving other phenomenal seafood dishes. Finish your meal with tart key lime pie, baked fresh daily. ■TIP➔ **Joe's famously refuses reservations, and weekend waits can be three hours long—yes, you read that correctly—so come early or order from Joe's Take Away next door.** ⑤ *Average main: $42* ⊠ *11 Washington Ave., South Beach* ☎ *305/673–0365, 305/673–4611 for takeout* ⊕ *www.*

6

joesstonecrab.com ⚏ *Reservations not accepted* ⊘ *No lunch Sun. and Mon. and mid-May–mid-Oct.*

★ **Fodor's**Choice ✕ **Michy's.** *Eclectic.* Even before multiple stints
$$$ on any and every great food show on TV, Miami's home-grown star and James Beard winner Michelle Bernstein was making national headlines with her self-named restaurant, Michy's. Bernstein's regulars often pack the small eatery, which serves exquisite Latin- and Mediterranean-influenced dishes at over-the-causeway (non–tourist trap) prices. The food is bold, eclectic, and beyond tasty—everything you'd expect from a culinary wizard. Can't-miss entrées include seared turbot with sweet shrimp, potato gnocchi, arti-choke *barigoule* (braised artichokes in a seasoned broth), and short ribs "falling off the bone." Both appetizers and mains (aptly termed Plates of Resistance on the menu) come in half and full portions, which makes dining here an even more amazing deal. Ⓢ *Average main: $26* ⊠ *6927 Biscayne Blvd., Upper East Side* ☎ *305/759–2001* ⊕ *www. michysmiami.com* ⊘ *Closed Mon. No lunch.*

$$ ✕ **News Café.** *American.* No trip to Miami is complete with-out a stop at this Ocean Drive landmark, though the food is nothing special. The 24-hour café attracts a crowd with snacks, light meals, drinks, periodicals, and the people-parade on the sidewalk out front. Most prefer sitting out-side, where they can feel the salt breeze and gawk at the human scenery. Sea-grape trees shade a patio where you can watch from a quiet distance. Offering a little of this and a little of that—bagels, pâtés, chocolate fondue, sand-wiches, and a terrific wine list—this joint has something for everyone. Although service can be indifferent to the point of laissez-faire and the food is mediocre at best, News Café is just one of those places visitors love. Ⓢ *Average main: $15* ⊠ *800 Ocean Dr., South Beach* ☎ *305/538–6397* ⊕ *www. newscafe.com* ⚏ *Reservations not accepted.*

★ **Fodor's**Choice ✕ **Perricone's Marketplace and Café.** *Italian.* Brick-
$$ ell Avenue south of the Miami River is burgeoning with Italian restaurants, and this lunch place for local bigwigs is the biggest and most popular among them. It's housed partially outdoors and partially indoors in an 1880s Ver-mont barn. Recipes were handed down from generation to generation, and the cooking is simple and good. Buy your wine from the on-premises deli, and enjoy it (for a small corking fee) with homemade minestrone; a generous antipasto; linguine with a sauté of jumbo shrimp, scallops, and calamari; or gnocchi with four cheeses. The home-made tiramisu and cannoli are top-notch. Ⓢ *Average main:*

$22 ✉ *Mary Brickell Village, 15 S.E. 10th St., Downtown* ☎ *305/374–9449* ⊕ *www.perricones.com.*

★ **Fodor'sChoice** ✕ **Yardbird Southern Table & Bar.** *Southern. Top*
$$ *Chef* contestant Jeff McInnis brings a helluva lot of Southern lovin' from the Lowcountry to South Beach at this lively and funky spot. Miami's see-and-be-seen crowd puts calorie-counting aside for decadent nights filled with comfort foods and innovative drinks. The family-style menu is divided between "small shares" and "big shares," but let's not kid ourselves—all the portions are huge (and surprisingly affordable). You'll rave about the pimento cheese jar, fried-green-tomato BLT, grilled-mango salad, 27-hour-fried chicken, and shrimp and grits. Oh, and then there are the sides, like the house-cut waffle fries with a buttermilk dipping sauce and bacon salt, and the super-creamy macaroni-and-cheese. Don't plan on hitting the beach in a bikini the next day. ⑤ *Average main: $18* ✉ *1600 Lenox Ave., South Beach* ☎ *305/538–5220* ⊕ *www.runchickenrun.com.*

WHERE TO STAY

South Beach is the center of the action in Miami Beach, but it's also expensive. If you are looking for a budget hotel, you'll almost certainly have to choose one that's a few blocks from the beach instead of being right across the street.

For expanded reviews, facilities, and current deals, visit Fodors.com.

$$ 🏨 **Angler's Boutique Resort.** *Hotel.* This enclave of upscale studios, bi-level duplexes, and villas captures the feel of a sophisticated private Mediterranean villa community, making it easy to forget that the hotel is on busy Washington Avenue, two blocks from the beach. **Pros:** gardened private retreat; excellent service. **Cons:** on busy Washington Avenue; beach is a 10-minute walk. **TripAdvisor:** "best of the best," "great location," "top notch." ⑤ *Rooms from: $299* ✉ *660 Washington Ave.* ☎ *305/534–9600* ⊕ *www. theanglersresort.com* ⇨ *24 rooms, 20 suites* ⊺◎⊺*No meals.*

$ 🏨 **Circa 39 Hotel.** This stylish yet affordable boutique hotel
★ pays attention to every detail and gets them all right. **Pros:** affordable; chic; intimate; beach chairs provided; art deco fireplace. **Cons:** not on the beach side of Collins Avenue. ⑤ *Rooms from: $169* ✉ *3900 Collins Ave., Mid-Beach, Miami Beach* ☎ *305/538–4900, 877/824–7223* ⊕ *www. circa39.com* ⇨ *96 rooms* ⊺◎⊺*No meals.*

$$$ ⚄ **King & Groves Tides South Beach.** *Hotel.* Formerly the crown jewel of the Viceroy Hotel Group, the Tides is an exclusive Ocean Drive art deco hotel of just 45 ocean-facing suites adorned with soft pinks and corals, gilded accents, and marine-inspired decor. **Pros:** superior service; great beach location; ocean views from all suites plus the terrace restaurant. **Cons:** tiny elevators; ubiquitous taxidermy. ⑤ *Rooms from: $339 ✉ 1220 Ocean Dr., South Beach, Miami Beach ☎ 305/604–5070 ⊕ www.kingandgrove.com/tides-south-beach ⇨ 45 suites ⎮◎⎮No meals.*

$$$ ⚄ **National Hotel.** *Hotel.* Unlike its neighbors, the National Hotel has maintained its distinct art deco heritage while also keeping up with SoBe's glossy newcomers with its beautifully renovated cabana wing. **Pros:** stunning pool; perfect location. **Cons:** tower rooms are really dated; neighboring hotels can be noisy on the weekends. ⑤ *Rooms from: $305 ✉ 1677 Collins Ave., South Beach, Miami Beach ☎ 305/532–2311, 800/327–8370 ⊕ www.nationalhotel. com ⇨ 143 rooms, 9 suites ⎮◎⎮No meals.*

$ ⚄ **Park Central.** *Hotel.* This seven-story, oft-photographed 1937 archetypal art deco building on Ocean Drive offers a wide range of somewhat dated, Old Florida–style rooms decorated with black-and-white photos of old beach scenes. **Pros:** spacious rooftop sundeck; comfy beds; perfect location for first trip to Miami. **Cons:** furnishings are so not South Beach; small bathrooms; most rooms have limited views. **TripAdvisor:** "excellent location," "art deco paradise," "great staff." ⑤ *Rooms from: $160 ✉ 640 Ocean Dr. ☎ 305/538–1611, 800/727–5236 ⊕ www.theparkcentral. com ⇨ 113 rooms, 12 suites ⎮◎⎮No meals.*

$$ ⚄ **The Standard.** *Resort.* An extension of André Balazs's trendy and hip yet budget-conscious hotel chain, the shabby-chic Standard is a mile from South Beach on an island just over the Venetian Causeway and boasts one of South Florida's most renowned spas and hottest pool scenes. **Pros:** free bike and kayak rentals; swank pool scene; great spa; inexpensive. **Cons:** slight trek to South Beach; small rooms with no views. ⑤ *Rooms from: $269 ✉ 40 Island Ave., Belle Isle ☎ 305/673–1717 ⊕ www.standard-hotel.com ⇨ 104 rooms, 1 suite ⎮◎⎮No meals.*

★ **Fodor's**Choice ⚄ **The Surfcomber.** In 2012 the legendary Surf-
$$ comber joined the hip Kimpton Hotel group, spawning a fantastic nip-and-tuck that has rejuvenated the rooms and common spaces to reflect vintage luxe and oceanside freshness, and offering a price point that packs the place with a young, vibrant, and sophisticated yet unpretentious

crowd. **Pros:** stylish but not pretentious; pet-friendly; on the beach. **Cons:** small bathrooms; front desk often busy. **TripAdvisor:** "amazing staff," "great property," "perfect location." ⑤ *Rooms from: $259* ✉ *1717 Collins Ave., South Beach, Miami Beach* ☎ *305/532–7715* ⊕ *www.surfcomber. com* ⇌ *182 rooms, 6 suites* ⑩ *No meals.*

$ ⛁ **Villa Paradiso.** *B&B/Inn.* One of South Beach's best deals, Paradiso has huge rooms with kitchens and a charming tropical courtyard with benches for hanging out at all hours. **Pros:** great hangout spot in courtyard; good value; great location. **Cons:** no pool; no restaurant. ⑤ *Rooms from: $149* ✉ *1415 Collins Ave., South Beach, Miami Beach* ☎ *305/532–0616* ⊕ *www.villaparadisohotel.com* ⇌ *17 studios* ⑩ *No meals.*

NIGHTLIFE

One of Greater Miami's most popular pursuits is barhopping. Bars range from intimate enclaves to showy see-and-be-seen lounges to loud, raucous frat parties. There's a New York–style flair to some of the newer lounges, which are increasingly catering to the Manhattan party crowd who escape to South Beach for long weekends. No doubt, Miami's pulse pounds with nonstop nightlife that reflects the area's potent cultural mix. On sultry, humid nights with the huge full moon rising out of the ocean and fragrant night-blooming jasmine intoxicating the senses, who can resist Cuban salsa with some disco and hip-hop thrown in for good measure? When this place throws a party, hips shake, fingers snap, bodies touch. It's no wonder many clubs are still rocking at 5 am. If you're looking for a relatively nonfrenetic evening, your best bet is one of the chic hotel bars on Collins Avenue.

How to get past the velvet ropes at the hottest South Beach nightspots? First, if you're staying at a hotel, use the concierge. Decide which clubs you want to check out (consult *Ocean Drive* magazine celebrity pages if you want to be among the glitterati), and the concierge will email, fax, or call in your names to the clubs so you'll be on the guest list when you arrive. This means much easier access and usually no cover charge (which can be upward of $20) if you arrive before midnight. Guest list or no guest list, follow these pointers: Make sure there are more women than men in your group. Dress up—casual chic is the dress code. For men this means no sneakers, no shorts, no sleeveless vests, and no shirts unbuttoned past the top button. For women, provocative and seductive is fine; overly revealing is not. Black is always right. At the door: don't name-drop—no one takes it seriously. Don't be pushy while trying to get the doorman's attention. Wait until you make eye contact, then be cool and easygoing. If you decide to tip him (which most bouncers don't expect), be discreet and pleasant, not big-bucks obnoxious—a $10 or $20 bill quietly passed will be appreciated, however.

SHOPPING

If you're over the climate-controlled slickness of shopping malls and can't face one more food-court "meal," you've got choices in Miami. Head out into the sunshine and shop the city streets, where you'll find big-name retailers and local boutiques alike. Take a break at a sidewalk café to power up on some Cuban coffee or fresh-squeezed OJ and enjoy the tropical breezes.

Give your plastic a workout in shopping the many high-profile tenants on the densely packed two-block stretch of **Collins Avenue** between 5th and 10th streets. Think Club Monaco, MAC, Kenneth Cole, Barney's Co-Op, and A/X Armani Exchange. Sprinkled amid the upscale vendors are hair salons, spas, cafés, and such familiar stores as the Gap, Urban Outfitters, and Banana Republic. Be sure to head over one street east and west to catch the shopping on Ocean Drive and Washington Avenue.

The eight-block-long **Lincoln Road Mall** is the trendiest place on Miami Beach. Home to more than 150 shops, 20-plus art galleries and nightclubs, about 50 restaurants and cafés, and the renovated Colony Theatre, Lincoln Road is like a larger, more sophisticated cousin of Ocean Drive. The "see and be seen" theme is furthered by outdoor seating at every restaurant, where well-heeled patrons lounge and discuss the people (and pet) parade passing by. An 18-screen movie theater anchors the west end of the street, which is where most of the worthwhile shops are; the far east end is mostly discount and electronic shops. Sure, there's a Pottery Barn, a Gap, and a Williams-Sonoma, but the emphasis is on art galleries and emporia with unique personalities, like En Avance, Chroma, Base, and Jonathan Adler.

HOMESTEAD

30 miles southwest of Miami.

Updated by Lynne Helm

In recent years Homestead has redefined itself as a destination for tropical agro- and ecotourism. At a crossroads between Miami and the Keys as well as Everglades and Biscayne national parks, the area has the added dimension of shopping centers, residential development, hotel chains, and the Homestead–Miami Speedway—when car races are scheduled, hotels hike up their rates and require minimum stays. The historic downtown has become a preservation-driven Main Street. Krome Avenue, where it cuts through the city's heart, is lined with restaurants, an arts complex, antiques shops, and low-budget, sometimes undesirable accommodations. West of north–south Krome Avenue, miles of fields grow fresh fruits and vegetables. Some are harvested commercially, and others beckon with "U-pick" signs. Stands selling farm-fresh produce and nurseries that grow and sell orchids and tropical plants abound. In addition to its agricultural legacy, the town has an eclectic flavor, attributable to its population mix: descendants of pioneer Crackers, Hispanic growers and farm workers, professionals escaping the Miami hubbub, and latter-day Northern retirees.

EXPLORING

ArtSouth. This groundbreaking project centered on a 3½-acre complex includes the historic First Baptist Church, 30 artist studios, galleries, workshops, sculpture garden, and stage. Watch artists at work, take classes, and enjoy concert performances. Check Second Saturdays opening exhibits, including free live entertainment, art demonstrations, self-guided tours, and refreshments 3–7 pm. ⊠ *240 N. Krome Ave.* ☎ *305/247–9406* ⊕ *www.artsouthhomestead. org* ⊠ *Free* ☉ *Tues.–Fri. 10–6, weekends noon–6.*

Coral Castle. Driven by unrequited love, 100-pound Latvian immigrant Ed Leedskalnin (1887–1951) built this castle in the early 1900s out of massive slabs of coral rock, a feat he likened to building the pyramids. Visitors can learn how he peopled his fantasy world with his imaginary wife and three children, studied astronomy, and created a simple home and elaborate courtyard without formal engineering education and with tools he mostly fashioned himself. Highlights of this National Register of Historic Places site include the Polaris telescope built to spot the North Star, a working sundial, a 5,000-pound heart-shape table featured in Ripley's *Believe It or Not,* a banquet table in the shape of Florida, and a playground Ed named "Grotto of the Three Bears." ⊠ *28655 S. Dixie Hwy.* ☎ *305/248–6345* ⊕ *www.coralcastle.com* ⊠ *$12* ⊙ *Daily 8–6.*

★ **Dante Fascell Visitor Center.** Go outside on the wide veranda
☯ to take in views across mangroves and Biscayne Bay. Inside the museum, artistic vignettes and on-request videos including the 11-minute *Spectrum of Life* explore Everglades National Park's four ecosystems, while the Touch Table gives both kids and adults a feel for bones, feathers, and coral. Facilities include the park's canoe and tour concessionaire, restrooms with showers, a ranger information area, gift shop with books, and vending machines. Various ranger programs take place daily during busy fall and winter seasons. On the second Sunday of each month from December through April, the Family Fun Fest program offers three hours of hands-on activities for kids and families. Rangers also give informal tours of Elliott and Boca Chita keys; arrange in advance. Outside are picnic tables and grills. A short trail and boardwalk lead to a jetty. This is the only area of the park accessible without a boat. ⊠ *9700 S.W. 328th St., Homestead* ☎ *305/230–7275* ⊕ *www.nps. gov/bisc* ⊠ *Free* ⊙ *Daily 9–5.*

WHERE TO EAT

★ **Fodor's**Choice ✕ **Bobbie Jo's Diner.** *Southern.* Head to Bobbie
$ Jo's with the locals for good, old, Southern-style home cooking. Burgers, sandwiches, and dinners—including chicken livers, chicken and dumplings, and fried clams— come with fresh-baked corn bread and a daily selection of sides such as okra with tomatoes, turnip greens, pickled beets, or onion rings. The Bobbie Jo burger comes with fries for under five bucks. Don't miss out on the changing selection of homemade soups and desserts. All this goodness comes cheap, but at the expense of anything-but-glamorous dining environs and often slow (albeit friendly) service. ⑤ *Average main: $10* ⊠ *1320 N. Krome Ave.* ☎ *305/246– 2990* ⊙ *No dinner Sun.*

$ ✕ **NicaMex.** *Mexican.* Among the local Latin population this 68-seat eatery is a low-budget favorite for Nicaraguan and Mexican flavors. It helps if you speak Spanish, but usually some staffers on hand speak English, and the menu is bilingual. Although they term it *comidas rapidas* (fast food), the cuisine is not Americanized. You can get authentic huevos rancheros or *chilaquiles* (corn tortillas cooked in red-pepper sauce) for breakfast, and specialties such as *chicharron en salsa verde* (fried pork skin in hot-green-tomato sauce) and shrimp in garlic all day. Hearty seafood and beef soups are best sellers. Choose among domestic or imported beers, and escape south of the border. $ *Average main: $10* ⊠ *32 N.W. 1st St., across from Krome Ave. bandstand* ☎ *305/247–0727.*

SPORTS AND THE OUTDOORS

AUTO RACING

Homestead-Miami Speedway. The speedway buzzes more than 280 days each year with racing, manufacturer testing, car-club events, driving schools, and ride-along programs. The facility has 65,000 grandstand seats, club seating eight stories above racing action, and two tracks—a 2.21-mile continuous road course and a 1.5-mile oval. A packed schedule includes GRAND-AM and NASCAR events. ⊠ *One Speedway Blvd.* ☎ *866/409–7223* ⊕ *www.home-steadmiamispeedway.com.*

BOATING

Homestead Bayfront Park. Boaters, anglers, and beachgoers give high ratings to the facilities at this recreational area adjacent to Biscayne National Park. The 174-slip marina, accommodating vessels up to 50 feet long, has a ramp, dock, bait-and-tackle shop, fuel station, ice, and dry storage. The park also has a tidal swimming area, a beach with lifeguards, a playground, ramps for people with disabilities (including a ramp that leads into the swimming area), and a picnic pavilion with grills, showers, and restrooms. ⊠ *9698 S.W. 328th St.* ☎ *305/230–3033* ⊇ *$6 per passenger vehicle; $12 per vehicle with boat Mon.–Thurs., $15 Fri.–Sun.; $15 per RV or bus* ☉ *Daily sunrise–sunset.*

SHOPPING

Krome Avenue. In the heart of Old Homestead, this popular shopping street with a brick sidewalk has art galleries and antiques stores, including Jacobsen's Antique Mall, which has multiple dealers. ⊠ *144 N. Krome Ave..*

6

FLORIDA CITY

2 miles southwest of Homestead.

Updated by Lynne Helm

Florida's Turnpike ends in Florida City, the southernmost town on the peninsula, spilling thousands of vehicles onto U.S. 1 and eventually west to Everglades National Park, east to Biscayne National Park, or south to the Florida Keys. Florida City and Homestead run into each other, but the difference couldn't be more noticeable. As the last outpost before 18 miles of mangroves and water, this stretch of U.S. 1 is lined with fast-food eateries, service stations, hotels, bars, dive shops, and restaurants. Hotel rates increase significantly during NASCAR races at the nearby Homestead–Miami Speedway. Like Homestead, Florida City is rooted in agriculture, with hundreds of acres of farmland west of Krome Avenue and a huge farmers' market that processes produce shipped nationwide.

WHERE TO EAT

$$ ✕ **Capri Restaurant.** *Italian.* Locals have come to this family-owned enterprise for affordable Italian-American classics since 1958. Interior dining areas have redbrick accent walls with plenty of round tables; the sunny courtyard has umbrella-covered tables. Tasty options range from pizza with a light, crunchy crust and ample toppings to broiled steaks and seafood-pasta classics; spaghetti comes 16 ways. Old Time Capri Favorites, at $12.95, include chop steak with mushroom gravy or sausage and pepper, with either soup or salad. Daily early-bird entrées (4:30–6:30 for $12–$14) include soup or salad and potato or spaghetti. The Tuesday family night (after 4 pm, $7.95) comes with all-you-can-eat pasta and salad or soup. Specialty martinis and fruity cocktails supplement the international wine list. $ *Average main: $16* ⊠ *935 N. Krome Ave.* ☎ *305/247–1542* ⊕ *www.dinecapri.com* ⊘ *No lunch Sun.*

$$$ ✕ **Captain's Restaurant and Seafood Market.** *Seafood.* A comfortable place where the chef prepares seafood with flair, this is among the town's best bets. Locals and visitors alike gather in the cozy dining room or outdoors on the patio. Blackboards describe a varied menu of sandwiches, pasta, seafood, steak, and nightly specials, plus stone crabs in season. Inventive offerings include a lobster Reuben sandwich and pan-seared tuna topped with balsamic onions and shallots. Specials sometimes include crawfish pasta. $ *Average main: $20* ⊠ *404 S.E. 1st Ave.* ☎ *305/247–9456.*

$ ✕**Farmers' Market Restaurant.** *Seafood*. Although this eatery
★ is in the farmers' market on the edge of town and serves
fresh vegetables, seafood figures prominently on the menu.
A family of anglers runs the place, so fish and shellfish
are only hours from the sea, and there's a fish fry on Friday nights. Catering to anglers and farmers, the restaurant opens at 5:30 am, serving pancakes, jumbo eggs, and
fluffy omelets with home fries or grits in a pleasant dining
room with checkered tablecloths. Lunch and dinner menus
have fried shrimp, seafood pasta, country-fried steak, roast
turkey, and fried conch, as well as burgers, salads, and
sandwiches. ⑤*Average main: $13* ✉*300 N. Krome Ave.*
☎*305/242–0008.*

$$ ✕**Mutineer Wharf Restaurant.** *Seafood*. Families and older
☾ couples flock to the quirky yet well-dressed setting of this
roadside steak-and-seafood outpost with a fish-and-duck
pond and a petting zoo for kids. It was built in 1980 to look
like a ship, back when Florida City was barely on the map.
Etched glass divides the bi-level dining rooms, with velvet-
upholstered chairs, an aquarium, and nautical antiques.
Topping the menu of about a dozen seafood entrées is the
stuffed grouper, Florida lobster tails, and snapper Oscar,
plus another half-dozen daily seafood specials, as well as
poultry, ribs, and steaks. Burgers and seafood sandwiches
are popular for lunch, as is weekday happy-hour buffet
until 7 in the lounge with purchase of a drink. You also
can dine in the restaurant's Wharf Lounge. Most Friday
and Saturday nights feature live entertainment and danc-
ing. ⑤*Average main: $16* ✉*11 S.E. 1st Ave. (U.S. 1), at
Palm Dr.* ☎*305/245–3377* ⊕*www.mutineerrestaurant.com.*

$ ✕**Rosita's Restaurante.** *Mexican*. With its growing Mexican
★ population, this area can boast the authenticity that you
just don't get in the Tex-Mex chains. Order à la carte spe-
cialties or dinners and combos with beans and rice and
salad. Breakfast, lunch, and dinner entrées are served all
day and range from Mexican eggs, enchiladas, and taco
salad to stewed beef, shrimp ranchero-style, and fried pork
chop. Food is on the spicy side, but if you like more fire,
avail yourself of the fresh-tasting salsa, pickled jalapeños,
or bottled habanero sauce on each table. Clean (with lin-
gering whiffs of bleach to prove it) and pleasant, with an
open kitchen, take-out counter, and Formica tables, this
place is a favorite with locals and guests at the Everglades
International Hostel across the street. ⑤*Average main: $12*
✉*199 W. Palm Dr.* ☎*305/246–3114.*

6

WHERE TO STAY

For expanded reviews, facilities, and current deals, visit Fodors.com.

$$ ⊞ **Best Western Gateway to the Keys.** *Hotel.* For easy access to Everglades and Biscayne national parks as well as the Florida Keys, you'll be well-placed at this two-story motel two blocks off Florida's Turnpike. **Pros:** convenient to national parks, outlet shopping, and Keys; business services; pretty pool area. **Cons:** traffic noise; fills up fast during high season. ⑤ *Rooms from: $135 ✉ 411 S. Krome Ave. ☎ 305/246–5100, 888/981–5100 ⊕ www.bestwestern.com/ gatewaytothekeys ⇄ 114 rooms ⦿ Breakfast.*

$ ⊞ **Comfort Inn.** *Hotel.* Amid an asphalt complex of hotels, gas stations, and eateries just off U.S. 1, this Comfort Inn has a friendly front desk offering tips on Keys or Everglades adventures or action at the nearby track. **Pros:** close to restaurants and services. **Cons:** no elevator; noisy location. ⑤ *Rooms from: $79 ✉ 333 S.E. 1st Ave. ☎ 305/248-4009, 888/352–2489 ⊕ www.comfortinn.com ⇄ 124 rooms ⦿ Breakfast.*

$ ⊞ **Everglades International Hostel.** *Hotel.* Stay in clean and spacious private or dorm-style rooms (generally six to a room), relax in indoor or outdoor quiet areas, and watch videos or TV on a big screen. **Pros:** affordable; Everglades tours; free services. **Cons:** communal living; no elevator; old structure. ⑤ *Rooms from: $25 ✉ 20 S.W. 2nd Ave. ☎ 305/248–1122, 800/372–3874 ⊕ www.evergladeshostel.com ⇄ 46 beds in dorm-style rooms with shared bath, 2 private rooms with shared bath, 2 suites ⦿ No meals.*

$ ⊞ **Fairway Inn.** *Hotel.* Two stories high with a waterfall pool, this motel has some of the area's lowest chain rates, and it's next to the Chamber of Commerce visitor center so you'll never be short of reading and planning material. **Pros:** affordable; convenient to restaurants, parks, and raceway. **Cons:** plain, small rooms; no-pet policy. ⑤ *Rooms from: $89 ✉ 100 S.E. 1st Ave. ☎ 305/248–4202, 888/340–4734 ⇄ 160 rooms ⦿ Breakfast.*

$$ ★ ⊞ **Ramada Inn.** *Hotel.* If you're looking for an upgrade from the other chains, this pet-friendly property offers more amenities and comfort, such as 32-inch flat-screen TVs, duvet-covered beds, closed closets, and stylish furnishings. **Pros:** extra room amenities; business clientele perks; convenient location. **Cons:** chain anonymity. ⑤ *Rooms from: $99 ✉ 124 E. Palm Dr. ☎ 305/247–8833 ⊕ www.hotelfloridacity.com ⇄ 124 rooms ⦿ Breakfast.*

$ ⊡**Travelodge.** *Hotel.* This bargain motor lodge is close to Florida's Turnpike, Everglades and Biscayne national parks, the Florida Keys, and the Homestead–Miami Speedway. **Pros:** pet-friendly for a $10 per night fee; convenience to U.S. 1; complimentary breakfast. **Cons:** small rooms; busy location. ⑤*Rooms from: $79* ⊠*409 S.E. 1st Ave.* ☎*305/248-9777, 800/758-0618* ⊕*www.tlflcity.com* ⇋*88 rooms* ⏇*Breakfast.*

SHOPPING

☺ **Robert Is Here.** This remarkable fruit stand sells vegeta-
★ bles, fresh-fruit milk shakes (try the key lime), 10 flavors of honey, more than 100 types of jams and jellies, fresh juices, salad dressings, and some 30 kinds of tropical fruits, including (in season) carambola, lychee, egg fruit, monstera, sapodilla, dragonfruit, genipa, sugar apple, and tamarind. The stand started in 1960, when seven-year-old Robert sat at this spot selling his father's bumper crop of cucumbers. Today, Robert (still on the scene daily with his wife and kids), ships all over the United States and donates seconds to needy area families. An odd assort-ment of animals out back—from goats to emus—adds entertainment value for kids. Picnic tables, benches, and a waterfall with a koi pond add some serenity to the experi-ence. The stand, on the way to Everglades National Park, opens at 8 am and stays open until at least 7. It shuts down between September and October. ⊠*19200 S.W. 344th St.* ☎*305/246-1592.*

Travel Smart Florida Keys

WORD OF MOUTH

"Our adult family of four will be traveling to Key West in January and we are wondering if we need to keep our rental car from the airport once we are in Key West."

—Sealight3

"You may choose to but you absolutely don't need to keep your rental car. There is a bus system on the island. One popular way of getting around is by bicycle, which is what I did."

—Daniel_Williams

GETTING HERE AND AROUND

Key West International Airport is the only airport in the Keys that accommodates commercial flights, and five major airlines and a few small companies serve the airport. Most visitors fly into Miami International Airport and either drive to their destination in the Keys or take an air shuttle to Key West. The drive is long and slow. It can be done in a half-day, but it's better to break up the drive and spend some time exploring the Keys outside of Key West.

■TIP➔ Ask the local tourist board about hotel and local transportation packages that include tickets to major museum exhibits or other special events.

▌ AIR TRAVEL

About 450,000 passengers use the Key West International Airport (EYW) each year; its most recent renovation includes a beach where travelers can catch their last blast of rays after clearing security. Because flights are few, many prefer flying into Miami International Airport (MIA) and driving the 110-mile Overseas Highway (aka U.S. 1).

AIRPORTS

The fittingly tiny, laid-back Key West International Airport (EYW) has greeted domestic passengers and overseas private planes since 1957. In 2009 the airport completed its four-year renovation, which includes a beach where travelers can catch their last blast

of rays after clearing security. The new McCoy Terminal sits atop a 475-car parking ramp.

The airport is a short drive from Old Town, so should your flight get delayed (it happens often enough), jump in a taxi and enjoy a few more hours of Key West freedom. Note that ⊕ *www.keywestinternationalairport.com* is not the official airport site; it is operated by an outside travel agency.

Airport Information Key West International Airport (EYW) ☎ *305/296–5439* ⊕ *www.keywestinternationalairport.com.* **Miami International Airport** (*MIA*). ☎ *305/876–7000* ⊕ *www.miami-airport.com.*

GROUND TRANSPORTATION

Airporter operates scheduled van and bus pickup service from all Miami International Airport (MIA) baggage areas to wherever you want to go in Key Largo ($50) and Islamorada ($55). Groups of three or more passengers receive discounts. There are three departures daily; reservations are required 48 hours in advance.

Greyhound Lines runs a special Keys shuttle two times a day (depending on the day of the week) from Miami International Airport (departing from Concourse E, lower level) and stops throughout the Keys. Fares run from around $25 for Key Largo (⊠*Howard Johnson, MM 102*) to around $45 for Key West (✉ *3535 S. Roosevelt, Key West International Airport*).

Keys Shuttle runs scheduled service six times a day in 15-passenger vans (nine passengers maximum) between Miami and Fort Lauderdale airports and Key West with stops throughout the Keys for $60 to $90 per person sharing rides.

SuperShuttle charges about $165 for two passengers for trips to the Upper Keys; to go further, you must book an entire 11-person van, which costs $250 to Marathon or $350 to Key West. For a trip to the airport, place your request 24 hours in advance.

Contacts Airporter ☎ *305/852-3413, 800/830-3413.* **Greyhound** ☎ *800/231-2222* ⊕ *www.greyhound.com.* **Keys Shuttle** ☎ *305/289-9997, 888/765-9997* ⊕ *www.floridakeysshuttle.com.* **SuperShuttle** ☎ *305/871-2000* ⊕ *www.supershuttle.com.*

FLIGHTS

Service between Key West International Airport and Miami, Fort Lauderdale/Hollywood, Fort Myers, West Palm Beach, Orlando, Tampa, Atlanta, and Charlotte, NC (seasonally) is provided by American Eagle, Cape Air, Delta (Express Jet), United (Silver Air) and US Airways.

Flying time from Miami is 50 minutes, from Orlando just over an hour, from Atlanta about 2 hours.

Airline Contacts AirTran.

AirTran to Miami, Fort Lauderdale, Fort Myers, Jacksonville, Key West, Orlando, Pensacola, Sarasota, Tampa, and West Palm Beach. ☎ *800/247-*

8726 ⊕ *www.airtran.com.* **American Airlines** ☎ *800/433-7300* ⊕ *www.aa.com.* **United** ☎ *800/864-8331 for U.S. reservations, 800/538-2929 for international reservations* ⊕ *www.united.com.* **Delta** ☎ *800/221-1212 for U.S. reservations, 800/241-4141 for international reservations* ⊕ *www.delta.com.* **US Airways** ☎ *800/428-4322 for U.S. and Canadian reservations, 800/622-1015 for international reservations* ⊕ *www.usairways.com.*

▌ BOAT TRAVEL

Boaters can travel to and through the Keys either along the Intracoastal Waterway (5-foot draft limitation) through Card, Barnes, and Blackwater sounds and into Florida Bay, or along the deeper Atlantic Ocean route through Hawk Channel, a buoyed passage. Refer to NOAA Nautical Charts Numbers 11451, 11445, and 11441. The Keys are full of marinas that welcome transient visitors, but they don't have enough slips for everyone. Make reservations in advance, and ask about channel and dockage depth—many marinas are quite shallow.

For nonemergency information, contact Coast Guard Group Key West; VHF-FM Channel 16. Safety and weather information is broadcast at 7 am and 5 pm Eastern Standard Time on VHF-FM Channels 16 and 22A. There are stations in Islamorada and Marathon.

Key West Express operates air-conditioned ferries between the Key West Terminal (Caroline and Grinnell streets) and Marco Island and Fort Myers Beach. The trip from Fort Myers Beach takes at least four hours each way and costs $86 one way, $146 round-trip. Ferries depart from Fort Myers Beach at 8:30 am and from Key West at 6 pm. The Marco Island ferry costs $86 one way and $146 round-trip, and departs at 8:30 am (the return trip leaves Key West at 5 pm). A photo ID is required for each passenger. Advance reservations are recommended.

Information Key West Express
✉ *100 Grinnell St., Key West, Florida, USA* ☎ *888/539-2628* ⊕ *www.seakeywestexpress.com.*

■ BUS TRAVEL

The City of Key West Department of Transportation has six color-coded bus routes traversing the island from 6:30 am to 11:30 pm. Stops have signs with the international bus symbol. Schedules are available on buses and at hotels, visitor centers, and shops. The fare is $2 one way.

The Lower Keys Shuttle bus runs from Marathon to Key West ($4 one way), with scheduled stops along the way.

Miami Dade Transit provides daily bus service from MM 50 in Marathon to the Florida City Walmart Supercenter on the mainland. The bus stops at major shopping centers as well as on-demand anywhere along the route during daily round trips on the hour from 6 am to 10 pm. The cost is $2 one-way, exact change required.

Bus Information City of Key West Department of Transportation
☎ *305/809-3910*
⊕ *www.kwtransit.com.*

■ CAR TRAVEL

By car, from Miami International Airport, follow signs to Coral Gables and Key West, which puts you on LeJeune Road, then Route 836 west. Take the Homestead Extension of Florida's Turnpike south (toll road), which ends at Florida City and connects to the Overseas Highway (U.S. 1). Tolls from the airport run approximately $3. Payment is collected via **Sun Pass,** a prepaid toll program, or with **Toll-By-Plate,** a system that photographs each vehicle's license plate and mails a monthly bill for tolls, plus a $2.50 administrative fee, to the vehicle's registered owner. Vacationers traveling in their own cars can obtain a mini-SunPass sticker via mail before their trips for $4.99 and receive the cost back in toll credits and discounts. The pass also is available at many major Florida retailers and turnpike service plazas. It works on all Florida toll roads and many bridges. For details on purchasing a mini-SunPass, call or visit the Web site. For visitors renting cars in Florida, most major rental companies have programs allowing customers to use the Toll-By-Plate system. Tolls, plus varying service fees, are automatically charged to the credit card used to rent the vehicle. For details, including pricing options at participating rental-car agencies, check the program Web site. Under no circumstances should motorists attempt to stop in high-speed electronic tolling lanes. Travelers can contact Florida's Turnpike Enterprise for more information about the all-electronic tolling on Florida's Turnpike.

The alternative from Florida City is Card Sound Road (Route 905A), which has a bridge toll of $1. Continue to the only stop sign and turn right on Route 905, which rejoins U.S. 1 31 mi south of Florida City.

Except in Key West, a car is essential for visiting the Keys. The best Keys road map, published by the Homestead–Florida City Chamber of Commerce, can be obtained for $5.50 from the Tropical Everglades Visitor Center.

Avis, Budget, Enterprise, and Hertz serve Marathon Airport. Avis, Alamo, Budget, Dollar, Enterprise, Hertz, National, and Thrifty serve Key West's airport. Enterprise also has an office in Key Largo. ■TIP➔ **Avoid flying into Key West and driving back to Miami; there could be substantial drop-off charges for leaving a Key West car there.**

GASOLINE
The deeper you go into the Keys, the higher the pump price goes. Gas stations in Homestead and Florida City have some of the most affordable prices in South Florida, so fill your tank in Miami and top it off in Florida City.

PARKING
The only place in the Keys where parking is a problem is in Old Town Key West. There are public parking lots that charge by the day (some hotels and B&Bs provide parking or discounts at municipal lots). If you arrive early, you can sometimes find spots on side

streets off Duval and Whitehead, where you can park for free—just be sure it's not marked for residential parking only. Your best bet is to bike or take a trolley around town if you don't want to walk. The trolleys allow you to disembark and reboard at will at several different stops. The Conch Train makes only two stops where you can board and disembark.

ROAD CONDITIONS
Most of the Overseas Highway is narrow and crowded (especially on weekends and in high season). Expect delays behind RVs, trucks, cars towing boats, and rubbernecking tourists. The section of highway that travels from the mainland to Key Largo is particularly slow and congested. Occasional passing lanes allow you to get past slow-moving trucks. The quality of local roads in Key West is good, though some side streets are narrow. Traffic in the historic district often becomes congested throughout the day and night.

CAR RENTAL
When you reserve a car, ask about cancellation penalties, taxes, drop-off charges (if you're planning to pick up the car in one city and leave it in another), and surcharges (for being under or over a certain age, for additional drivers, for additional insurance, or for driving across state borders or beyond a specific distance from your point of rental). All these things can add substantially to your costs. Request car seats and extras such as a GPS when you book.

CAR RENTAL RESOURCES

LOCAL AGENCIES		
Continental (Fort Lauderdale and Orlando)	800/221–4085 or 954/332–1125	www.continentalcar.com
Sunshine Rent A Car (Fort Lauderdale)	888/786–7446 or 954/467–8100	www.sunshinerentacar.com
MAJOR AGENCIES		
Alamo	877/222–9075	www.alamo.com
Avis	800/331–1212	www.avis.com
Budget	800/527–0700	www.budget.com
Hertz	800/654–3131	www.hertz.com
National Car Rental	800/227–7368	www.nationalcar.com

Rates are sometimes—but not always—better if you book in advance or reserve through a rental agency's Web site. There are other reasons to book ahead, though: for popular destinations, during busy times of the year, or to ensure that you get certain types of cars (vans, SUVs, exotic sports cars).

■TIP➜ Make sure that a confirmed reservation guarantees you a car. Agencies sometimes overbook, particularly for busy weekends and holiday periods.

Unless you fly into Key West and decide to stay in Old Town for your entire vacation—perhaps with a bus trip to another Key or some water sports excursions—you will need a car. Rentals of all makes and models are available at the Miami International Airport, Key West International Airport, and rental agencies throughout the Keys. Reserve your car early during big events such as Home-

stead Miami Speedway races (Key Largo is often affected), October's FantasyFest in Key West, and the Christmas and Easter holidays.

▮ TAXI TRAVEL

Serving the Keys from Ocean Reef to Marathon, A1 Luxury Limousine has luxury Hummers and limos that seat up to eight passengers, as well as vans and buses. It'll pick up from any airport in South Florida.

Florida Keys Taxi & Group Transportation operates around the clock in Key West. The fare for two or more from the Key West airport to Old Town is $8 per person. Otherwise meters register $2.75 for first 1/5 mi, $8 per mile.

ESSENTIALS

▌ ACCOMMODATIONS

The most characteristic type of lodging in the Keys is a small, family-owned place, whether it be a guesthouse in Key West or a dive lodge in Key Largo. The islands do have their share of franchised operations and big destination resorts, but intimate lodging is still quite easy to find throughout the Keys. This is particularly true in Key West's Old Town, where many of the historic Victorian homes have been transformed into B&Bs. Most serve only Continental breakfast (a restaurant license is required to serve hot food).

Most hotels and other lodgings require you to give your credit-card details before they will confirm your reservation. If you don't feel comfortable e-mailing this information, ask if you can fax it (some places even prefer faxes). However you book, get confirmation in writing, and have a copy of it handy when you check in.

Be sure you understand the hotel's cancellation policy. Some places allow you to cancel without any kind of penalty—even if you pre-paid to secure a discounted rate—if you cancel at least 24 hours in advance. Others require you to cancel a week in advance or penalize you the cost of one night. Small inns and B&Bs are most likely to require you to cancel far in advance. Most hotels allow children under a certain age to stay in their parents' room at no extra charge, but others charge for them as extra adults; find out the cutoff age for discounts. Many of Key West's guesthouses do not allow children under a certain age.

APARTMENT AND HOUSE RENTALS

Although short-term rentals are available throughout the Keys, Key West has the largest inventory, and several rental companies can hook you up. *See Lodging Alternatives in the Key West chapter for local vacation-rental agencies.* National agencies, Home Away, Interhome, and Villas International are also good resources in finding a vacation rental in the Keys.

Contacts Interhome. Daytona Beach, Miami, Orlando, Sarasota, Florida Keys, Lower Gulf Coast, Tampa Bay Area ☎ *954/791–8282, 800/882–6864* ⊕ *www.interhome-usa.com.* **Villas International.** Miami, Orlando, Broward County, Florida Keys, Lower Gulf Coast, Palm Beach County, Tampa Bay Area ☎ *415/499–9490, 800/221–2260* ⊕ *www.villasintl.com.*

▌ COMMUNICATIONS

INTERNET

Internet access is the norm in smaller guesthouses, lodges, motels, and resorts. Typically it's Wi-Fi and often free, although not always available in every room, especially in older concrete-block or tin-roof structures. The larger resorts often charge for the service.

▌ EATING OUT

The variety of restaurants in the Keys is vast, but if you were to ask a visitor what is typical, you would probably hear about the colorful seaside fish houses, some with more character than others. Seafood comes so fresh you'll be spoiled for life. Pay special attention to local catches—especially snapper, mahimahi, grouper, lobster, and stone crab. Florida spiny lobster is local and fresh from August to March, and stone crabs from mid-October to mid-May.

Also keep an eye out for authentic key lime pie. The real McCoy has yellow filling in a graham-cracker crust and tastes pleasantly tart. (If it's green, just say "no.") Cuban and Bahamian styles influence local cuisine, so be sure to sample some black beans and rice and conch fritters.

Restaurants may close for a two- to four-week vacation during the slow season—between mid-September and mid-November.

MEALS AND MEALTIMES
Unless otherwise noted, the restaurants listed in this guide are open daily for lunch and dinner.

PAYING
Most restaurants accept the major credit cards. Some of the small, family-owned operations do not.

WORD OF MOUTH

Was the service stellar or not up to snuff? Did the food give you shivers of delight or leave you cold? Did the prices and portions make you happy or sad? Rate restaurants and write your own reviews or start a discussion about your favorite places in the Travel Talk Forums on www.fodors.com. Your comments might even appear in our books. Yes, you, too, can be a correspondent!

RESERVATIONS AND DRESS
It's a good idea to make a reservation if you can. We only mention them specifically when reservations are essential or not accepted. For popular restaurants, book as far ahead as you can, and reconfirm as soon as you arrive. (Large parties should always call ahead to check the reservations policy.) Online reservation services make it easy to book a table before you even leave home.

WINE, BEER, AND SPIRITS
If the Keys have a representative tipple, it is the margarita. Kelly's Caribbean Bar & Brewery in Key West is the Keys' only microbrewery, and it sells bottled product.

▌ EMERGENCIES

Keys Hotline provides information and emergency assistance in six languages. Florida Marine Patrol maintains a 24-hour telephone service to handle reports of boating emergencies and natural-resource violations. The Keys have no 24-hour pharmacies. Hospital pharmacists will help with emergencies after regular retail business hours. Fishermen's Hospital, Lower Florida Keys Health System, and Mariners Hospital have 24-hour emergency rooms.

▌ MONEY

ATMs are common throughout the Keys if you need to get cash, so there's no need to carry a large amount of money on your person.

CREDIT CARDS

We cite information about credit cards only if they aren't accepted at a restaurant or a hotel. Otherwise, assume that most major credit cards are acceptable.

It's good to inform your credit-card company before you travel to prevent it from putting a hold on your card owing to unusual activity—not a good thing halfway through your trip. Record all your credit-card numbers—as well as the phone numbers to call if your cards are lost or stolen—in a safe place, so you're prepared should something go wrong.

Both MasterCard and Visa have general numbers you can call if your card is lost, but you're better off calling the number of your issuing bank, since MasterCard and Visa usually just transfer you to your bank; your bank's number is usually printed on your card.

Reporting Lost Cards American Express ☎ *800/528–4800* ⊕ *www. americanexpress.com.* **Diners Club** ☎ *800/234–6377* ⊕ *www.dinersclub. com.* **Discover** ☎ *800/347–2683* ⊕ *www.discovercard.com.* **Master-Card** ☎ *800/622–7747* ⊕ *www.mastercard.com.* **Visa** ☎ *800/847–2911* ⊕ *www.visa.com.*

▌ TIME

The Florida Keys are in the Eastern Time Zone. The Dry Tortugas lie in the Central Time Zone, but the ferries and seaplanes run according to Eastern time. During daylight saving time, some operations stay open later.

▌ TIPPING

Tip at restaurants (15% is sufficient except at the most fancy, expensive places, where a larger tip of around 18% is more common). It's common courtesy to leave a dollar or two per night for the housekeeper at your hotel (unless you are staying at a B&B that's run by the owners); leave the money each morning before your room is cleaned.

▌ VISITOR INFORMATION

There are several separate tourism offices in the Florida Keys, or you can try the web site of Visit Florida as well for general information and referrals to local agencies.

Contacts Big Pine and the Lower Keys Chamber of Commerce ✉ *MM 31 OS, 31020 Overseas Hwy., Big Pine Key, Florida, USA* ☎ *305/872-2411, 800/872-3722* ⊕ *www.lowerkeyschamber.com.*

Greater Key West Chamber of Commerce ✉ *510 Greene St., Key West, Florida, USA* ☎ *305/294-2587, 800/527-8539* ⊕ *www.keywestchamber.org.*
Greater Marathon Chamber of Commerce and Visitor Center ✉ *MM 53.5 BS, 12222 Overseas Hwy., Marathon, Florida, USA* ☎ *305/743-5417, 800/262-7284* ⊕ *www.floridakeysmarathon.com.*
Islamorada Chamber of Commerce & Visitors Center ✉ *MM 83.2 BS, 83224 Overseas Hwy, Upper Matecumbe Key, Islamorada, Florida, USA*

☎ *305/664-4503, 800/322-5397* ⊕ *www.islamoradachamber.com.*
Key Largo Chamber of Commerce ✉ *MM 106 BS, 10600 Overseas Hwy., Key Largo, Florida, USA* ☎ *305/451-4747, 800/822-1088* ⊕ *www.keylargochamber.org.*
Visit Florida ☎ *850/488-5607, 866/972-5280* ⊕ *www.visitflorida.com.*

INDEX

PHOTO CREDITS

NOTES

NOTES

NOTES

NOTES

FODOR'S IN FOCUS FLORIDA KEYS

Editorial Contributors: Chelle Koster Walton, Teri Evans, and Michael de Zayas

Series Editor: Douglas Stallings

Editor: Douglas Stallings

Editorial Production: Jennifer DePrima

Maps & Illustrations: David Lindroth, *cartographers*; Rebecca Baer, *map editor*; William Wu, *information graphics*

Design: Fabrizio La Rocca, *creative director*; Tina Malaney, Chie Ushio, Jessica Ramirez, *designers*; Melanie Marin, *associate director of photography*; Jennifer Romains, *photo research*

Cover Photo: (The Artist House, Key West) Susanne Kremer/Fototeca 9x12

Production/Manufacturing: Angela L. McLean

COPYRIGHT

3rd Edition

ISBN 978-0-89141-937-2

ISSN 1942-7328

SPECIAL SALES

This book is available for special discounts for bulk purchases for sales promotions or premiums. Special editions, including personalized covers, excerpts of existing books, and corporate imprints, can be created in large quantities for special needs. For more information, write to Special Markets/Premium Sales, 1745 Broadway, MD 3-1, New York, NY 10019, or e-mail specialmarkets@randomhouse.com.

AN IMPORTANT TIP & AN INVITATION

Although all prices, opening times, and other details in this book are based on information supplied to us at press time, changes occur all the time in the travel world, and Fodor's cannot accept responsibility for facts that become outdated or for inadvertent errors or omissions. **So always confirm information when it matters,** especially if you're making a detour to visit a specific place. Your experiences—positive and negative—matter to us. If we have missed or misstated something, **please write to us.** Share your opinion instantly through our online feedback center at fodors.com/contact-us.

PRINTED IN THE UNITED STATES OF AMERICA

10 9 8 7 6 5 4 3 2 1

ABOUT OUR WRITERS

Chelle Koster Walton admits she's a "fair-weather writer"—her specialty is travel and cuisine in Florida, the Caribbean, and other tropical locales. She has written for such publications as *Family-Fun, Bridal Guide,* the *Los Angeles Times, National Geographic Traveler, USA Today,* the *Miami Herald,* and www.FoxNews.com. A resident of Sanibel Island, Florida, for more than 25 years, she is the author of and contributor to several Florida and Caribbean guidebooks and mobile device apps, including *The Sarasota, Sanibel Island & Naples Explorer's Guide*; the Sanibel & Captiva Islands Selective & Seductive app; *Fun with the Family in Florida*; *The Bahamas Explorer's Guide;* and the Nassau Selective & Seductive app. Walton also contributes annually to Fodor's Florida and Bahamas guidebooks, and is a Southwest Florida Explorer writer-producer for WGCU Public Television. Her love affair with the Florida Keys began more than 20 years ago, when she and her husband Rob began their diving-camping trips to Long Key State Park. More recently, Walton introduced her son Aaron to Key West, and they co-authored a teen-travel article about their visit to the island and the Dry Tortugas.

Paul Rubio updated the Miami chapter of *Fodor's Florida,* and Lynne Helm updated the Everglades chapter of *Fodor's Florida,* from which material is excerpted in "Gateways to the Keys."

Acknowledgments

Chelle wishes to express her appreciation to her mindful editor, Douglas Stallings, and to the following Keys residents and experts whose spirit and knowledge helped her infuse this book with that indefinable Keys flavor: Carolina Bustamante, Carol Shaughnessy, Captain Victoria Rose Impallomeni, Shannon O'Malley, Claire Kunzman, and Bill and Jaye Boswell. Thanks also to my sister-in-law, Mindy Koster, who has been a huge help with fact-checking through the years this book has developed. Final hugs to Robert and Aaron Walton for their forbearance during the completion of this project and for their shared love of the Florida Keys.